and *Elisha Bliss*

by HAMLIN HILL

UNIVERSITY OF MISSOURI PRESS

Columbia · Missouri

817
C625xh

PUBLICATION OF THIS BOOK
HAS BEEN AIDED BY THE FORD FOUNDATION PROGRAM
TO SUPPORT PUBLICATION,
THROUGH UNIVERSITY PRESSES, OF WORK IN THE
HUMANITIES AND SOCIAL SCIENCES

For Arlette, Cynthia, Scott, and Sondra

SOMETIMES WITHOUT WHOM

AND SOMETIMES IN SPITE OF

PREFACE

*B*ooks about Mark Twain have been pouring off presses for the last few years at a dizzying rate, adding to our understanding of various aspects of his amazingly complex position as man and writer. The present volume concentrates on Twain's business relationship with Elisha Bliss and the American Publishing Company. The decade during which Twain was Bliss's most important author was germinal, I think, to Twain's later career as a publisher and businessman and significant, in ways that have never been fully explored, to his aims, techniques, and development in writing.

In a sense the picture of Mark Twain presented here is fractional and thereby distorted. Several volumes—notably Kenneth Andrews' *Nook Farm: Mark Twain's Hartford Circle*, Franklin Rogers' *Mark Twain's Burlesque Patterns*, Walter Blair's *Mark Twain & Huck Finn*, and Henry Nash Smith's *Mark Twain, The Development of a Writer*, and of course Paine's biography—have thoroughly explored various facets of Twain's life and work in the 1870's, and the repetition of those biographical facts and critical evaluations has seemed unnecessary. On the other hand, selectivity does not imply, I hope, oversimplification; though the influence of Bliss and the

American Publishing Company on Twain was enormous, it was only one of a number of vital influences that shaped the career and the craft of Mark Twain.

An earlier version of this study was submitted as a doctoral dissertation at the University of Chicago in 1959. For assistance then I was indebted to librarians at the University of Chicago Library, the Georgetown University Library, the Connecticut Historical Society, the Connecticut State Library, the Watkinson Library of Reference, and the Library of Congress; to Mr. Newton Brainard, Mrs. Frances Edwards, and Mr. Frederick S. Hoffer, all of Hartford, the late Frank C. Willson, Melrose, Massachusetts, and Mr. Jacob Blanck and Mr. Cyril Clemens, Kirkwood, Missouri, all of whom supplied valuable information.

Four major collections of unpublished Mark Twain material provided the bulk of the documentation for the dissertation and for this revised version. To Mr. Donald Gallup, American Literature Collections, Yale University Library; Mr. John D. Gordan, the Henry W. and Albert A. Berg Collection of The New York Public Library; Mr. Clifton Waller Barrett, whose collection has since been deposited in the Alderman Library, University of Virginia; and Professor Henry Nash Smith and Mr. Frederick Anderson, the Mark Twain Papers in the General Library of the University of California at Berkeley, I am grateful for generous permission to examine, cite, and quote materials in their possession. The trustees of the Estate of Samuel L. Clemens (Mark Twain), Deceased, also granted liberal permission to quote previously unpublished Mark Twain material.

Professors Walter Blair, Paul Baender, and Napier Wilt and Mr. Franklin Meine all assisted in the birth pangs of the dissertation and provided encouragement when it was vital.

Since then, some of the material from the dissertation has appeared in *American Literature,* the *Bulletin of the New York Public Library,* and *American Quarterly* in different form. To the Duke University Press, the New York Public Library, and the American Studies Association I am grateful for permission to utilize herein parts of those articles.

In order to reduce considerably the documentation of the present volume, I have used the following abbreviations in the footnotes and occasionally in the text:

Autobiography	*Mark Twain's Autobiography,* edited by Albert B. Paine (New York, Harper and Brothers, 1924).
Business Man	*Mark Twain, Business Man,* edited by Samuel C. Webster (Boston, Little, Brown & Company, 1946).
CWB	The Clifton Waller Barrett Collection, University of Virginia, Charlottesville, Virginia.
Eruption	*Mark Twain in Eruption,* edited by Bernard DeVoto (New York, Harper and Brothers, 1940).
FCW	The Frank C. Willson–Mark Twain Collection, University of Texas, Austin, Texas.
Letters	*Mark Twain's Letters,* edited by Albert B. Paine (New York, Harper and Brothers, 1917).
Love Letters	*The Love Letters of Mark Twain,* edited by Dixon Wecter (New York, Harper and Brothers, 1949).
Mrs. Fairbanks	*Mark Twain's Letters to Mrs. Fairbanks,* edited by Dixon Wecter (San Marino, California, Huntington Library, 1949).

MTP   The Mark Twain Papers, General
                     Library, University of California,
                     Berkeley.

NYPL   The Henry W. and Albert A. Berg
                     Collection of The New York Public
                     Library.

Paine   Albert B. Paine, *Mark Twain, A
                     Biography* (New York, Harper and
                     Brothers, 1912).

Twain-Howells Letters   *Mark Twain–Howells Letters: The
                     Correspondence of Samuel L.
                     Clemens and William D. Howells,
                     1869–1910,* edited by Henry Nash
                     Smith and William M. Gibson
                     (Cambridge, Mass., Harvard Uni-
                     versity Press, 1960).

Yale   The Mark Twain Collections, Yale
                     University Library, New Haven.

Permission to quote from copyright materials was granted
by the following: Harper & Row, Publishers, for Albert B.
Paine, *Mark Twain, A Biography;* Albert B. Paine, editor,
Mark Twain's Autobiography, Mark Twain's Letters, and
Mark Twain's Notebooks; Bernard DeVoto, editor, *Mark
Twain in Eruption;* Dixon Wecter, editor, *The Love Letters of
Mark Twain;* and for *Mark Twain's Speeches* (1910); the
Huntington Library for Dixon Wecter, editor, *Mark Twain's
Letters to Mrs. Fairbanks;* the President and Fellows of
Harvard College and the Mark Twain Company for Bernard
DeVoto, *Mark Twain at Work;* the President and Fellows of
Harvard College, the Mark Twain Company, and Mildred
Howells and John Mead Howells for Henry Nash Smith and
William M. Gibson, editors, *Mark Twain–Howells Letters: The*

Correspondence of Samuel L. Clemens and William D. Howells, 1869–1910; and Mrs. Doris Webster for Samuel C. Webster, editor, *Mark Twain, Business Man.* The frontispiece photograph of Elisha Bliss is reproduced with the permission (and assistance) of the Mark Twain Library and Memorial Commission, Hartford. The University Research Committee of the University of New Mexico provided a grant for clerical aid in the preparation of the manuscript.

A final word, perhaps as a kind of defense. The massive scholarship which will be involved with the forthcoming Manuscript Edition of Mark Twain will include a more thorough, more meticulous study of the composition, publication, and contemporary reception of the major Mark Twain volumes than was realistically feasible in the present book. Undoubtedly, the editors of *Innocents Abroad, Roughing It, Tom Sawyer,* and *A Tramp Abroad,* Professors Leon Dickinson, Franklin Rogers, John Gerber, and Roger Asselineau, will fill in blank spots, correct errors of fact, and revise many of the conjectures contained in this volume. I am convinced, however, that the main thesis—that Mark Twain was shaped in his aims, techniques, and craft by the influence of the American Publishing Company and his subscription audience—will find further, more convincing support in the scholarly analysis and reconstruction of his subscription works.

HAMLIN HILL

The University of New Mexico
Albuquerque, New Mexico
August, 1963

CONTENTS

"For a book is always written for somebody to read, and . . . the patron is not merely the paymaster, but also in a very subtle and insidious way the instigator and inspirer of what is written."

VIRGINIA WOOLF
"The Patron and the Crocus"
The Common Reader

CHAPTER I

THE ONLY WAY
TO SELL A BOOK

*W*HEN MARK TWAIN stepped off the *Quaker City* in 1867, no one would have predicted for him a career as author (rather than journalist), publisher, or speculator, but by 1880, when he made a contract with James R. Osgood to publish *The Prince and the Pauper,* he was already all three. The change, a growth of qualities that had been a part of Sam Clemens for a long time, is significant, for Mark Twain's disasters in the 1880's and 1890's were in large part a result of Twain's experiences in the 1870's. Economically, anyway, it was Charles L. Webster and Company and, of course, the speculation in the Paige typesetter that brought on bankruptcy and at least some of the disillusionment and pessimism of the last years of Twain's life.

The journalist who returned to New York City in 1867 was in the process, unconsciously perhaps, of refining his craft by a number of devices that scholars have scrutinized closely in the past few years. The newspaper reporter had already published one book, *The Jumping Frog*, and made remarks in his letters about the format and typography that suggested a latent desire to castigate typesetters, printers, or anyone who tampered with his material. The humorist who had, as he was later to claim in the dedication to *Roughing It*, been a millionaire for twelve days, was always hypnotized by the thought of barrels full of money to be earned by a courageous gamble. The journalist had been aware a few years earlier of the distinction between popular humor and the literature that would secure fame and honor and had committed himself reluctantly and wistfully to the former.[1] All that was needed was a catalyst, a spark, that would show him how to combine his desires to write enduring literature, to earn an impressive income, to adapt his journalistic background, and to continue writing the humor which came from natural instinct and over a decade of apprentice training.

The spark came, on November 21, 1867, in the form of a letter from Elisha Bliss of the American Publishing Company of Hartford, "perhaps," Bliss boasted with more bravado than truth, "the oldest subscription house in the country." Mark Twain should write a subscription book, Bliss said, but Mark Twain, in addition to being flattered by the suggestion, was puzzled. He apparently did not know for certain just what a subscription book was. Horace Greeley published by subscription, though, and so did Albert D. Richardson, and Twain went to both of them to find out about the possibilities of the method. Finally, the humorist made a trip to Hartford the week of January 24, 1868, and came away with a contract that was "splendid" for a book of *Quaker City* material for which he was to receive a royalty "a fifth more than they have paid any author, except Horace Greeley"—whom the American Publishing Company had never paid anything, because they did not issue his books.

Twain thus made a commitment for a book with the most

energetic, but far from the oldest, publisher in a field that was relatively new, that would die out by the end of the nineteenth century, and that would have a profound effect on Twain's methods of writing, his attitude toward his books, and his almost paranoid suspicion that people were trying to swindle him. If it was not a classic example of the sheep stepping into the wolf's den, it was fairly close.

A late arrival in the business, the American Publishing Company incorporated in Hartford on April 10, 1865, to "Print, Publish, Manufacture, and Sell Books, Maps and Charts." An 1889 announcement that the company traced its "lineage to the origin of the subscription business"² rests, somewhat precariously, on its descent from Lucius Stebbins, who first proposed the name. In an article on "The Press" in *The Memorial History of Hartford County,* Charles H. Clark, editor of the *Hartford Courant,* tried to explain the genealogy:

> The most remarkable development of the subscription business traces back to the work of Lucius Stebbins, who at first colored geographies, published by Mr. Robinson. As the school-book business moved to New York he began publishing historical and descriptive works, illustrated with colored wood-engravings, and sold by travelling agents. . . . Stebbins adopted the name of the American Publishing Company, and in 1859 sold this business to the firm of Hurlbut and Kellogg, who kept the name of the American Publishing Company; but no such company actually existed until April, 1865.

Stebbins did occasionally use the name "American Subscription House" and distributed Jane E. Stebbins' *Moses and the Prophets; Christ and the Apostles; Fathers and Martyrs . . . Embracing a Period of More Than 2000 Years* under that imprint. The American Publishing Company judiciously changed the title to *Illustrated History of the Bible* when it reissued the book.

Seven stockholders established the company and divided up the 2,000 shares of $25 stock. Five of the seven had experience in business already. William N. Matson, first president, was a member of S. S. Scranton and Company, which was one of the "not less than eight subscription houses [that] grew up out of the establishment started by Mr. Stebbins." John B. Burr was the owner of J. B. Burr and Company, which published an edition of Barnum's *Struggles and Triumphs* in 1869, several subscription editions of Thomas W. Knox's *Underground* in the 1870's, and Matthew H. Smith's *Sunshine and Shadow* (1868) and *Twenty Years Among the Bulls and Bears of Wall Street* (1870). Thomas Belknap was also a publisher, responsible for such subscription works as Signor Antonio Blitz's *Fifty Years in the Magic Circle*, D. J. Kirwan's *Palace and Hovel*, and half a dozen historical works by Benson J. Lossing. Sidney Drake and J. G. Parsons owned a bookbindery at 150 Asylum Street. The two other stockholders, Henry French and E. G. Hastings, apparently had no prior experience with the mechanics of publishing.

The American Publishing Company's location in Hartford provided several distinct advantages. It was at the center of the subscription book industry in the United States, so that paper manufacturers, printers, and binders were right at hand, a factor that was to become vital when it was necessary to "keep six steam presses & a paper mill going *night & day*" in an attempt to catch up on orders for *Innocents Abroad*. Apparently because of Stebbins, Hartford had become, as a writer in *The Trade Circular Annual for 1871* put it, "the headquarters for this kind of trade, no less than twelve or fourteen firms in that city being engaged in it."

> In the eight years, 1861–1868, there were issued from Hartford alone about 30 subscription books, the other cities publishing, perhaps, enough more to make 100. The business in Hartford amounted during that time to $5,000,000, and employed 10,000 agents in disposing of 1,426,000 copies.[3]

Not only were facilities for publication plentiful; costs were much less than they were in other publishing centers. "Printing, binding, stationery, etc., are said to be done cheaper there than they can be elsewhere. Even the paper is manufactured within a stone's throw of Asylum-st., on which nearly all the publishing houses stand."

At least as propitious as the location of the new company was the year of incorporation, 1865. The Civil War, as the writer for the *Trade Circular Annual* caustically pointed out, "furnished not only popular subjects for book-making, but also a host of cripples to act as agents." Though the veteran was not the only person solicited to act as salesman,

> the greatest reservoir of manpower for canvassing was the soldiers of the late war. No sooner, it seemed, had the armies of Grant and Sherman passed in review along Pennsylvania Avenue . . . than the ex-soldier without a job would be skirmishing through every four corners and hamlet in the land with Joseph T. Headley's *The Great Rebellion* (sales: 150,000), or Greeley's *American Conflict* (250,000).[4]

One contemporary speculated that "at least 50,000 agents must be employed by the Hartford firms in the course of a year, and more than 1,000,000 circulars distributed through the country."[5] Under the control of a regional supervisor or general agency, "the agents would penetrate into the thinly settled communities. . . . Contracts were signed on the basis of sample dummies, the required number of copies periodically supplied on a cash basis, and delivery made on a second visit."[6] The agent received a percentage of the retail price: The Union Book and Bible House, for instance, gave 40 per cent on regular books and 50 per cent on Bibles and albums.

The sample dummy, or prospectus, was in most cases the key to the sale of a subscription book; not very many of the authors were as familiar as Twain or Marietta Holley. This prospectus contained samples of pages from the book itself, including the full-page illustrations, the table of contents, and about fifty random leaves of the text, bound in a cover identical to the cloth cover of the book. At the back were strips of the alternative, higher-priced bindings and blank pages for prospective customers to sign. Unfortunately, though, the description was apt to be a high-pressure one which alienated customers so thoroughly that one publisher recommended concealing the prospectus until the agent managed to get inside the house (see *Helpful Hints . . .* , reprinted as Appendix A). The canvassers' semiscrupulous methods caused George Ade to complain that they "supplemented their specious arguments with private tales of woe. . . . Nobody," he claimed, "really wanted these books. They were purchased because the agents knew how to sell them." [7]

By contrast, James S. Barcus, who as the head of a subscription house issued a booklet entitled *The Science of Selling for Canvassers, Drummers, and Clerks* (1917), praised his agents rather extravagantly as dedicated men:

> The rank and file of book salesmen that go up and down the highways and byways carrying good tidings of knowledge and erudition to the masses . . . are men of integrity and moral purpose—men who have chosen to do this work from as high-minded motive and pure intent as prompt the establishment of a factory, the building of a mercantile house, or the preaching of the gospel.

Most of this is sheer nonsense, of course, but one phrase in Barcus' eulogy had a familiar ring. When he claimed that canvassers carried knowledge and erudition to the masses, he was echoing the subscription dealers' standard defense against the attacks of the "regular trade." All through the 1870's the subscription publisher and author were the targets of constant abuse from the book publishers. The 1871 *Trade Circular Annual,* for example, truculently insisted that subscription books are often absolutely worthless, and this is not only true with regard to the nature of their contents, but also extends to their manufacture, in which paper, print, and binding are usually of the commonest and worst description. How buyers can be found for such books is a puzzle, for beyond their title, there is nothing attractive about them, and yet they sell by thousands.

The author who might be in danger of succumbing to the lure of mere profit was austerely reminded by S. R. Crocker, editor of the *Literary World*, in his August, 1874, issue, that subscription books

> cannot possibly circulate among the better class of readers, owing to the general and not unfounded prejudice against them as a class. Consequently an author of established reputation, who resorts to the subscription plan for the sake of making money, descends to a constituency of a lower grade and inevitably loses caste.[8]

Several explanations have been suggested for the vitriolic antagonism of the regular trade. "Under the subscription system, complimentary review copies were not distributed."[9] Subscription volumes, dependent on door-to-door canvassing, "would take no advertising space"[10] in newspapers and magazines. Subscription publishers were guilty of "working off antiquated works in new disguises [or] flooding the country with flashy books produced overnight on some spectacular event."[11] Though these explanations may have had something to do with the enmity, the obvious reason was that the author who published by subscription was making money at a rate that dazzled the regular trade. It was difficult for a bookseller not to be envious when he saw reports of sales of 100,000 copies of a book and realized that not one of them had been sold through a bookstore, or not legally at any rate.

The subscription publisher had a complicated arrangement whereby he and his canvassers both agreed not to sell books to bookstores, and by 1897 A. D. Worthington and Company, publishers of Mary A. Livermore's *The Story of My Life*, cited two U. S. Circuit Court decisions in Ohio and Pennsylvania which gave subscription publishers the right to sue booksellers who offered their works in trade stores.[12] Nevertheless, publishers who felt that the subscription market for a book was near saturation would "dump" books into the trade, and individual peddlers would also sell to stores surreptitiously. All this chicanery meant that trade dealers had to indulge in "dishonesty in order to obtain for their shelves copies of a book 'sold only by subscription.' "[13] The system was one in which the agent was his own middleman, and the bookseller resented "the loss of business which properly belongs to him."[14]

The subscription publishers replied as best they could to the attack. Feigning injured innocence, they combined their noble aim of bringing knowledge and erudition to the masses with the argument that they served a customer who had no bookstore available to him. F. E. Compton, publisher of a present-day encyclopedia, explains:

> Probably ninety per cent of the book buyers of that time never entered a bookstore. They were far removed from bookstores, physically or spiritually, and most of them would never have bought a book if the subscription business had not "sold" them the idea and brought the book to them.[15]

The subscription publishers did not have the same opportunity to publish their views as the trade, but at least the short-lived magazine of the American Publishing Company, *The American Publisher*, lasted long enough to print a defense of colportage, in which the Reverend John Todd, D.D., lauded the system whereby books were supplied to "mechanics and farmers . . . in places wholly unexpected, and where, a few years ago, a new book would very seldom be found." He predicted that the number of readers of subscription books would increase "ten-fold, within a few years."[16] In 1873 the

American Publishing Company attempted to answer the charges of unreasonable prices and dishonesty:

> It has been claimed that books sold by Agents are higher in price than those of equal value sold at book-stores. This belief often prevents a person from buying of an Agent. So far as our books are concerned, there is no foundation for such a claim. Please consider the following statements:
>
> FIRST. The most expensive books issued are those which have the engravings worked in with the text. The reasons are these:—To make the cuts effective, it requires a great many and a large outlay. We have expended on the plates for this book [*The Gilded Age*] nearly $10,000. . . .
>
> SECOND. We claim that we sell you books with from two hundred to three hundred engravings, finely printed on extra fine paper, and most firmly bound, as low as you can buy any book equal in *weight, size,* and *popularity,* containing but few if any cuts, at any bookstore; while you will be asked there for books illustrated as are our $3.50 ones (if they have any such) at least $5 or $6. . . .
>
> We allow our Agents exactly the discount on our price, that publishers allow the regular trade, and *no more;* and as through our Agents we sell ten times more of our books than do the trade publishers, we can afford a better book for a given sum.
>
> THIRD. We furnish only Agents who enter into written agreements with us, pledging themselves not to put any books into stores; and it is only through dishonest Agents that they are ever seen there. The greater popularity of our works and their ready sale make it an object for the trade to get them; and they have in many instances used unfair means to obtain the works from us. This we know and have proof of.[17]

A year later Elisha Bliss, who probably wrote the statement above, released for publication in the *New York Tribune* what was probably the most eloquent plea for colportage, as it was operating out of Hartford, when he piously celebrated the

"hundreds of thousands of little libraries" that subscription
book buyers were amassing throughout the country:

> In the little towns where there are no bookstores the book
> agent induces people to buy. One book thus sold is read
> with avidity by the whole household, and when another
> agent comes it is ready to buy another book. In that way,
> a nucleus is formed for hundreds of thousands of little
> libraries throughout the country, which never would
> have existed except for the book agent. After a few books
> are bought by subscription the people go to the book-
> stores, if there are any in their neighborhood. . . . There
> is a large field covered with people that have no oppor-
> tunity to buy books except in the way we sell them. . . .
> These are the people our agents seek out and induce to
> purchase books.[18]

The unctuous phrasings of Barcus and Bliss can best be
relegated to the pigeonhole marked "Bombast." Nothing in the
history of subscription publishing suggests that it was moti-
vated by sublimated evangelism or that Bliss was impelled by
the noble urge to spread light where there was only darkness
before.

It is true, though, that the subscription book industry had a
highly specialized function, well recognized by those publishers themselves and even grudgingly conceded occasionally
by trade publications. "The subscription business," one of the
early reviews of *The Gilded Age* pointed out, "more than the
'regular,' must suit a widely-dispersed average of customers." [19]
The "regular trade" author consoled himself on the compara-
tively insignificant sales with the thought that he was at least
circulating "among the better class of readers" while the
subscription author sacrificed prestige to popular appeal and
profit. Obviously, with specialized methods of manufacture,
sales, and distribution, and with a specialized audience, the
subscription author produced an extremely specialized kind of
book.

By and large, the subscription book was patently subliterary.

As Clemens told Joel Chandler Harris, "Mighty few books that come strictly under the head of *literature* will sell by subscription." During the early days of the business "religious books, embracing a 'Cottage Bible,' medical works, and books for making every man his own lawyer, represent what may be called the natural staple of the subscription business," [20] but the post-Civil War canvasser had a much wider choice of books to peddle. As the subscription companies expanded, they began looking for histories, autobiographies, reminiscences, first from the Civil War and then from any area of interest or author that might command respectable sales. Horace Greeley's *The American Conflict*, first published by O. D. Case, appeared even before the conflict was decided. Case followed Greeley with Junius H. Browne's *Four Years in Secessia* in 1865. Albert D. Richardson's *The Secret Service: Field, Dungeon, and Escape* (1865) and his *Personal History of U. S. Grant* (1868) were staples of the American Publishing Company. J. B. Burr ran Thomas W. Knox's *Underground* through several editions, beginning in 1873; T. Belknap issued Benson J. Lossing's *Pictorial Field Book of the Civil War* (1874). Hurlbut, William and Company issued the first volume of Headley's *The Great Rebellion* in 1863, and the American Publishing Company brought out the second in 1866. Civil War books were still going strong as late as the 1880's, when Allan Pinkerton's *Spy of the Rebellion* (1883), a reissue of Richardson's life of Grant, and half a dozen volumes of autobiography published by Twain's company appeared on the market.

Other reminiscences and travel accounts also sold. In addition to Twain's *Innocents Abroad, Roughing It,* and *A Tramp Abroad,* the American Publishing Company printed Junius H. Browne's *Sights and Sensations in Europe* (1871), Thomas W. Knox's *Overland through Asia* (1870), Richardson's *Beyond the Mississippi* (1867, 1869), Charles Dudley Warner's *Moslems and Mummies* (1876), and Julia A. Stone's *Illustrated*

India (1877). Other typical offerings were Mary Livermore's *The Story of My Life*, George Bidwell's *Forging His Chains*, Fanny Kelly's *Narrative of My Captivity*, Blitz's *Fifty Years in the Magic Circle*, Barnum's *Struggles and Triumphs*, Matthew Smith's *Twenty Years Among the Bulls and Bears of Wall Street*, Mrs. Francis Victor's *The River of the West*, Albert S. Evans' *Our Sister Republic*, George M. Dutcher's *The Story of My Life*, S. S. "Sunset" Cox's *The Diversions of a Diplomat in Turkey*, and *The Life and Letters of Roscoe Conkling*.

Biblical and religious works apparently commanded a sizable audience. In addition to Jane Stebbins' *Illustrated History of the Bible*, her *Our Departed Friends, or, Glory of the Immortal Life* found a publisher—L. Stebbins Company. Conybeare and Howson's *Life of St. Paul*, W. L. Gage's *The Land of Sacred Mystery, or The Bible Read in the Light of Its Own Scenery*, and Gage's *The Home of God's People* were all hawked by subscription.

Topical books that exploited current events rolled from the presses at fantastic rates. For example, when Mormonism became a popular topic, *The Exposé, or Mormons and Mormonism, The Past, Present and Future of Mormonism*, *"Tell It All:" The Story of a Life's Experience in Mormonism*, and *Lament of a Mormon Wife* appeared. Between the time of Stanley's commission to find Livingstone in 1869 and the first few years of the 1870's, various houses issued *The Last Journals of David Livingstone*, *Africa and Its Explorers, or Livingstone Lost and Found*, and *Livingstone's Life Work*. In the midst of the Nares, Nordenskiöld, *Polaris*, and *Jeannette* polar expeditions of the early 1870's, canvassers peddled *Our Lost Explorers*, *The Frozen Zone and Its Explorers*, and a reprint of Elisha Kane's *Arctic Exploration*. Even at the end of the century publishers dashed off volumes for sale "by subscription only" about the assassination of McKinley, the death of Victoria, and the history of the Spanish-American War.

Obviously, the subscription book was usually a nonfictional, first-person narrative that allowed for some kind of sensational—or at least popular—appeal. Howells' recollection of his and Aldrich's plan to write a book for subscription publication contains as much astute logic as facetiousness; the proposed title, *Memorable Murders,* suggests both the factual basis and the sanguinary nature of most subscription books. It was not until 1873 that a subscription house, the American Publishing Company, ventured to publish a novel, *The Gilded Age.*

In part, the trouble with fiction was that it was only rarely long enough for subscription requirements. As a reviewer of *The Innocents Abroad* put it, "no man ever saw a book agent with a small volume in his hand." [21] The typical volume was an ugly duckling that trade journals sniped at with a humor obviously flavored with more than a dash of resentment:

> A gorgeous binding, usually in very bad taste, thick but cheap paper, outrageously poor wood-cuts, the largest type with the thickest leads, add up into a very big, gaudy book which a glib tongue or persistent boring cheats folks into buying at five dollars, when the reading matter which it contains, if worth anything, would make about a dollar-and-a-half book in the regular trade.[22]

Frank Bliss, who took over the management of the American Publishing Company from his father in 1880, explained the situation this way: "People in those days would not pay for blank paper and wide margins. They wanted everything filled up with type or pictures." [23] Part of the subscription book's appeal was bulk, "that intrinsic worth of bigness and durability which commends itself to the rural economist, who likes to get a material return for his money," Bret Harte styled it.

One way to expand a book to the necessary length was to saturate it with illustrations, usually woodcuts that looked as if they might have been engraved with a tablespoon. "Cheap engravings meant a big saving in production costs," notes DeLancey Ferguson, "and most subscribers wouldn't know the difference anyway." [24]

Illustrations alone were not enough, of course, to make up the necessary 600-plus pages. Manuscript equivalent to approximately two volumes of the regular length was necessary, and "if a man had only a book and a half in him, that was too bad; he had to get up the half somehow or throw in the towel."[25] One alternative was to throw in a second, shorter, somehow related manuscript at the end of a book and add "Together with . . ." to the title page. Thus Richardson added a biographical sketch of Schuyler Colfax to his *Personal History of U. S. Grant;* Mrs. Victor's *Eleven Years in the Rocky Mountains and a History of the Sioux War* contained an added biography of Custer. Headley's *Illustrated Life of Washington* threw in "an interesting account of Mount Vernon" by Lossing, and Charles D. Brownell's *Indian Races* included an account of the "Indian Massacres in Minnesota" by Headley. Stebbins blithely ignored mathematics, added an appendix to his *Eighty Years' Progress in the United States* (1861), and reissued it in 1872 as *One Hundred Years' Progress of the United States.* Twain, too, was to use the device in *Roughing It, A Tramp Abroad,* and *Life on the Mississippi* in appendixes containing material "borrowed" from other authors.

The publisher and the peddler had many ways of indulging in shady practices under the subscription system, and it was the unsavory "hard sell" that caused Julian Hawthorne to complain that agents "are trained to talk a man into a state of imbecility, and then, under guise of giving him something he does not want, to rob him of his money."[26] They dumped books in bookstores. They reserved the first spaces on their order blanks in the prospectuses for the most prominent men in the community and copied these names into the next prospectus when they had used up all the order pages. They sold for five dollars retail books that cost fifty-five to seventy cents to manufacture. They used engravings over and over again and then bragged about the cost of illustrations. They canvassed a book under one title until they had exhausted the market and then reissued it under a new title and "sold" the customers as well as the volume. Joaquin Miller's *Paquita,* to cite just one example, appeared under that title, *Unwritten History,* and *Life among the Modocs* at various times in the first decade after its issue.

The American Publishing Company, though it was perhaps the most respectable of the subscription houses, was far from virgin pure, at least after Bliss took over its management. In its first two years, the pre-Bliss years, the company published three books: Richardson's *The Secret Service,* the second volume of Headley's *The Great Rebellion* (and a 1,200-page one-volume issue of the complete book), and a family Bible so arranged that "Family Portraits may be preserved within its sacred lids." Both Richardson's and Headley's books were also published in German translations. Then, in 1867, Elisha Bliss moved to Hartford.

Bliss had been born in Springfield, Massachusetts, in 1822 and worked in the retail dry goods business there. He became a dry goods jobber in New York City, lived in New Jersey, and at forty-five, through some kind of agreement or connection I have been unable to reconstruct, replaced S. S. Scranton as the secretary of the American Publishing Company. He held that post until 1870, when he became president. From 1871 to 1873, he was secretary again, and from 1873 through the decade, he was president.

The misconception that "until Bliss had become manager, the Company had dealt mainly in works of a heavily evangelical cast, which may have laid up treasure in Heaven, but had paid few dividends" [27] is certainly not true. *The Secret Service* and *The Great Rebellion* were not by any stretch of the imagination pious, and though accurate figures are not available for the company's sales in its first two years, estimates for both books have gone as high as 100,000. What Bliss did bring to the company was a remarkably shrewd business acumen, the courage to gamble on vast expansion, the willingness to publish a whole list of books at once, and the gargantuan diplomacy necessary to handle authors like Mark Twain. As his obituary in the *Hartford Courant* set forth,

> Mr. Bliss was a man of great business energy, a thorough master of the subscription book business and an excellent organizer of agencies. He was a good judge of what would suit the popular mind, and his quick perception well fitted him to select the proper agents to bring his publications before the public.[28]

Bliss began by replacing several of the older general agents with his relatives—in Newark and Trenton—and making his son treasurer. Before long, he attempted a couple of magazines, *The American Publisher* and *The American Monthly: A Mirror of the Age*, mainly in order to print excerpts from and advertisements for his own books. By the early 1870's he was publishing subscription books under a string of imprints, including Belknap and Bliss, R. W. Bliss, F. C. Bliss, the Mutual Publishing Company, and the Columbian Book Company. As Mark Twain told Howells, "If you want to write the Mutual Pub. Co., address the American Pub. Co.—the former is buried in the stomach of the latter." [29]

The American Publishing Company operated in its first two years on the cardinal principles of subscription publishing: maximum promotion of a very limited number of books ("two books at a time," Twain told his mother), and canvassing for those two books only after they were actually published. Bliss learned early that for the vast majority of subscription books the advance sales and those in the very first months after publication were the most important. When reviews and journals deigned to notice subscription books at all they rarely had a single good word, and the purchaser of most of the books would have had to be gullible indeed if he remained unaware that the volume was not quite the product advertised. To quote Twain once more, "a subscription harvest is *before* publication, (not *after*, when people have discovered how bad

one's book is)." Twain's diagnosis is borne out by a stock
ledger of books which the American Publishing Company
received from its binderies. Almost without exception the
market was exhausted within six months of the publication. So
Bliss began emphasizing pre-publication sales, bragging to
Twain of the 41,000-copy advance sale of *Beyond the Mississippi.* Occasionally it was necessary to canvass for five or six
months in order to secure a satisfactory sale.

Then to compensate for an intensive canvass, Bliss began
turning out books at what was a fantastic rate for a subscription
house. In the first ten years of his management of the company,
Bliss issued well over fifty books, including those published by
the Mutual Publishing Company, Columbian Book Company,
and other subsidiary imprints. Activity became so frenetic in
1876 that Twain suggested Bliss reduce the company's business
by two-thirds in order to concentrate on just one or two
books—*Tom Sawyer,* of course, among them. He insisted that
"we publish books so fast that canvassers are likely merely to
skim the cream of a district & then 'lay' for the next
new book." [30] Twain knew that the system worked fine for the
company, since it kept profits rolling in, kept the name of the
American Publishing Company constantly before the public,
and allowed the company to move into what Twain thought
were much too sumptuous offices and to buy its own printing
office and presses. But it did not suit at least one author who
felt that *his* books ought to be canvassed alone, with the full
force of the company behind him, for at least nine months.

Another departure, probably the most important one that
Bliss made from standard subscription technique, was to
experiment with fiction and even poetry. As Twain remembered telling Grant, "Not many books were suitable to that
method of publishing, but . . . the memoirs of such illustrious
persons as Sherman and Grant were peculiarly adapted to that
method." [31] When Bliss asked Twain specifically for a book
"*humorously inclined,*" he was taking an enormous risk, but it

was a gamble that paid off. The success of *Innocents Abroad* sent Bliss scurrying for other humorists who might have a book to publish by subscription. By the 1880's Bliss had books by not only Mark Twain but also Bret Harte, Palmer Cox, Marietta Holley, Josh Billings, Robert J. Burdette, August Berkeley, Dan DeQuille, Charles H. Webb, and even an anthology called *The World of Wit and Humor* for sale. Whatever else may account for the spectacular success of the American Publishing Company, its policy of printing popular humor and fiction was a large contributing factor. And it was something more than luck, too. Maybe Bliss knew the public taste better than most of the other companies' directors. All the evidence points to the conclusion that Bliss exploited his customers, teased their curiosities, flattered their rural insularity, and promised them humor that would strike a responsive chord.

It would be nice to imagine Bliss as the genial publisher who pictured the "farmer and mechanic" coming home after an eighteen-hour day and picking up one of those stubby brown volumes with "American Publishing Company" stamped in gilt on the spine, and who found his reward in the idea that he was bringing a few moments of light-hearted joy into the pastoral scene. It would be nice, but it wouldn't be Elisha Bliss. He was coldly calculating, he was happy to cheat both authors and customers with a repertory of the worst tricks of salesmanship, and he apparently juggled books with the skill of a master accountant. Twain once compared Bliss with a general who had an army of canvassers spread out over the country attacking the customers. It was to take over a decade for Twain to realize that the authors of the books Bliss published were under attack, too.

This was the publishing world into which Twain stepped. It was unrespectable to the "literary" author; it was indifferent to the customer, except as he represented cash in the agent's pocket; it paid allegiance to a business ethic that was nowhere more clearly condemned than in Twain's and Warner's *The*

Gilded Age, even though, paradoxically, Twain himself was to use many of the American Publishing Company's techniques and shady tactics when he set up Charles L. Webster and Company. As he became more and more immersed in the mechanics of subscription publishing, the Missouri humorist moved to Hartford, became a director of the company, and made himself a self-proclaimed authority on its method. In many ways, it was a fortunate alliance; for a popular humorist, it was the ideal outlet. The subscription technique was as crassly commercial as Twain often was; the profits played a vital part in soothing the author's ego. Further, he was always certain of his audience because it was largely the same one for whom Twain had written newspaper columns during the preceding decade. Both Twain and the industry were young, brash, even experimentally inclined. What Twain gave Bliss can be measured in dollars and cents: so much money, a grand new office in 1876, a skyrocketing rise in the value of the company's stock, and a reputation as "the most prosperous subscription-book concern in the country." [32]

On the other hand, publication by subscription aggravated some of the problems Twain faced as a writer. It required him to be "funny," it made him the target of cultural snobs like Croker who intensified his misgivings about the merit of his art, and it widened even further the kinds of gulfs that Henry Seidel Canby points out separated Twain from Henry James. For Twain, money poured in—$105,000 for subscription books between 1869 and 1881, lecture halls packed, interviewers swarmed; but *The Prince and the Pauper* and *Joan of Arc* would have to be published anonymously or the audience would not take them seriously, Twain thought. The *Atlantic* audience was the only one that did not insist on Twain's performing antics like the King in "The Royal Nonesuch," and Livy Clemens rankled because her husband was "so persistently glorified as a mere buffoon, as if that entirely covered my case." [33] James's most popular book, *Daisy Miller,* sold less than Twain's least successful subscription volume; and *his* statement that Twain and Poe appealed to primitive minds was as much a rationalization of his lack of popular appeal as Twain's famous 1889 letter to Andrew Lang was a clue to his desire for acceptance by the cultivated reader. James standing in front of the marquee of a theater running an Oscar Wilde play and incapable of comprehending why the audience flocked there rather than to his own presentation down the street was the opposite side of the coin from Twain, who in his last years wore the Oxford robes on every possible occasion as the visible sign of the imprimatur of "literary" acceptance that he had sought for half a century.

And it all began, for Mark Twain at any rate, on November 21, 1867.

CHAPTER II

THE PEOPLE'S AUTHOR

CRITICS AGREE that Mark Twain had a tough time writing *Innocents Abroad*. The book was to some extent crucial in deciding which turn his career would take, because it meant that for the first time he was faced with the composition of a lengthy work with at least some degree of structure and unity—the exact degree is still a matter of debate. He had to decide whether to use the old *Alta California* letters in the book or whether even to write a book about the *Quaker City* trip. He had to attempt to gauge the taste of the audience for whom he was supposed to write, and there were several ways that his yardstick measured incorrectly.

Artistically, the book was to be an anomaly of embarrassing chauvinism and the purplest prose, with more than a dash of burlesque at other authors who wrote no more floridly than Twain himself had. Relying on some techniques that had served him well in Nevada and California journalism helped quite a bit, and borrowing passages—even pages—from other authors filled out some of the interminable quota of manuscript that he had contracted to supply Bliss. When he finished writing and the book was published, Twain gave no hint that he was aware that he had composed a volume whose date of publication would be used to mark the beginning of American realism or to signal the cutting and tying of America's umbilical cord to Europe (though some of Whitman's admirers would date the latter event about fourteen years earlier).

Mechanically, the book was a nightmare, too. Twain was busy lecturing, writing for newspapers, courting Livy while the book went through the process of printing, proofreading, and revising, and Bliss, who tried to keep up with Twain's schedule in order to send proof to him, must have breathed much easier when the humorist made one of his stopovers in Hartford.

But Twain was simply not yet an author. Writing was less a craft than a livelihood; it was always to remain important as a source of income, no matter to what extent Twain developed an "art" of writing. The wandering journalist, though he did little to impede the publication of *Innocents* by his nomadic activity, was apparently just not very much interested in *book* publication. For this reason, his move to Hartford in 1871, his sale of his interest in the Buffalo *Express*, and his resignation from the staff of the *Galaxy* at the same time represent a significant about-face—a deliberate destruction of his journalistic commitments and a move to not only the respectability of Nook Farm but also to the offices of the American Publishing Company. Whatever else may have prompted the Clemenses' move, clearly Bliss's publication of *Innocents Abroad* and *Roughing It* persuaded Twain that he could be a writer of books by subscription without sacrificing profit or popular appeal. The move to Hartford is as significant for Twain's literary career as Howells' move to New York over a decade later is for American literary history: before *Innocents Abroad* was published, Twain was a newspaperman, and after *Rough-*

ing It was published, he was on a more "literary" path. Bliss's share in determining the change in direction was tremendous, and the publishing history of these first two major books contains important clues to the reasons for the shift.

Exactly what persuaded Bliss to offer Twain a contract at all is still conjectural. Twain told Mrs. Fairbanks that his own *Quaker City* letters, published in the *New York Tribune,* had resulted in "several" book offers, but Leon Dickinson's suggestion that an editorial in the *Tribune*—published the same day Bliss wrote his first letter to the humorist—was responsible seems more logical. Bliss's ears would have pricked up at the suggestion, "We are not aware whether Mr. Twain intends giving us a book on this pilgrimage, but we do know that a book written from his own peculiar standpoint, giving an account of the characters and events on board ship and of the scenes which the pilgrims witnessed, would command an almost unprecedented sale." [1] Bliss specified merely "a work of some kind, perhaps compiled from your letters from the East." Twain, when he replied eleven days later, on December 2, 1867, agreed that the *Alta* material, which he may have planned to compile even before he left on the *Quaker City* trip and which he had considered dramatizing a month earlier, would "make a volume that would be more acceptable in many respects than any I could now write." Such a volume would be easier for the humorist to complete, but Twain wanted assurance that even this minimal delay would not damage his journalistic money-making: "I have other propositions for a book, but have doubted the propriety of interfering with good newspaper engagements, except my way as an author could be demonstrated to be plain before me." [2]

Apparently it took almost two months before his way as an author was spelled out in dollars and cents, for until the week of January 24, 1868, when he went to Hartford to "cut the matter short by coming up here for a *talk*," [3] he showed only moderate interest in Bliss's proposition. But he talked over the financial aspects of subscription publication with Albert D. Richardson and Horace Greeley, concluded that the 5 per cent royalty Bliss was offering was worth his trouble, and made a "splendid" contract that he acknowledged in a letter to Bliss on January 27. Not until almost nine months later, long after the manuscript had been turned over to Bliss, was the formal contract signed, but it included one clause that would become important the next summer when Clemens accused Bliss of violating their agreement. The publisher agreed "that the work shall be electrotyped during the next 4 months and be ready to place in the hands of their Agents very early next spring." [4]

Even after he made his contract Twain did not rush into the job of reworking his material. The last of the *Alta* clippings he requested from his mother did not arrive in Washington, D. C., until February 21.[5] On January 30, after apparently doing some figuring on the back of a letter he wrote Will Bowen on January 25,[6] Twain discovered that the job of writing the book was going to involve more than merely revamping the *Alta* letters. Even with the profusion of illustrations typical in the subscription books, the letters would make up only 250 pages. Suddenly his splendid contract became an albatross around his neck. He asked Mrs. Fairbanks for copies of her letters to the *Cleveland Herald* and hoped to get ideas from the *Quaker City* material of Dr. Abraham R. Jackson and Colonel J. H. Foster. By mid-February he had begun writing, and elated with the simplicity of the book-writing he had so wholesomely feared, he decided that the *Alta* letters were so bad he would write the entire volume, provided he did not "get too much pushed for time." Craftsmanship, unity, and structure played no part in his plan: it was the time element, the deadline, that was to determine the course of composition.

Then Joe Goodman, Twain's old crony from *Territorial Enterprise* days, sent word that the *Alta California* had copyrighted the *Quaker City* letters and intended to bring them out in book form. That changed Twain's mind again.

Now, he told Mrs. Fairbanks, Bliss wanted a completely new book "but *that* won't do." [7] The letters that he had not liked the month before were now so integral to the volume that (as Twain told his brother Orion) if the *Alta* published the letters, the new book would never get published. In part, Twain may have thought the printing of his "wretched, slangy letters, unrevised" would ruin him; but to anyone who knows much about his vitriolic temperament, there is another obvious consideration. Hell's furies were little more than social discomforts compared to Mark Twain scorned, and now that the *Alta* had refused permission to use the letters, they became indispensable. And on March 12 Mark Twain left for San Francisco on the *Henry Chauncey.*

His negotiations were successful: the *Alta* waived its right to the letters if Twain would acknowledge and thank the *Alta* for being so generous. He did acknowledge, but as he noted in his *Autobiography* thirty-five years later, he refused to thank.

More important, though, to the completion of the book was Twain's renewing his friendship with Bret Harte. In spite of having counted words and pages a dozen times and of announcing his plans for the composition of the book, before he got to San Francisco Twain usually was talking about his writing in the future tense except when he told Orion that he had completed "the first ten chapters of the sixty or eighty" [8] just before leaving. In his *Autobiography* the humorist recalled having written most of the book, 200,000 words, during two months in California.

Even excepting the lengthy section of new material on France in Chapters X to XV, which may have been written on board the *Henry Chauncey,* since Harte had them in time to put them in the July issue of the *Overland Monthly,* most of the book was written while Twain was in close contact with Harte. Leon Dickinson has provocatively asked, "Did Harte influence Mark Twain in his work of revising the *Alta* letters for publication in book form?" "The point," Dickinson adds,

"cannot be proved," but he suggests that the addition, in
revision, of the passages satirizing Lamartine and Prime
follows a suggestion Harte made in his review of John F.
Smith's *Going to Jericho* in the July *Overland Monthly*.[9] And
since the passage about Prime in *Innocents Abroad* is the first
instance of Twain's habitual method of "padding"—quoting
extensive passages from other authors—the possibility of
Harte's having suggested its use assumes interest not only
for *Innocents Abroad* but also for *Roughing It, A Tramp
Abroad,* and *Life on the Mississippi*.

After the final volcanic explosion between them in 1876,
Twain would hardly have acknowledged Harte's assistance,
but earlier, in November, 1870, he *did* admit to Charles H.
Webb that Harte had taken an editorial hand in the revising of
Twain's manuscript. "Harte read all the MS of the 'Innocents' &
told me what passages, paragraphs & chapters to leave out—& I
followed orders strictly." [10] Twain did not specify just what
the orders were, and his wording suggests that Harte offered
advice only about excisions. But if Twain's claim that Harte
"trimmed and trained and schooled me patiently until he
changed me from an awkward utterer of coarse grotesque-
nesses to a writer" has any relevance to *Innocents Abroad,* then
it seems quite probable that Harte made some of the suggestions he had embodied in a current review to a friend who was
writing a similar kind of book.

The additions to the *Alta* letters exploited at least three
techniques for which Harte might deserve some credit. First of
all, they utilized quotations not only from W. C. Prime's *Tent
Life in the Holy Land* but also from W. H. Neligan's *Rome: Its
Churches, Its Charities, and Its Schools* and C. W. E.'s *Life in
the Holy Land*. Second, the use of these sentimental writers—
and the contrast between their sanctimonious tears and Twain's
dry-eyed realistic vision—provided the first sustained use of
the serious-comic alternation that was to be one of Twain's
most dependable structural methods (and that, admittedly, he

had used earlier in the Mark Twain-Mr. Brown dichotomy in
the Sandwich Islands letters). Finally, a surprisingly large
percentage of the new material was moralistic in its tone.
Twain needed no instruction in preaching; after all, he had
been the "Moralist of the Main" in San Francisco in the
mid-60's. But Harte, who was learning the ingredients in
writing necessary for Eastern approval long before Twain and
who was deprecating the lack of seriousness in contemporary
American humor as early as 1875, might well have suggested
the value of sections ridiculing France, the Héloïse and
Abélard story, Europeanized Americans "who have actually
forgotten their mother-tongue in three months," and the
"Pilgrims."

Whatever the source, Twain began experimenting in *Innocents Abroad* with the various devices which would help him
accumulate the number of pages necessary for a subscription
book. Even with half his total manuscript already available in
the *Quaker City* letters, the job was not an easy one—and it
would become even more difficult when, in later travel books,
he had even less material to begin with. He used his own
notebooks to add matter about the glove purchase in Gibraltar,
the description of his trip through the Zeb Dana Valley, the
story of Joseph, and the speculations on the Nazarenes'
attitude toward Jesus. Much of the material between Gibraltar
and Naples almost surely came from a notebook which was
later lost, and the expository sections on France, Rome, Venice,
Florence, and the Capuchin Convent have the guidebookish
sound of measurements and statistics. From his *Alta* letters of
the spring and summer of 1867, reprinted as *Mark Twain's
Travels with Mr. Brown*, he lifted the anecdote about his stay
at the "Benton House," in reality the Heming House in Keokuk
(from his letter of April 19, 1876), and the quotations about
the early life of Christ from the Apocrypha (from his letter of
June 2). Some of his new material showed Twain's straining:
the handbill and newspaper account of a contest in the

Coliseum, for example, is one spot where the reader senses what Frank Baldanza has called "a flagging of his energies here and there." [11] But at least it was a speedy process. By June 17 Twain had reached Chapter LVIII, manuscript page 2343, and he reported to Mrs. Fairbanks that he expected to have enough extra manuscript to "cut out a vast deal that *ought* to perish. I mean only to *glance* at Spain & the islands of the return voyage." [12] On July 6 he left San Francisco, and on August 1 he presented Elisha Bliss with his manuscript.

But Bliss was in no rush to get it. On July 29 he wrote Twain that there was no need "to press this business unless you wish it"; the company, in the midst of a big campaign to sell Richardson's new biography of U. S. Grant, was in no position to begin the preliminary work on Mark Twain's volume. Whether it was a deliberate delaying move or not, Bliss offered to read the manuscript and volunteer his ideas about alterations to the author. "I mean of course *minor ones* such as arrangements of chapters, styles etc." [13] (One can only guess what Bliss would have called a major alteration.) At any rate, Twain agreed, and it cost him seven months' time. The author bowed to Bliss's chopping out items about Samson, the Jaffa Colony, and Twain's Temperance Society experience.[14] And he agreed to include his oyster shell suppositions which form the basis of Chapter XXXIX in the book.[15] This suggests, incidentally, that part of the manuscript of *Innocents Abroad* (presumably not extant) consisted of the actual *Alta* letters, perhaps pasted to blank pages. Had Clemens rewritten his *Quaker City* letters, Bliss would have had no opportunity to pass judgment on material that Twain had excluded from the revised version. Only if he had made corrections on the letters themselves would Bliss have been able to suggest retaining the "oyster shell" paragraphs. The point becomes important to a consideration of the writing of *Roughing It*.

So from August, 1868, to February, 1869, Clemens heard little about his book and did nothing to assist its publication.

Then, in February Bliss announced, "We are about ready to Electrotype." He had another idea, too. "What do you say," he offered, "to our getting a good *grammarian* and proof *reader here* to revise, that is read and correct proofs? With a permission on your part to cut out a line in an *unimportant paragraph* when needed to make them come out right on the pages." [16] Twain agreed, and then raised a furor two months later when the "infernally unreliable" [17] proofreader ignored Twain's own corrections. The author read proof himself, too, as best he could. In early March he went to Hartford to read with Bliss. Later that month he went to see Livy in Elmira, planning to read proof for the entire book before he left.[18] On March 30 he asked Bliss to send proofs as quickly as possible. But with all this activity, he had reached only page 300 in his correcting by the middle of April. Bliss apologized: "Printers slower than the d——l. I wish I was a type-setter I'd push it." [19] In May Twain went back to Hartford to read the last of the proof, but again he was disappointed; he had read, as he reported back to Livy, "one little trifle of a few pages." [20] Finally, on June 4, he wearily told Mrs. Fairbanks,

> To-day the *last* chapters of the proof came & tomorrow we shall finish reading & be done with the tiresome book forever. I am ever so glad of it, & I do not want another such task like it shortly.—I lost very nearly all my interest in it, long ago. It makes just about 650 or 660 pages, & so is not too bulky, after all.[21]

Ten months from delivery of manuscript to correction of proof, with no indication that Twain was responsible for any of the delay. Combined with the other slowdowns that plagued the book, though, it was to result in Twain's first major altercation with Bliss.

The other delays involved the illustrations and the title for the book. Twain had expected *Innocents Abroad* to issue in March and had publicly announced that date. But on March 13 he had seen proofs of only 80 of the 234 illustrations.[22] In

April and May he commented again on the illustrations, pleased that they were costing $7,000—or so Bliss said.[23] Twain's eye for art—which he knew was bad enough to make humorous hay with in *Innocents Abroad* and *A Tramp Abroad*—was never more myopic. Even if the proof had come in promptly, the illustrations would have caused the publication of the book to be put off.

Twain had first hit on a title for the book back in January, 1868: "The Modern Pilgrim's Progress or Cruise of the *Quaker City*." By October he had changed his mind only slightly. "Not knowing what else to name it," he wrote his California audience, "I have called it 'The New Pilgrim's Progress,' " [24] and in the winter of 1868–1869 Bliss even began advertising the book as *The New Pilgrim's Progress*.[25] Then, just before March 13, 1869, when the mechanics of publication were in full swing, the directors of the company balked at the irreverence of the title. Sidney Drake, president of the company that year, begged to be released from the contract, according to Twain's recollection in his autobiography. They were afraid that people "will shudder at that [title], as at least taking the name of a consecrated book in vain & perhaps burlesquing it, within." [26] And then Bliss stood up and threatened to resign from the company and publish the volume himself should the company refuse to. E. S. House, who claimed he got the story from Charles Dudley Warner, printed a version of Bliss's speech in the *New York Evening Mail* the year of Twain's death.

> "Well, gentlemen," he [Bliss] said, "you have all had an opportunity to express your opinion as to whether or not our company should publish this work, and your collective opinion, based on your individual views, seems to be decidedly against the publication of it. Now that you have had an opportunity to publish this book, and have rejected it, I want to say to you that I shall immediately enter into negotiations with Mark Twain for the purpose of publishing the book on my personal account. . . . I

am willing to risk a considerable amount of my personal means to publish it, for I am satisfied that it will prove a most profitable venture for me." [27]

Perhaps the basic facts of the story are true, though one wonders how the directors of the company could contemplate reneging on a book that was not only legally contracted for but even in the process of having proof pulled. At any rate, Clemens was looking for a new title again in March.

After judiciously rejecting weird titles proffered by Mrs. Fairbanks—"Alonzo & Melissa," "The Loves of the Angels," and "that other rubbish you propose"—he first suggested "The Innocents Abroad, or The New Pilgrim's Progress" as a possibility. On March 30 he sent this title and "The Exodus of the Innocents, or The New Pilgrim's Progress" to Bliss,[28] who thought very little of either. "Keep up a d——l of a thinking & *maybe* (it is about time for them) you will get something better if not either will do," Bliss moaned.[29] Nothing better came along, though, and on April 20 Twain made his choice final.[30]

Bliss had begun setting up the book as the corrected proof came back, rather than waiting for all the proofreading to be finished. In the middle of May Twain told Livy that 20,000 copies of the book were ordered, and three days later he commented that "the printing is proceeding, & the bright, clean pages look handsome." [31] It looked as though the problems had ironed themselves out and the book was ready to appear. And then came the explosion.

Twain, remember, had first expected the book to appear in March, and Bliss had told him in February that "you will see that the spring arrangement has been a good one for you." [32] Then spring slipped by in the rush of preparation, and Twain looked for his book to come out in the summer. But on July 12 Bliss tried to soothe the humorist into not planning on the release of *Innocents* until autumn. "Unfortunately we have been delayed too long to make a summer Book of it—but *unavoidably* we propose to make a fall book of it with every advantage of full preparation & an early start." [33] Twain's reply of July 22, which he remembered fairly accurately in his autobiography, was a masterpiece of ironic sarcasm:

> Mr. Bliss, are you not making a mistake about publishing this year? The book was to have been ready peremptorily just a year ago exactly. Then as it was necessary to make room & a market for Grant's biography, it was judged much better to delay this book of mine a month or two. Then to be up with a rival publisher & make capital out of a rival book, it was thought best to make a *spring* book of mine, in order to give the "Metropolis" a chance. And then in order once more to fight a rival book & a rival house, it was considered best to make mine a *summer* book, & give the "Mississippi" a fresh boost. And now that the further delay of my book will encourage agents to continue to labor for the "Mississippi" (I only just barely suppose this from hearing you tell a new agent he could have my book when issued *if* he would work on the "Mississippi" until that vague & uncertain event transpired) it is deemed best to hold it back & make a *fall* book of it. Do not misunderstand. I am not complaining. I am not contending that there is any occasion for you to comply with that portion of a contract which stipulates that the book shall be issued "early in the spring." I am not pretending that there is a *community* of interest here which would make it improper for you to take the liberty & the responsibility of departing from the letter of a contract in order to subserve your interest without first inquiring for form's sake whether it will be satisfactory all round—or whether it will be equally profitable all round. I am not contending that I am hurt unto death simply because the delay for "Grant" damaged my interests likewise, or because the delay necessary to make me a spring vegetable damaged my interests or because the delay in order to open up the "Mississippi" again damaged my interests; or because the further delay to bail the "Mississippi" dry is *still* damaging my interests. *No. . . .*
>
> All I desire is to be informed from time to time what

future season of the year the publication is postponed to
& why—so I can go on informing my friends intelligently—I mean that infatuated baker's dozen of them
who, faithful unto death, still believe that I *am* going to
publish a book. But, seriously, I object to any further
delay & hereby enter my protest against it. These delays
are too one-sided. Everyone of them has had for its object
the furthering of the Am Pub Co's interest— & to compass
this *my* interests have been entirely disregarded. We
both know what figure the sales were expected to reach if
due & proper diligence were exerted in behalf of the
publication. If that result is not achieved shall you be
prepared to show that your tardiness was not the cause?
& failing this, shall you be prepared to recompense me for
the damage sustained? Those are grave questions. I have
ceased to expect a large sale for a book whose success
depended in a great measure upon its publication while
the public were as yet interested in its subject, but I shall
feel entirely justified in case the sales fall short or
reasonably short of what we originally expected them to
reach. I think you will do me the justice to say that I have
borne these annoying & damaging delays as patiently as
any man whose bread & butter & reputation were at stake
could have borne them. I cannot think that I have been
treated just right.[34]

Bliss's response to the attack was a combination of injured
innocence and violent counterattack. In this, only the first of a
number of head-on collisions, Bliss set a characteristic pattern
in which, unlike Charles Webster and Frank Bliss, and very
much like Mark Twain, he admitted no error in judgment, no
possibility of having been wrong.

The first reply was curt:

Your communication is rec'd. I cannot to day reply to it
as I wish. I will do so in a day or two. In mean time I
have the honor to send you 3 Vols of "The Innocents,"
one for yourself, & one each for the papers in Elmira
which please deliver with extra sheets also—We did not
propose to send to the press until next month for valid
reasons, but we shall send at once, hoping that the effects

may not all be lost by notices appearing at a most
inauspicious time when most people are busy or away
from house—. . . .[35]

Then on August 4, having worked up sufficient steam, Bliss
elaborated:

> I have been intending to reply fully to your last
> letter—but must say, that I could not get myself into the
> right humor for it. I felt very much annoyed & hurt, at
> what was therein written, as I had not dreamed such a
> construction was placed upon what I was doing. . . .
> I will only refer to one statement in yours which was
> that the Book was to be out promptly on the *1st of Aug.
> 1868*—Now you will recollect you arrived in N. Y. from
> Cal. on the 25th of July & only placed the mss. in our
> hands sometime *in Aug.* & therefore you could not
> certainly expect the Book to be published before we had
> the mss. The first delay, was to give time to *illustrate* it
> not to give room for Grant. . . .
> The delay this Spring has been by the great quantity of
> illustrating put in & other causes. You must know that I
> tried hard to get it out early as possible—I did *not sham
> it.* . . . So I don't lay up anything you said—only hope
> you will hereafter, if you want to say such things to me
> again, just come out plain & call me a d——d cheat &
> scoundrel—which will really it seems to me cover the
> whole ground & be a great deal more brief. Now let's let
> the thing drop & *sell the Book.* . . .[36]

It was exactly right. And Twain, who had conceded the
wickedness of his letter, admitted that "perhaps you had very
good reasons for delaying the book till fall which I did not
know anything about."[37] Flushed with the success of the book
and impressed with Bliss's sales techniques, Twain became
unbelievably docile. "I was in Elmira yesterday," he wrote on
August 12, "and saw the book, and my faith in it has all come
back again. It is the handsomest book of the season and you
ought to be proud of your work. . . . I like the circulars, I like
the book, I like you & your style & your business vim, & believe

the chebang will be a success." [38] Nevertheless, ten years later he was to tell Frank Bliss, Elisha's son, that the elder Bliss had delayed *Innocents* in direct violation of their contract in order to publish other books.[39]

Twain, a neophyte still to many of the aspects of subscription publication, was dazzled at the "machinery" of selling.

> What with advertising, establishing agencies, &c., you have got an enormous lot of machinery under way and hard at work in a wonderfully short space of time. It is easy to see, when one travels around, that one must be endowed with a deal of genuine generalship in order to maneuvre a publication whose line of battle stretches from end to end of a great continent, and whose foragers and skirmishers invest every hamlet and besiege every village hidden away in all the vast space between.[40]

Before long, though, the astonished spectator was to appoint himself a general and to differ sharply with Bliss on military strategy. He suggested that Bliss had sent review copies to the newspapers too early,[41] and he proposed to Frank Bliss that the company "issue prospectuses & startling advertisements now while I am stirring the bowels of the communities"[42] on a lecture tour. Bliss, who thought well of the idea of publicizing *Innocents* in conjunction with the author's personal appearances, asked for a list of his New England lecture engagements because "we think we can make use of the knowledge to our mutual benefit,"[43] and even planned to send long advertising material to California "to be there by the *time* you *are*" when Twain contemplated a trip.[44] The humorist used both the Buffalo *Express* and his *Galaxy* column to the book's advantage.[45] He proposed a Mrs. Barstow of Alexandria, Virginia, as an agent.[46] And he concocted, overenthusiastically, a plan for a giant oyster supper to celebrate the sale of the 100,000th copy of *Innocents*.[47]

Whatever other value Twain's help may have had, it at least gave him the first taste of a high-pressure sales campaign

which, with the experience of the coming decade, persuaded
him that he could sell his own books better than anybody else.
As anyone who has read Twain's letters to Charles Webster
knows, plans and strategies were subject to change and
cancellation at a minute's notice, but the difference between
Bliss and Webster was that the earlier publisher trusted his
own business sense and not Twain's.

Consider, for example, Twain's directions during the 1870's
to Bliss about the value of newspaper and magazine publicity.
With *Innocents* he thought it would have been better to delay
sending books to newspapers. But in 1873, he explained the
relative failure of *Roughing It* because of "the original lack of
publicity and notoriety" which was necessary "for a book the
instant it is issued." [48] But in the very same letter he asked Bliss
not to announce *The Gilded Age*. In 1880, then, he thought
that the newspaper publicity had ruined the sales of *The
Gilded Age* and told Bliss "to keep my books strictly out of the
newspapers and we'll find our profit in it." [49] And, finally, in
March, 1881, he told James R. Osgood, his new publisher, that
Bliss had lost half the possible sales of *A Tramp Abroad* by
failing to utilize the newspapers properly.[50] In part, Twain was
plagued with the copyright problem and felt that any excerpts
appearing in newspapers were an intrusion on his rights, but
his vacillations put Bliss in the position of never being right.
Using the newspapers destroyed sales, and not using them
destroyed sales, too. Unsurprisingly, Bliss endured and continued to go his own way in spite of anything Mark Twain
suggested.

Following typical subscription technique, Bliss advertised
for agents for *Innocents Abroad* well in advance of its release.
In the earliest advertisement for the book, on the final page of
The Great Metropolis, Bliss announced that territory would be
awarded to agents on March 1, 1869. The agents had something
of a wait, however, if they planned on taking orders that soon.
The first prospectuses, the indispensable tool of the subscrip-

tion canvasser, were not ready until July 12. As indications of
what Bliss thought would appeal to the audience, as gauges of
his perception of the qualities in Twain that would sell, the
various prospectuses are invaluable. Made up of pages from
the books with advertising notices and order blanks, they
indicate better than anything else the bases of Mark Twain's
popularity.

At first Bliss included pages 19–20, 33–48, 289–304, and
529–44 of the first edition in the prospectus (a copy is at
Yale), so the customer saw a facetious account of the Atlantic
crossing, one on "guide baiting" in Rome, and one of Holy
Land description and burlesque of W. C. Prime. The passages
notably accented fairly low humor and burlesque of sentimentality, highfalutin airs, and erudition. They were Mark
Twain at his most raucously anti-intellectual. The appeal, in
other words, was to the popular reader, and Bliss calculated
with great perception that the average man would rather have
his guidebook laced with humor and iconoclasm than with
piety and a sermon. It is curious how often the American
Publishing Company relied upon ocular images to advertise
Mark Twain. His vision, Bliss was telling his readers in
advertising copy, is *your* vision, not a stuffy literary figure's.
Innocents contained "a description of the Countries, Nations,
Incidents and Adventures, seen and passed through by the
party, as they appeared to the eyes of the AUTHOR, *Differing
materially in several points from* descriptions usually given." [51]
Or again:

> This work is not one of an ordinary nature, traveling
> over paths trodden by hundreds of others, treading with
> greatest care and caution in their very footsteps, and
> seeing only what they saw, praising only what they
> praised, and condemning only what they condemned,
> but the author has here given a new and entirely original
> view of persons, places and things abroad, describing
> them as they appeared to him. . . .
> . . . No one will rise from its reading without having a

better and clearer knowledge of the countries it describes than ever before, and more ability to judge between truth and fiction in what he may read respecting them in the future.[52]

In an advertising broadside Bliss boasted that Twain was "The People's Author as no writer has ever been able so fully to interest all classes and ages."[53]

Significantly, in a later issue of the prospectus Bliss removed pages 19 and 20 and substituted the famous passage on the Sphinx from page 629 of the text and eight pages of reviews of the book and the lecture, "The American Vandal Abroad." Although either Bliss or Clemens might have proposed the addition of the Sphinx passage—it was highly esteemed by contemporary reviewers and readers as an example of "the beautiful and the sublime" that *Innocents* contained—it suggests that by 1872 there was a growing awareness on somebody's part of more "literary" values, of Mark Twain's appeal to an audience who wanted at least a tiny taste of the merits of acceptable, cultivated literature. Since it was in the 1870's, after his marriage to Livy, when Twain became perturbed about his status as a writer, the inclusion of the Sphinx passage might be the first suggestion of Twain's stirring interest in an audience that would not expect him to paint himself striped and turn cartwheels.

The book, at any rate, struck the right note. Among those 1,200 reviews of *Innocents* of which Twain boasted in his Buffalo *Express* column were accolades ranging from the Northern Tier (Pa.) *Gazette* to the Greenport (R. I.) *Republican Watchman*. The thirty-nine reviews reprinted in the 1872 prospectus followed Bliss's line in reviewing the book: its original point of view, its humor, its instruction, and its high moral tone all made it a fine family book, "permanently adapted for home reading aloud, [which] will invariably call up around the fireside a spirit of mirth and congeniality."[54] Twain thought that "the irreverence of the volume appears to

be a tip-top good feature" and Bliss did advertise the book as
"racy" and "spicy," but it was the irreverence that thumbed its
nose at sober "Pilgrims" and sacred shrines that constituted
Innocents' real value to its readers and reviewers.

Bliss and Twain knew the value, too, of exaggerating the
actual sales. Bliss usually exaggerated the popularity of Twain's
books by one-third, and his reports have been the basis of
present-day estimates of the humorist's sales and incomes. Like
contemporary salesmen, Bliss felt there was no danger in
suggesting that a book was a best seller even before it really
was. Twain got the habit, and, as he told Bliss about *Innocents,*
he was smug about "keeping fine large stories afloat about our
sales." [55] In fact, because of these publicity stories, the accounts
of Twain's book sales have been as exaggerated as those of his
death.

On July 20, 1869, Bliss received the first copies of *Innocents*
from his bindery: 68 cloth copies, 60 gilt-edged, 250 Leather
Library, and 25 half-morocco. From then to the end of 1869,
just over 31,500 copies were bound and 1,231 prospectuses
delivered. Twain's statement to Mrs. Fairbanks that "we sell
about as many as $5 apiece as at $3.50" [56] was reasonably
accurate: 16,910 of these copies were in the cloth binding. For
the first three months of 1870 sales averaged about 9,000 copies
a month, but they slowed down to about 3,000 in April. By its
first anniversary, 69,156 copies of *Innocents* had come from the
bindery, and after its birthday, sales dropped down to 1,000
to 1,500 copies a month and sold at that rate for two years. In
November, 1870, sixteen months after publication, copies
bound equaled just over 77,800—not the 85,000 Clemens
reported. [57] At the end of two full years just a few copies under
90,000 had been bound, but it took another full year for sales to
pass the 100,000 mark. From then to the end of the decade,
sales averaged 3,500 copies a year. On December 31, 1879,
125,479 copies had been delivered to the American Publishing
Company: 88,124 of these were plain cloth and the rest the

higher-priced bindings. Bliss had received 2,061 prospectuses, 2,000 of them by July, 1872.

A comparison of these actual statistics with the "fine large stories" of Twain and Bliss shows amazing discrepancies. In 1872 the *Dictionary of American Biography* listed the two-year sale as 100,000, and in 1874 Bliss gave the sales as 150,000. In 1875 Duyckinck's *Cyclopedia of American Literature* claimed that 125,000 of *Innocents* had been marketed in three years. *Appleton's Journal*, on July 4, 1874, gave the five-year sale as a whopping 241,000.

The real test of the book for Mark Twain, though, was the royalty check. The impending decision to write books for a living depended on the kind of living he could make. And there was no reason for disappointment.[58] Extant receipts suggest his own estimate that the book earned him $1,200 to $1,500 monthly [59] was reasonably accurate for the first year or so. On January 31, 1870, Twain received a check for $4,309.42,[60] and there had been at least one earlier payment in November, 1869. On May 1, 1870, he received another royalty statement which came to $3,914.65 [61] and on April 1, 1872, another which totaled $1,220.22.[62] It was an initial success startling enough for Twain to want to duplicate, and almost immediately he began considering the possibilities of another subscription book.

Albert Bigelow Paine has stated that right after the publication of *Innocents Abroad* Twain had not yet made definite plans for a second subscription book, that he still saw newspaper reporting as his major profession and was still committed to a lifetime of journalism.[63] Then, in early July, 1870, according to Paine, it was Bliss who "proposed a book which should relate the author's travels and experiences in the Far West." [64] Actually, Twain had been working long before then toward the book that would become *Roughing It*. As early as October 11, 1869, Twain had responded to an invitation of the New

York Society of California Pioneers with a letter that reminisced about his mining days in Nevada and California. In December he printed a stream of articles in the Buffalo *Express*, articles like "Baker's Cat," "Exorbitant Rates (The Sex on Exhibition)," "Pocket Mining," "Silver Land Nabobs," and others that would be used later in the book. On January 6, 1870, Twain told Mrs. Fairbanks that he was planning to write a book during the coming summer. He received his old files of the *Territorial Enterprise* from his family on March 26. Finally, in May, he told Mrs. Fairbanks, "I doubt if I could do better than rub up old Pacific memories & put them between covers along with some eloquent pictures." In addition, Twain was planning a Noah's Ark book which he expected to be "a lightning-striker" when he got it finished, and a new edition of his sketches "on a different and more 'taking' model" [65] than *The Jumping Frog.*

Finally, as the humorist recalled in his autobiography, immediately after the publication of *Innocents* "proposals were coming in now from several other good houses. One offered fifteen per cent royalty; another offered to give me *all* of the profits and be content with the advertisement which the book would furnish the house." [66] One of the offers was from the *Galaxy*, which wanted him to write a humorous column which the magazine would retain "the privilege of issuing . . . in book form at the end of the year in a $1.50 book . . . & pay me a royalty of 20 cents on each copy sold." [67] Next he reported to Bliss in early May that a Philadelphia subscription house had made him an offer. [68] Just a few weeks later, Appleton's asked him to furnish two-line captions for a book of cartoons. [69] This flirting with other publishers not only struck fear into Bliss's heart; it also meant that in large part Twain's decision to become an author rather than a journalist was fairly concrete as a result of the public acceptance of *Innocents Abroad.*

Bliss took the bait and got Twain's signature on a contract on

July 15, 1870. As a matter of fact, Bliss completed every
agreement he ever made with Twain, three further contracts,
within a few years of the contract for *Roughing It*. The Old
Fox, as Twain once called him, was saddling his star author
with contracts from which it would take Twain a full decade to
unburden himself.

The *Roughing It* contract is interesting for several reasons.
First, it specifies merely "a book upon such subject as may be
agreed upon," [70] not upon Far Western material. To some
extent Twain was still not sure of his subject, but, more
important, he and Bliss were trying to keep the topic a mystery
so that other publishers could not dash off competing volumes.
"The subject of it is a secret," Twain told Orion in July,
"because I may possibly change it. But as it stands, I propose
to do up Nevada and Cal." [71] The contract also stipulated that
Clemens was to publish no book with another publisher until
Roughing It issued, and that clause was to create trouble when
Sheldon published *Mark Twain's (Burlesque) Autobiography
and First Romance* in the spring of 1871. Orion, who was in
Hartford editing *The American Publisher*, reported to his
brother that Bliss was unhappy because Sheldon's book was
going to be published in muslin:

> Against that Bliss protests. He says that makes it a book.
> He will not object to a pamphlet at 30 or 40 cents, but
> does to one at 50¢; and especially to the muslin. He says
> that if you let that be printed in muslin he will not come
> down on you with the contract, but he will always feel
> like you haven't treated him right. His company enjoys
> the prestige of being the sole publisher of Mark Twain,
> which they use with their agents, and the advantage of
> this prestige they will lose if a book of yours comes out by
> somebody else. [72]

Twain was not impressed with the argument, and as if to
underline his indifference, the book not only appeared in cloth
but in a rainbow choice of colors: green, terra cotta, and

purple. A final point was that the contract raised Twain's share from 5 to 7½ per cent of the retail price. Bliss was forced by those competing bids from other houses to increase his royalty, but he chided Twain for even considering the disloyalty of publishing with someone else. Regardless of other bids, Twain explained, "I would merely have asked you to climb along up *as near that figure as you could & make money,* but I wouldn't have asked anything more."

> Whenever you said that you had got up to what was a fair divide between us (there being no *risk*, now, in publishing for me, which there *was,* before,) I should have closed with you on those terms. I have never had the slightest idea of publishing with anybody but you. (I was careful to make no promises to those folks about their bid.)
>
> You see you can't get it out of your head that I am a sort of rascal, but I ain't. I can stick to you just as long as you can stick to me, & give you odds. I made that contract with all my senses about me, & it suits me & I am satisfied with it. If I get only half a chance I will write a book that will sell like fury provided you put pictures enough in it.[78]

It would not be long, however, until this blissful togetherness faded into talk of breach of contract, consultations with lawyers, and plans for the lawsuits that were to destroy the subscription publishing industry in the United States.

On July 15, the date of the contract, Twain wrote Orion that he "began" the book "today," and asked if Orion had "a memorandum of the route we took—or the names of any of the Stations we stopped at? Do you remember any of the scenes, names, incidents or adventures of the coach trip?—for I remember next to *nothing* about the matter." Two weeks later, though, after Orion's memorandum book had arrived, he told his family that he would not begin on the new book for another month. As with *Innocents,* he apparently spent some time collecting, reading, organizing material. "I have got my work ciphered down to *days,*" he wrote his sister in August, "and I haven't a single day to spare between this and the date which, by written contract I am to deliver the M. S. of the book to the publisher [January 1, 1871]." [74] Finally, on September 4, he was able to tell Bliss that in the preceding week he had written the first four chapters of the book and to predict that "it will jump right strait into continental celebrity the first month it is issued." Two weeks later he had reached Chapter VII or VIII and told Bliss, "Am up to page 180—only about 1500 more to write." [75]

Then later that autumn Langdon and Livy both became ill, and complicated plans for his book of sketches and a volume known as the "Riley Diamond Mine" book interrupted Twain's work on *Roughing It*. On January 24, 1871, Twain wrote Bliss about a publishing schedule:

> Orion says you hardly know whether it is good judgment to throw the Sketch Book on the market & interfere with the Innocents. I believe you are more than half right—it is calculated to do more harm than good, no doubt. So if you like the idea, suppose we defer the Sketch Book till the *last*. That is, get out the big California & Plains book first of August, then the Diamond book first March or April 1872—& *then* the Sketch book the following fall. Does that strike you favorably? [76]

Three days later, he decided that he would "write night & day & send you 200 pages of ms every week (of the big book on California, Nevada, & the Plains) & finish it all up the 15th of April if you can without fail *issue* the book on the 15th of May." [77]

The next progress report—on March 10, 1871—announced to Orion that Twain had sent 160 pages of manuscript to be copied and would forward them the next week with a chapter that could be used in *The American Publisher,* Bliss's magazine. He asked Orion to write him "in minute detail" everything Orion could remember about Slade so he could write a chapter which he would also let Orion use in *The American Publisher*.

Orion's reply, a long letter from Hartford on March 11, allows a revealing look at the way Mark Twain worked over factual material for fictional purposes. Orion's account was hesitant, confused, equivocating:

> I don't think we heard of Slade till after we had left Rocky Ridge Station—the last one before reaching South Pass Station where the lands looked so low, where we saw the first snow, and where a spring with waters destined for the Atlantic stood within a man's length (or within sight) of another spring whose waters were about to commence a voyage to the Pacific. There was nothing then in a name to attract us to Slade, and yet I remember something of his appearance while totally forgetting all the others. Perhaps the driver's description caused the difference. We got there (to R R station) about sun up. There were a lot of fellows, young and rough in a room adjoining that in which we sat—if indeed it was not in the same room. They were washing in a pan, joking, laughing and chaffing each other, and kept it up at the table. I don't remember what they said, or anything they said, but I believe the subject was their hostelry and silly trifles. I think Slade got to the table after every body else did, and showed good appetite for the bacon slices, &c. I think he was about your size, if any difference rather shorter and more slender. He had gray eyes, very light straight hair, no beard, and a hard looking face seamed like a man of 60, though otherwise he did not seem over thirty. I think the sides of his face were wrinkled. His face was thin, his nose straight and ordinarily prominent—lips rather thinner than usual—otherwise nothing unusual about his mouth, except that his smile was attractive and his manner pleasant. Nothing peculiar about his voice. It does not leave a pleasant recollection—but I don't know in what respect—it was neither very fine nor very coarse.[78]

Out of Orion's ambiguities, Twain compressed only a sentence or two of physical description:

> He was so friendly and so gentle-spoken that I warmed
> to him in spite of his awful history. . . . And to this
> day I can remember nothing remarkable about Slade ex-
> cept that his face was rather broad across the cheek
> bones, and that the cheek bones were low and the lips
> peculiarly thin and straight.

But Twain also juggled the chronological facts so that the two
Overland passengers heard gory tales of Slade for days before
they actually met him, rather than learning of his history *after*
the breakfast. Thus Twain heightened the humor of the
completely fictional account of the breakfast with Slade and
his terror over accepting the last cup of coffee.

Twain took even broader artistic liberty with the stories
about Slade that Orion could remember. Orion relayed this
anecdote:

> Once Slade had a quarrel with a huge teamster, and in an
> apparent excess of courage dared the latter to fight.
> Whether the teamster had got him "covered" first, or
> whether Slade was afraid of the result on some other
> account, he proposed that each should throw away his
> pistol and fight a fair fist fight. The teamster agreed and
> the pistols were flung one side; but the moment the
> teamster's pistol left his hand Slade sprang for the pistols,
> obtained both and shot the teamster dead.

Twain omitted Orion's equivocations from the account, removing "apparent excess of courage," the two uses of "whether,"
and the "or some other account." He uncluttered the story by
stating simply that Slade "had an angry dispute with one of his
wagon drivers." He proposed definitely that the teamster
"was the quicker artist," and in his version only the driver
threw away his pistol. And thereby Slade, whom Twain was
portraying as a paradoxical "bloody, desperate, kindly-man-
nered, urbane gentleman," was bestowed with a superior ingenuity and cunning. Again, Orion wrote concerning Slade's
capture by some Spaniards:

> Once they got him fastened up in the station by fastning
> the door when he was in mounting guard and giving him
> half an hour to prepare for death. He entreated them to
> permit him to bid farewell to his wife. They finally
> consented that he might send for her by the pony express
> which seems to have come along about the right time.
> She came immediately by horseback and was allowed to
> enter his room. For a wonder he seems to have been
> caught without his arms, and that he only needed a visit
> from his wife to supply the deficiency, for soon after her
> arrival he issued with her from the station, having a pistol
> in each hand, with which he defied his guards, and
> mounting the horse with his wife galloped away.

Twain wisely canceled the opportune pony express and
straightened out the final sentence. More important, he substituted for Orion's unadorned, "she came immediately by
horseback," two sentences: "She was a brave, loving, spirited
woman. She jumped on a horse and rode for life and death."
Twain's version foreshadowed much more appropriately than
Orion's the emotional death scene, which Twain quoted
directly from Dimsdale's *The Vigilantes of Montana*.

The Slade chapters, IX and X, follow immediately the ones
he reported finishing the previous September; this means that
either he made no continuous progress in the interval or that
he had been at work on some other part of his book.
Intriguingly, Twain wrote Bliss a week later that he had "hardly
written a page of manuscript" [79] in the past three months. In
addition, he had written Orion on March 4 that "right in the
first chapter I have got to alter the whole style of one of my
characters and rewrite him clear through to where I am
now." [80]

These various reports create a mystery. As Franklin Rogers
points out, "One would have to assume that between September 19, 1870, and the middle of March, 1871, Twain wrote only
one or two chapters, a maximum of 2,700 words." [81] Professor
Rogers advances the hypothesis that Twain had actually

reached Chapter XIX before he began the revision he started
on March 4, the spot at which he relied most heavily upon
letters written in 1861 and 1862 to the Keokuk, Iowa, *Gate
City*, letters which suggested the tenderfoot-oldtimer per-
sonae that most critics have believed the revision emphasized.
There are some indications, though, that Twain may have been
at work instead, or in addition, on the Sandwich Islands
material that is at the very end of *Roughing It*, a section of that
book that is decidedly inferior and that has been explained
away by most of Twain's apologists as a last-minute straw at
which the humorist clutched in order to fill out the necessary
length.

A number of facts, unconvincing separately, merge to
suggest that Twain had planned to use the Sandwich Islands
letters fairly early and that he was working through them
during the winter of 1870 when he could make no progress on
the earlier chapters of the narrative. First, Twain had already
prepared his Sandwich Islands letters for publication in
acceptable enough form to send to Dick and Fitzgerald in
1867.[82] Next, remember that Twain usually included printed
material in the text when he decided to add from the work of
others or from his own earlier published writing. He probably
included the *Alta California* letters in the manuscript of *Innocents* in some such fashion (see p. 28) and was to paste torn
pages from another's work into *Tom Sawyer* and *Life on the
Mississippi*. Suppose he had the 1867 clippings of Sandwich
Islands letters before him when he calculated the composition
of the book. He would obviously contemplate writing a great
deal less manuscript than the 2,400 pages the earlier book had
required. And all along, he envisioned a book that would
require only 1,500 or so pages of his writing. In September,
1870, he had figured on 1,680 pages; by the following May he
was two-thirds done, with 1,200 pages; and in August, 1871, he
told Livy that he had thought "just a little over 1,500 pages
would be enough."[83] Even the final number of manuscript

pages, 1,830, does not, I think, include the Sandwich Islands section. At the ratio of four manuscript pages to one printed page,[84] these 1,830 pages would have produced just 460 printed pages. The Sandwich Islands letters begin on book page 454.

More suggestive, Clemens mentioned the Liar Sketch, which appeared in Chapter LXXVII of the book, to Orion in a letter on March 4, 1871. The story appeared in the April, 1871, *Galaxy* under the title, "About a Remarkable Stranger, Being a Sandwich Island Reminiscence," and with the explanation that it was "a chapter from the book I am writing." [85] At the very least this shows that Twain was at work in some fashion upon the last chapters of the book at the same time that he was composing the Overland trip section.

Another point, the suggestion that the Sandwich Islands section was among the first manuscript Twain sent Bliss, will be examined later. And further progress reports—for example, his telling Orion in July that he had completed the manuscript to Chapter LVI and would be finished with the book (an additional twenty-two chapters, or over 170 printed pages) in two or three weeks [86]—allow no time for the task of revising the Hawaiian Islands letters.

In one sense the whole question is academic, for whenever Twain decided to add the last chapters, he made a mistake. Structurally, they do violence to the first half of the book with its theme of the initiation of the tenderfoot into Western society. But criticism has implied that the sin belonged more to the American Publishing Company than to Twain. Because they were appropriated at the last minute to fill out the necessary subscription volume, critics say, the last chapters ought to be dismissed as not really a part of the book. One popular paperback series has even printed *Roughing It* without the Sandwich Islands material. If, however, the suggestion that their inclusion was a fairly early idea of Twain's is correct, then, for once, Bliss does not deserve the blame. Twain's development as a literary craftsman, so far as evidence shows, had not refined itself by the writing of *Roughing It* to the point that he saw the Overland trip as art and the Sandwich Islands material as filler; he even wistfully hoped that he had enough manuscript to omit not the Hawaiian Islands chapters, but instead, the Overland material.[87]

Whatever he had done by March, it was not enough to encourage Twain, but in the next few months he made several significant decisions that not only helped the writing of *Roughing It* but also committed him even further to his career as an author. In a series of symbolic gestures he cut himself loose from his "Memoranda" column in the *Galaxy* in April, sold out his interest in the Buffalo *Express*, and waged a battle royal with Bliss and Orion about his duties as newspaper contributor to *The American Publisher*. Orion had been taken on as editor of the journal, little more than an advertisement for Bliss's books with excerpts from current publications and advertisements for agents, in order to keep Twain from "deserting to other publishers; &, 2d, get an occasional article out of me for the paper." [88] Twain had even had first chance at the job of editor, but turned Bliss down. In January Orion had conveyed Bliss's offer of $5,000 for Twain "to write exclusively for this paper, if you will give him all your books, which he thinks you ought to do—let him do all your publishing, and just write books and for the paper. He wants you to write something on insurance for the next paper and he will pay you for it." [89] In March Twain asked Orion, "Now do try and leave me clear out of the Publisher for the present, for I am endangering my reputation by writing *too much*—I want to get out of the public view for a while." [90] On March 11, after getting yet another request for material, he wrote Orion a savage letter, demanding that Orion and Bliss stop insisting on new material:

> I have never tried to crowd the Company—but here the Co. is trying to crowd *me*.

I will never enter into even the most trifling business agreement hereafter without having it in writing with a revenue stamp on it. . . .

Drop all advertisements about my writing *"exclusively"* for the Publisher, for I want no manacles on me. And put this paragraph in prominently:

Correction

An item has appeared in several of the papers to the effect that I am to write *regularly* for the Publisher. It would be wrong to let this error go uncorrected. I only propose to write occasionally—nothing more. I shall doubtless appear less frequently than any other contributor.

MARK TWAIN

With amazing judiciousness, Twain left the letter for two days before he mailed it, just to see if his anger would cool. But in the postscript it was obvious that he needed more than two days to survive being ordered to publish in Bliss's magazine. He launched into Orion again:

. . . Now *why* did you suppose I would appear *constantly* in the Publisher under a mere vague understanding that I was to be *paid* for it? (for I *never* promised it.)

Is it because I am under obligations to the American Publishing Co.? To decide that, it will be necessary to *examine the accounts and see which of us has made the most money out of the other.*[01]

Orion gave Elisha the letter, as Twain no doubt knew he would, and Bliss dashed off another of those remarkable letters that succeeded in keeping Twain in line for an entire decade. This one was twelve pages long:

Friend Clemens. Your brother has handed me your letter. I cannot conceive what we have done to draw your fire so strongly. . . . You say in yours *"drop all advertisements about my writing exclusively for the Publisher."* Will you do me the favor to say whether you have seen any

advertisements of ours to that effect? We have
never . . . hinted or said such a thing that we are aware
of: Again you say *"Say nothing more about my appearing
in the paper on any other footing than occasional like the
other authors."* Have you ever seen anything from us that
has placed you in any difficult position. . . . In any advt
or card issued by us your name has appeared *with the
others* & nothing said specifically about you.[92]

A few days later, Twain relented slightly and told Bliss "The
Pony Express" selection from *Roughing It* could appear in the
magazine. Since it was "by all odds . . . the finest piece of
writing I ever did," Twain wanted to be sure it was credited as
from his new book. He told Bliss to look it up "from along
about the 16oth to 170th page of the MS." [93]

Bliss made the mistake of pressuring again in April, suggesting that further chapters from the book would "whet the
people's appetite for more of the same," but Twain threatened
the conspirators "my wife will read my Hartford letters & if
they are of the same nature, keep them out of my hands." The
threats apparently worked, and Bliss and Orion had to content
themselves with mainly secondhand material. With two exceptions, further chapters from *Roughing It* appeared in the
magazine only after the book issued.[94]

By early April, Twain, with manuscript complete to Chapter
XXV, found he had to call on Orion again for help:

In moving from Buffalo here I have lost certain notes &
documents—among them what you wrote for me about
the difficulties of opening up the Territorial government
in Nevada & getting the machinery running. And now
just at the moment that I want it, it is gone. . . . Have
you time to scribble something again to aid my memory.[95]

Work was galloping along, aided by the inspiration of Joe
Goodman, Twain's old editor on the *Territorial Enterprise,*
who served as a catalyst during April. Twain was so pleased
with his progress that he completely abandoned his plan to go

back to the beginning of the book and revise it. Whatever his intention may have been—and critics have built up strong conjectural cases—the fact is that Mark Twain *never* returned to the opening chapters to rework his material. He did *not* alter a character to fit an initiation motif. For on April 8, he wrote Orion an extremely important letter: "Tell Bliss to go ahead & set up the MSS & put the engravers to work. My copy is down at the house & I am up here at the farm." Later in the same letter he repeated the instructions: "Tell Bliss to go ahead setting up the book just as it is." In the first place, Bliss already had a large segment of manuscript—through Chapter VIII. Twain had told Bliss earlier to look up "The Pony Express" in the manuscript, and in the present letter he gave Orion instructions about "Bemis and the Bull" ("It don't altogether suit me, but I shall alter it *very little,* anyway"), and the Jack and Moses anecdote:

> *Leave out* the yarn about Jack & "Moses." It occurs about 117th page. Close the chapter with these words "and when they tried to teach a subordinate anything that subordinate generally "got it through his head"—at least in time for the funeral.

Even more specifically though, he commented, "I am to the 570th page & booming along. And what I am writing now is so much better than the opening chapters, or the Innocents Abroad, that I do *wish* I could spare time to re-vamp the opening chapters, & even write some of them over." A postscript to the letter announced progress to page 610.[96] In short, Twain chose to pile up pages rather than to take time to carry out his intended revision, but the theme of tenderfoot-oldtimer must have been present all along and not an afterthought which credits Twain with conscious revision of a high order.

Toward the end of April though, the inspiration died out. Twain, who was so discouraged that he told Mrs. Fairbanks he was working but convinced that the book would fail, had reached only page 750 by April 30 (after piling up from page 160 to 610 in a month's time while Goodman was visiting). He thought *Roughing It* would be a "tolerable success." Four days later he figured he was half done, and by the middle of May he had 1,200 pages of manuscript, "enough . . . to make (allowing for engravings) about 400 pages of the book—consequently am two-thirds done." [97]

Again in June the task began to drag, forcing Twain to cancel a trip to Cleveland to visit the Fairbankses. "This book has been dragging along just 12 months, now, & I am *so* sick & tired of it. If I were to chance another break or another move before I finish it I fear I never *should* get it done." [98] Even when Bliss made public announcement in July that he had "in hand manuscript for a new book by Mark Twain, . . . a lively account of travel and a stirring recital of adventures in the Far West," [99] the book was not finished. On July 2 the bedeviled author was finishing Chapter LVI and planned to be through in a few weeks. [100] But even as late as August he wrote a chapter (probably XLVI, XLVII, or LIII) to be inserted in "the middle of the book," [101] and was at work on the revision of his 1,830 manuscript pages, discouraged because he could not leave out all of the Overland trip. The book was substantially complete, except for the rewriting of Chapter XX. One of Bliss's subordinates lost the original manuscript of the chapter; Clemens said in October that it would take him two weeks to rewrite it because he could "remember the heavy work it was to write it before and I wish that man had the ms stuffed into his bowels that lost it." [102] At about the same time, he wrote Horace Greeley to ask if the Hank Monk story were true, so perhaps he appropriated that old anecdote to fill out the lost chapter. [103] On October 3 Orion told his wife that Twain's "book is just going into the printer's hands," and as early as the end of October Twain, on a lecture tour stopover in Milford, Massachusetts, wrote Livy, puzzled because he had received no proof from Bliss. [104]

In writing *Roughing It* Mark Twain continued to utilize the methods of composition that had served to expand the *Alta* letters into *Innocents Abroad*. From his own earlier material he appropriated the Sandwich Islands letters, the "Moses Who?" story supposedly from his Holy Land notebook, and the anecdote of "Jim Townsend's Tunnel" from an *Alta* letter. In addition to the Buffalo *Express* articles from the winter of 1869–1870, he dredged up and included eight *Territorial Enterprise* articles for verisimilitude and description. Most of the old clippings were expository—reports of shootings (Chapter XLIX), statistics on silver mining (Chapters LII and LVII), and descriptions of a caved mine (Chapter LII) and of the Chinese section of Virginia City (Chapter LIV). But one *Enterprise* article, "Concerning a Frightful Assassination that Was Never Consummated," by an old friend of Twain's, Conrad Weigand, went into an appendix at the end of the book. The place Twain chose to put this particular abortive attempt at humor is significant. For the first time, in *Roughing It* he employed the appendix as a means of padding out a travel volume, and until *Following the Equator* he was to use the technique in all the travel narratives. It was especially convenient, because it removed the toilsome burden of trying to work the material into the context of the main narrative.

Twain used a paragraph from the *New York Times* describing a fifteen-hour, three-hundred-mile train ride from Omaha to the North Platte (Chapter IV). He took a long passage from Dimsdale's *The Vigilantes of Montana* with acknowledgment, but he paraphrased a lot of Dimsdale's material and even transcribed one passage verbatim without citing his source. He borrowed from the Mormon Bible in Chapter XVI, quoting several long passages with a running humorous commentary on the language, style, and syntax of the book. Finally, he found Mrs. Catherine V. Waite's *The Mormon Prophet and His Harem* useful in a couple of places. For his first two appendixes he paraphrased facts from her first chapter and quoted directly her description of the Mountain Meadows massacre.

It was while he was writing *Roughing It,* then, that Twain first faced the rigors of writing a book for a subscription audience. He had no *Alta* letters to rely on for half a book, and even though Orion's memorandum book may have helped in writing the first twenty-one chapters, and the Sandwich Islands letters gave him 30,000 words of material for the final chapters, "Mark Twain . . . was for the first time trying his hand at inventing a long narrative." [105] Consequently, the book was studded with anecdotes, especially the Overland trip section with the tales of Bemis and the Bull, the Slade breakfast, the coyote passage, the Hank Monk-Horace Greeley yarn, and the "Moses Who?" tale. The separate material written late in 1869 and early in 1870 provided most of the interest in the first section of the book, but Twain, obviously finding it difficult to get from anecdote to anecdote, marred the middle part with the clippings from the *Enterprise* and the descriptions of the intricacies of mining. Finally, his Sandwich Islands letters, whether they were revised early or late in the course of composition of the book, provided a relatively long section of varied material. Even here, though, he added three anecdotal chapters, on the Admiral (Chapter LXII), Horace Greeley's letter (Chapter LXX), and the Liar Sketch (Chapter LXXVII). And he finished the book with two "tales," of his first lecture and the fake robbery. Whether he consciously composed the early anecdotes of 1869 and 1870 to serve the dual function of separate publication and inclusion in his book, he must have noted the facility of writing with the earlier "sketches" available.

Roughing It was therefore an anomaly. Since many of the anecdotes were written earlier than the narrative plank, they were fresher, more ably constructed, and less obviously strained than most of the anecdotes in *Innocents Abroad.* But they were used in the book with less precision. In *Innocents,* since Twain had a complete narrative written beforehand, he could add material selectively. He could manipulate his desultory material methodically and with a certain amount of precision. In *Roughing It*, with the agonies of sustained composition always before him, he relied on so many from his available reservoir of sketches in the first half of the book that the second half lost both coherence and variety. And in his travel narratives from *Roughing It* on, except for *Following the Equator*, Twain was to work in the same manner—compiling sketches, tales, and anecdotes to string onto a slender narrative thread—and to fail to solve the problem of having enough of this material to carry the books, *A Tramp Abroad* and *Life on the Mississippi*, to completion.

Even though Bliss had been supervising the mechanics of publication ever since he got the first batch of *Roughing It* manuscript from Twain, there were still niggling delays of the sort that plagued *Innocents*. The first publication date had been set for August, 1871, and then it was moved up to March, 1871. Next, Twain wanted Bliss to issue the book by May 15, and ultimately it would not appear until January 30, 1872.

As with *Innocents*, there was a problem with the title. When Mrs. Fairbanks asked what the name of the book was to be, Twain replied, "My book is not named yet. Have to write it first—you wouldn't make a garment for an animal till you had seen the animal, would you?" [106] In July, 1871, Bliss asked the same question. "What is to be the title—This is a matter of some importance you know & necessary for the Prospectus unless we say we don't know it yet & call it the '*Unnamed*' & wait for developments to christen it." Finally, according to Paine, it was Bliss himself who gave the book its name. [107]

Work on the illustrations began shortly before July 4, 1871, when Orion wrote:

> Some of the artists' drafts for the pictures have come. I told Frank to take the tree out of Carson and put the auctioneer on the horse. He said he would take the tree

out, but people here wouldn't understand the idea of an
auctioneer on a horse. Another has him taking his rider
over a pile of telegraph poles—another bucking—and
another going through a gate, raking his rider off the top
beam. He is a ragged looking horse.[108]

On December 6, 1871, the illustrations were not yet finished;
Bliss complained that he had "set up to page 300 but plates not
finished of yet. They are finishing as we have begun to print.
We are kept back by here and there a cut not yet done." [109]
Perhaps the delay at this late date made it necessary for Bliss
to borrow illustrations from other American Publishing Company books, but this was a habitual practice with Bliss. In
Roughing It Bliss used pictures from at least two other books,
Thomas W. Knox's *Overland through Asia* (1870) and Albert
D. Richardson's *Beyond the Mississippi* (1869). From these
two books alone there were seventeen illustrations that showed
up in Twain's book either unaltered or changed only slightly,
and it is more than likely that other cuts were patched up in
order to fit into the context of *Roughing It.*[110]

With the printing begun in December and the title page
deposited in the Library of Congress on December 6, *Roughing
It* was almost ready to be sold. On January 30, 1872, Bliss's
bindery sent out the first copies, 52 Leather Library volumes.
The next day 252 cloth copies and 404 prospectuses arrived at
149 Asylum Street, and the campaign was on.

Back in May, 1871, the Washington, D. C., *National Republican* announced that Mark Twain "so far from proposing to
retire from the literary field, contemplates the publication of a
fresh volume, similar in size and style to the 'Innocents
Abroad.' " [111] The squib was picked up and carried in other
papers, as was the announcement in *The American Publisher*
in July: "The American Publishing Company of Hartford, has
in hand manuscript for a new book by Mark Twain. It is a
lively account of travel and a stirring recital of adventures in
the Far West. He was a miner and reporter, and had some

experiences, which, though sober reality, will tax credulity." [112] These announcements at least told the public that a new Mark Twain book was on the way.

The humorist assisted in the sales in a number of ways. By allowing Bliss to print sections of the book in *The American Publisher*, he whetted the people's appetite—or at least the appetites of those who read the 5,000 papers on the exchange list of the *Publisher*.[113] His lecture on *Roughing It*, first presented the day after Bliss wrote that printing had begun, and offered until February, 1872, undoubtedly helped, too. Twain was also instrumental in having H. H. Bancroft removed as the West Coast general agent for his books and A. Roman entered as a substitute. Bancroft, who had acted as general agent for *Innocents*, had refused to send a review copy to Harte for the *Overland Monthly*, and when he wrote asking Twain to help him get the agency for *Roughing It*, Twain declined.[114]

Most important, though, was his help in the preparation of the prospectus. He explained to Bliss in January, 1871, that "my popularity is booming, now & we ought to take the biggest advantage of it," but Bliss replied in April that he did "not think there is as much of a claim to see another book from you as there was 3 months ago. Then anything offered would sell—people would subscribe to anything of yours without . . . looking at it much. Now they will inspect a Prospectus closer & buy more on the strength of *it*." [115] So Clemens was persuaded to offer constant advice and assistance in the matter of choosing selections. He proposed the Bemis and the Bull story, the Slade chapters, and an unspecified chapter at page 750 of the manuscript for the dummy.[116] Then he decided that he would select the prospectus chapters himself, but by May he was too thoroughly interested in his work to go to Hartford with the sample chapters. Bliss replied on May 17,

> I think it would be well to have Prospectus out *soon as practicable* as agents are anxious for it. . . . I have no

doubt you have ample matter now to select from.
Therefore suppose you do as you suggest. Send another
batch on of *selected* chapters if you think best & I will get
right to work—Suppose you send on such a lot marked
with what in your opinion is particularly good & let me
then make up prospectus matter from it and get engraving for it underway.[117]

A month later Twain was jubilant about the magic charm the
agents' dummy was going to have. As he told Orion, "When the
prospectus is out I believe Bliss will sell 50,000 copies before
the book need be actually issued." [118] And later in the year he
told Livy,

I think Bliss has gotten up the prospectus book with taste
& skill. The selections are good, & judiciously arranged.
He had a world of good matter to select from, though.
This is a better book than the Innocents, & *much* better
written. If the subject were less hackneyed it would be a
great success.[119]

Interestingly, the matter that Bliss selected from the chapters
Twain had sent him was almost all from the Overland trip
narrative and the Sandwich Islands letters.

From the Overland trip Bliss chose the first two chapters (he
had told Twain earlier, "Your first chap. is *splendid* smacks of
the old style"),[120] the description of the jack rabbit, some of the
Bemis and the Bull story, the description of the pony express,
some of the Slade selection, the description of South Pass, all of
Chapter XV satirizing Mormons, and the tarantula anecdote.
From the rest of the book, selections illustrated the fire at
Tahoe, the Mexican Plug story, "Colonel Jack and Colonel
Jim," "The Aged Pilot Man," a selection of Sandwich Islands
description, and the "First Lecture."

Actually there are two states of the prospectus, an earlier
version, a copy of which is at Yale, and a later one, a copy of
which is in the Mark Twain Papers. Basically, the contents of
both issues are the same, though the order is slightly changed.

But the pagination of the two copies suggests Twain's progress in composing the narrative. In both prospectuses the material is from four sections of the book: pages 19–183 (The Overland Trip), 325–28 ("Colonel Jack and Colonel Jim"), 369–75 ("The Aged Pilot Man"), and 544–63 (Sandwich Islands and "First Lecture"). "Colonel Jack and Colonel Jim" had been written in 1869 and appeared in the Buffalo *Express* on January 8, 1870, under the title, "Silver Land Nabobs." According to Twain "The Aged Pilot Man" had been written in Nevada. In other words, if Twain took up Bliss's suggestion and sent along chapters for the prospectus in May, 1871, he chose consecutive narrative up to page 183, two sections of separate material that he planned to include somehow in the book, and the Sandwich Islands material. This suggests, once more, that the Hawaiian Islands letters were available at a fairly early period in the composition. More significant, in the Morse prospectus Bliss was unable to assign page numbers to the material beyond page 102. All later selections are either not numbered or have code numbers, "22–5," "16–2 to 16–8," and "1–73 to 3–73," for example. This can mean only one thing: when Bliss first chose prospectus material, he knew that only through page 102 was Twain's book in its final form. From there on, the material still needed to be worked into a unified narrative, so Bliss attempted to judge roughly the position of the material with the code numbers. For example, "22–5" meant the fifth page of the twenty-second chapter (actually page 166, the tenth of Chapter XXI); "1–73–3–73" signified the first three pages of Chapter LXXIII (really pages 544–46, the first three pages of Chapter LXXVI).

The later prospectus corrected the speculations in the earlier ones as far as possible—in other words, for as far along as Twain had shaped his manuscript in final form. The code numbers for chapters "17," "22," "24," "16," and "25" were replaced in the pagination with accurate page numbers for material that finally appeared in Chapters XVI, XXI, XXIII,

XV, and XXIV, respectively. Correct paging now went through page 375, but Bliss could not yet assign pagination to the Sandwich Islands matter, because even when the later prospectus was printed (undoubtedly from page proofs), Twain had not completed the manuscript. The prospectuses thus become important bibliographical evidence, and the Morse prospectus especially lends support to the theory that Twain did not appropriate the Sandwich Islands letters at the last moment to fill out his book.

The advertising pages in the prospectus attempted to link *Roughing It* to *Innocents Abroad* by suggesting that it, too, presented material from a fresh viewpoint. In a passage humorous in its own right, the prospectus proclaimed:

> Mark Twain's new book, Roughing It is a companion volume to The Innocents Abroad, and like it is filled with descriptions of people and things seen by the author himself, with his own eyes, which differ in some respects from those of others; related in his own style, which if in no other way meritorious, is at least an original one.
> It is suited to the wants of the old, the young, the rich, the poor, the sad, and the gay. "There is a time to laugh," and those who buy this book, will see clearly that the time has arrived.

Assuming that it was the author's descriptions and not his eyes to which the prospectus was calling attention, this was an attempt to suggest that the same freshly irreverent spirit which permeated *Innocents* was also an important feature of the new volume. Twain's deflating treatment of "the noble red man," for instance, was undoubtedly considered identical in tone to his treatment of the Old Masters. The copywriter for the prospectus (probably Bliss) was also aware of the book's historical character. *Roughing It,* he suggested,

> will be found to contain not only matter of an amusing character, but to be a valuable and correct history of an intensely interesting period.

> Recording facts and statistics relating to one of the most eventful periods of our nation's history, this volume will most worthily fill a place on the historical shelf of the library, hitherto void.

A contemporary estimate of the book which present-day critics frequently echo!

A year after *Roughing It* issued, Bliss continued to advertise it, capitalizing on Twain's delivery of the Sandwich Islands lecture in February, 1873, and on the play, "Roughing It." In *The American Monthly: A Mirror of the Age*, the short-lived, three-issue successor to *The American Publisher*, Bliss proclaimed

> "Roughing It" has been dramatized, and is playing at the Broadway Theater, New York. Steinway Hall overflows night after night to hear Twain's lecture on the Sandwich Island, which is embodied in "Roughing It," and the whole world is laughing over what they read and hear from him.[121]

Bliss apparently felt that this urban acceptance of *Roughing It* would be a sales point for rural buyers.

The first full month of sales looked well for *Roughing It*. By the end of February, 1872, 10,855 copies were bound, and Bliss needed 15,000 a month in March and April. At the end of May 46,122 copies had been sold (not the 62,000 that Twain reported to Howells), and two months later the figure had risen to 59,297 (not the 73,000 reported by the *Chicago Tribune* on July 21). But sales plummeted to around 1,000 a month, and at the end of one full year totaled 65,376. At the end of October, 1874, when Bliss enthusiastically announced the sales as 110,000, they had actually dropped to a few hundred a month, and the total demand had been just over 76,000 copies. At the end of 1879 *Roughing It* had sold 96,083 copies: 68,436 cloth, 2,066 gilt-edge, 23,831 Leather Library, 1,710 half-morocco, and 40 in other special bindings. Bliss had needed 1,637 prospectuses.

Though Mark Twain exaggerated his sales to the public, the humorist admitted his disappointment to Bliss. On receiving a royalty payment from Bliss, he mused:

> So Roughing It sells less than twice as many in a quarter as Innocents, a book which is getting gray with age. The fault is mainly in the engravings & paper, I think.—That, & the original lack of publicity. I believe I have learned, now, that if one don't secure publicity & notoriety for a book the instant it is issued, no amount of hard work & faithful advertising can accomplish it later on. When we look at what Roughing It sold in the first 3 & 6 months, we naturally argue that it would have sold full 3 times as many if it had gotten the prompt & early journalistic boost and notoriety that Innocents had.[122]

In part, Twain was still grumbling about a *New York Tribune* review of *Roughing It* by a man who, according to Twain's taste, anyhow, was as incompetent to review a book of humor as "Josh Billings to write a critique on the Iliad." [123] But in placing the primary blame on the quality of the paper and the illustrations, Twain was pouring salt into a wound that Orion had opened a month after *Roughing It* was published.

Orion discovered soon after he became editor of *The American Publisher* that Bliss expected him to do a considerable amount of office-boy work, addressing wrappers for the magazine and running after proof instead of "walking to think in the fresh air and [staying] at home after meals to polish up what I had written." [124] Unhappy with these "girlish duties," Orion either quit or was fired in March, 1872, and the same month he wrote a letter to Twain, making allegations about the manufacture of *Roughing It*. Twain's reply—Orion's letter apparently does not survive—made it clear that Orion had savagely attacked his former boss: "I cannot let you think that I overlook or underestimate the brotherly goodness & kindness of your motive in your assault on Bliss." [125] But he suggested that Orion's accusations were indefensible just the same. Even so, Orion succeeded in making Twain suspicious that he was being cheated—a fairly easy suspicion to arouse in the humorist.

Twain had made his contract with Bliss with the understanding that his share represented half the profits on the book—profits figured after the costs of printing, illustrating, engraving, and binding—and Orion's letter caused him some worry. He finally went in to see Bliss and came away—so he told Bliss—convinced that the contract was being fulfilled, that 7½ per cent of the price was the equivalent of half of the profits:

> The more I think over our last Tuesday's talk about my copyright or royalty, the better I am satisfied. But I *was* troubled a good deal, when I went there, for I had worried myself pretty well into the impression that I was getting a smaller ratio of this book's profits than the spirit of our contract had authorized me to promise myself; indeed, I was so nearly convinced of it that if you had not been so patient with my perplexities & taken the pains to show me by facts & figures & arguments that my present royalty gives me fully half & possibly even more than half the net profits of the book, I would probably have come to the settled conviction that such was not the case, & then I should have been dissatisfied. I am glad you convinced me, for I would be sorry indeed to have come away from your house feeling that I had put such entire trust & confidence in you to finally lose by it. But everything is plain & open, now. After thinking it over, I feel that, the result being the same, you will readily assent to the altering of our contract in such a way that it shall express that I am to receive half the profits.[126]

But Bliss did not alter the old contracts, and even if Twain had a temporary assurance of the honesty of his publisher, the misgivings returned. So, as he told the story a few years later to Charles H. Webb, he went to see his lawyer:

> My contract on "Roughing It" was strongly drawn, but when 90,000 copies had been sold I came to the conclu-

sion that an assertion of Bliss's which had induced me to submit to a lower royalty than I had at first demanded, was an untruth. I was going to law about it; but after my lawyer (an old personal friend & the best lawyer in Hartford) [Charles Perkins] had heard me through, he remarked that Bliss's assertion being only verbal & not part of a written understanding, my case was weak—so he advised me to leave the law alone—& charged me $250 for it.[127]

Then Orion, who made a habit of being helpful, found out about Twain's conference with Perkins and offered his own legal strategy: Twain should exercise his rights and break his contracts (contracts Twain had already signed for future books), and gather testimony in preparation for a trial.

Imagine the effect . . . on Bliss when he finds Hinckley [Bliss's bookkeeper] subpoenaed to testify as to borrowed engravings, the amount of paper received from the paper mill for Roughing It; the testimony of the paper man as to its quality; of the Churchman pressman as to the country newspaper style of printing the cuts, &c of the binder as to the quality of the binding, and how many he bound so. Bliss can see then that there is only needed to be added the testimony of some prominent engravers, book-binders, and book publishers in the trade, at Boston and New York, to overwhelm with devastating ruin the subscription business and the American Publishing Company in particular—besides inevitably beating them if they should sue your case would be one of the *causes celebre.* It would be seized upon with keen relish by newspapers favorable to the trade, and the testimony published. All this Bliss must foresee when he sees the course indicated as soon as an excuse offers to "perpetuate the testimony" of—say Hinckley. This indirect quiet threat would be so terrible that he would never bring a suit against you if you simply went quietly along and wrote your next book which you have contracted with him to publish, and put it into the hands of somebody else to publish just as if you had never made any contract at all with Bliss to publish it.[128]

Orion very probably knew his facts; at least, the seventeen illustrations from *Overland through Asia* and *Beyond the Mississippi* substantiate his charges of borrowed engravings. What apparently happened was that Bliss used two sets of books with *Roughing It,* one of which exaggerated the cost of paper, binding, and illustrating, and thus persuaded the author that there was a much smaller profit to divide in half than there actually was. Twain did not follow up Orion's suggestion, perhaps because he realized that even if he was not receiving half-profits he was making more on his books than any of his literary friends were receiving from trade publication. Nevertheless, he began looking for another publisher, and except for *The Gilded Age,* he never made another contract with Bliss after Orion warned him of the double-dealing of "the Old Fox."

Roughing It was a success, then, and the writing and publishing of it and *Innocents* were instrumental in the humorist's shift from journalism to literature. They persuaded him not only that he could make a living out of "book writing," but also that, publishing by subscription at least, he could reach an audience for whom his talents were admirably suited. By May, 1872, he claimed he had made $25,000 from *Innocents* and $10,500 from *Roughing It,*[129] an auspicious beginning. More important, he began to make comparative judgments. If *Roughing It* had been a more difficult book to write, it was the better volume. "I am at last easy & comfortable," he told Bliss,

> about the new book. I have sufficient testimony, derived through many people's statements to my friends, to about satisfy me that the general verdict gives "Roughing It" the preference over "Innocents Abroad." This is rather gratifying than otherwise. The *reason* given is, that they like a book about America because they understand it better. It is pleasant to believe this, because it isn't a great deal of trouble to write books about one's own country.[130]

Perhaps Twain had forgotten that *Roughing It* had been much more difficult to compose than *Innocents,* but even more significant, perhaps he was becoming aware this early of his unique position as recorder and interpreter of the nineteenth-century American common man. His offhand comment to Bliss casts shadows, in other words, on *Tom, Huck, Life on the Mississippi, The Connecticut Yankee, Pudd'nhead Wilson,* and all the qualities that Howells summed up as making Twain the Lincoln of our literature.

CHAPTER III

A LOT OF CIPHERING

*B*ETWEEN 1868 and 1873 Mark Twain's life changed its
course significantly. He and Livy settled down more or less
permanently in the Nook Farm community of Hartford, first in
the house he rented from John Hooker for $100 a month, and
after April, 1874, in the big gingerbread house whose architec-
ture somehow matched Twain's own piebald personality. The
match he made with the Langdons was not just respectable,
but startlingly impressive. And when Livy's father bought the
young couple the house in Buffalo, Mark Twain had his first
permanent address since he left Hannibal. Then the move up
to Hartford constituted a young Captain Stormfield's entering
Heaven.

New England represented, to at least one facet of Twain's
mind, a kind of Parnassus; if its people accepted him as one of
them, it signified that they saw something important, durable,
and maybe even "elevating" about his literature. The present-
day reader can only blush with embarrassment at Twain's

humility before some of the all-but-forgotten patriarchs of
decaying Brahminical New England. His letters back home
and to Orion and Mollie, who preceded him into the Genteel
Tradition's valley of death, reflect a mixture of reverential awe
and flattered vanity. Except for a few who disapproved of his
incessant smoking and thought his gait and his drawl could
only mean he was drunk, they liked him, accepted him, even
invited him into their homes. The Wild Humorist of the Pacific
Slope began to edge—sideways, to be sure—into the area of
(capital L) Literature. It was his special version of the Great
Unknown, and Literature never ceased to confuse and frustrate
his genius, to be a no man's land where he wandered, guided in
part by the precepts of his neighbors and in part by the
contradictory suggestions of his own magnificent instinct.

Thus he faced the publication of *The Gilded Age* with fear,
because "when a man starts out in a new role, the public
always says he is a fool and won't succeed"; he spoke of *Tom
Sawyer* as an experiment, told Howells in 1879 that he lacked
the faculty to write a novel, and even in 1884 referred to *Huck*
as "my last experiment." [1] In other words, though Nook Farm
could accept Mark Twain without more than a slight flinching,
as Kenneth Andrews has convincingly shown, Mark Twain was
unsure what his function as an accepted member of the elite
was, or how Literature should look, or how an Author should
act. He endured Mrs. Aldrich's ungracious insults, was rankled
when Joe Twichell's congregation suggested that Twain's
paying his minister friend's way to Europe and back in 1878
was gauche, and finally "committed" the Whittier Birthday
Dinner speech. So, although Nook Farm could accept Twain, it
could never really convince him of the fact.

Another part of the humorist did not change very much,
anyway. If he gave up the *Express,* the *Galaxy,* and *The
American Publisher* in order to concentrate on books, he was
still very much a businessman who measured both literary and
nonliterary achievement by the dollar mark even though he

felt certain, probably erroneously, that Nook Farm had a different yardstick. He cluttered up his life and energy during the 1870's and 1880's with so many projects for making himself a stereotype Horatio Alger that his literary work suffered. Even if he had an address, he was away from it as often as he was at home, on lecture trips, to Europe, up to Boston or down to New York, back to Keokuk, or off for the summer in Elmira. It is impossible not to stare in awe at Clemens' sheer physical energy during the Hartford period or to wish ruefully that a little more of it had been expended in literary activity. It is also indicative that Journalist Mark Twain, even if he had risen above the $20 letter of the sort the *Alta California* commissioned, was constantly dashing off letters to newspapers. In short, Mark Twain, to his glory, could never become a Charles Dudley Warner.

It is perhaps noteworthy, though, that the first sustained work he was to complete after arriving in Hartford was undertaken in collaboration with Warner, editor of two Hartford newspapers, author of quiet, calm sketches, and apotheosis of the Genteel Tradition; also, that it was to be one of those works of fiction toward which Twain felt such misgivings. (Perhaps it is noteworthy, too, that Warner agreed to the publication of the collaboration by the subscription method which produced, he told Helen Hunt Jackson, "such ill conditioned volumes.")

At any rate, Twain conceived the idea sometime in 1872 of using James Lampton as a character in a future work—the quixotic James Lampton whom George W. Cable instinctively called "Colonel" when they met in 1884 because of Lampton's similarity to Colonel Sellers.[2] To his sister, Twain wrote:

> I wish you would get all the gossip you can out of Mollie about Cousin James Lampton & Family, *without her knowing it is I that want it.* I want every little trifling detail, about how they look & dress, & what they say, & how the house is furnished—& the various ages & charac-

ters of the tribe. . . . I wish to write the whole thing
up—but not publish it for a great many years. That is, if
the story I write from it could be recognized by him or
the family.[3]

Since, as Twain oversimplified it in his *Autobiography*, Sellers
was based on Lampton, this letter suggests that he was
collecting ideas that would be put to use a lot sooner than "a
great many years."

Paine tells the familiar story of the conception of *The Gilded
Age*, reminiscent of James Fenimore Cooper:

> At the dinner-table one night, with the Warners present,
> criticisms of recent novels were offered, with the usual
> freedom and severity of dinner-table talk. The husbands
> were inclined to treat rather lightly the novels in which
> their wives were finding entertainment. The wives natu-
> rally retorted that the proper thing for the husbands to
> do was to furnish the American people with better ones.
> This was regarded in the nature of a challenge, and as
> such was accepted—mutually accepted: that is to say, in
> partnership. On the spur of the moment Clemens and
> Warner agreed that they would do a novel together, that
> they would begin it immediately.[4]

The dinner party took place in the winter of 1872, probably in
December, since Twain had been in England from August
through November. "But we were not able to get seriously at
work on it," Warner told Whitelaw Reid, "till some time in
January." Probably because of Twain's and Bliss's fear of the
competing houses getting out a similar volume, the composition
of *The Gilded Age* was shrouded in secrecy. Only the two
wives, Warner told Reid, knew anything about the project.

Scholars have, of course, studied the composition of the
book and attempted to unravel the mysteries of authorship.
Twain, we know, began the book and wrote in rapid-fire order
the first eleven chapters of the book—399 pages, 55 of which he
remembered composing in one sitting. Twain's first impulse
was to write a burlesque similar to "The Double-Barrelled

Detective Story," as a deleted fragment from the first few paragraphs suggests:

> The Squire was contemplating the morning. The air was balmy, the cornstalks were bending under their rich freight, the guano-beds were in bloom, the sycamores were distilling their fragrant gums, the faint flashings of innumerable fire-flies starred the sunny distances, & high in the zenith three or four indolent flying-squirrels were floating on drowsy wing.[5]

But on January 31, he saw the issue of the *New York Tribune* that headlined the Pomeroy scandal and also contained the review of *Roughing It* to which he violently objected, and presumably *The Gilded Age* turned into political satire as a consequence.

Twain receives general credit for Chapters I through XI, XXIV through XXXVII, and LVI through the Appendix, and Warner for XII through XXIII, XXXVIII through XLI, XLVI through L, and LIV and LV, though both Ernest E. Leisy and Bryant Morey French [6] have shown that each author worked over the material of the other. In the process of extremely close collaboration, the two authors also exchanged ideas. As Twain put it, Warner supplied the fiction and he provided the facts.

Warner told Twain, for example, about an Escol Sellers who lived in Bowlesville, Illinois, a strange inventor who held patents for a hill-climbing locomotive and a pulp-paper process, for converting steamboats to coal and removing brine from salt water. Sellers had even spent twelve years at a woodyard called Sellers' Landing, which he expected to mushroom into a large real estate project. Warner had learned of Sellers from a Dr. J. H. Barton, a close friend of both Warner and the branch of the Sellers family that lived in Philadelphia. However much Colonel Sellers derived from James Lampton or Jesse Leathers—the "rightful" Earl of Durham—or John Marshall Clemens, who also had a real estate speculation going on the Salt River during his son's youth, Escol Sellers saw definite aspects of his own character in the Colonel, and was to make trouble once *The Gilded Age* was published.

On April 16 Twain wrote Mrs. Fairbanks, apologizing for not corresponding sooner:

> . . . Chas Dudley Warner & I have been belting away every day on a *partnership novel.* I have worked 6 days a week—good full days—& laid myself up, once. Have written many chapters twice, & some of them three times—have thrown away 300 clean pages of MS. & still there's havoc to be made when I enter on final polishing. Warner has been more fortunate—he won't lose 50 pages.
> Three more chapters will end the book.[7]

With their wives acting as critics, the collaborators read their manuscript aloud in the evenings, and after the women voiced their approval of the plot, or plots, both authors spent some time revising their material separately before they began the task of cementing the two parts together. On April 26 Twain wrote Mrs. Clemens,

> I have finished trimming & revamping all my MS, & to-day we began the work of critically reading the book, line by line & numbering the chapters & working them in together in their appropriate places. It is perfectly fascinating work.[8]

Warner inserted three paragraphs into Twain's Chapter VI; Warner wrote Chapter XVIII, using material Twain "mapped out," and rewrote Twain's Chapter XXXV, utilizing some of his partner's manuscript. Warner apparently wrote the first draft of Chapter XLIII. Twain added two sections to Warner's Chapter LVIII. Both men wrote a version of the "boss" chapter, LX, and the wives voted to accept Twain's: "So my heroine, Laura, remains dead," he told Mother Fairbanks.[9]

The pagination of extant manuscript affirms that the two authors worked independently for the most part, numbering each chapter separately and then juggling the parts together in some kind of sequence. Chapter numbers are canceled and raised or lowered three or four times. Warner, who sensed better than Twain the aimlessness of the novel, attempted to work out a chronology from about Chapter XXV on, for Twain's benefit. Bumeroy—the original name for Senator Dilworthy, and more recognizably Pomeroy—would be exposed, Ruth would die, and the book "would leave the reader with the idea that Phil is some time to marry Alice." Obviously, Warner was at work on a sentimental novel and Twain on something not too far removed from his original burlesque notion. Eschol Sellers was originally named "Rollin Stone," and Senator Balloon, based on James Nye of Nevada, was originally "Bly." But Twain was as mawkishly maudlin as Warner on some occasions—Laura's death scene, for example. Chapter XXXIII on Washington society shows a great deal of revision, prompted most likely by the wives' superior knowledge of etiquette, and Twain's descriptions of Dilworthy's oily sanctimoniousness, which tended to mock enthusiastic religion in general, were toned down, possibly as a result of the wives' suggestions.[10]

The work of revising went rapidly, so rapidly that both authors were asking Reid to announce the book in the *Tribune* in April, and on May 3 Twain called for Bliss: "We shall doubtless be ready to talk business by about Tuesday, Wednesday, or at the latest, Thursday—and we shall be in a hurry too—shan't have long to talk. So, think it all over—Sheldon & Co. think we will make a serious and damaging mistake if we try to sell a novel by subscription."[11] Two days later he told Orion that "we finished revamping & refining the book tonight—ten day's labor. It is near midnight & we are just through."[12]

Bliss was not dissuaded by the argument of Sheldon & Company, who were wrangling for the right to publish *The Gilded Age.* Even though subscription houses had never undertaken to issue a novel before, Bliss completed the contract on May 8 which gave each author a 5 per cent royalty, a figure he told Twain three years earlier would leave the company a profit of less than $5,000.

With the book complete and in the hands of the American Publishing Company, Twain bundled up and left on May 17 for England and Routledge, the English publisher. Apparently he was to supervise the English publication, which was to depend on Bliss's sending page proof to London as soon as possible, and Warner was left to see about the American edition. Perhaps Twain felt, wisely as it turned out, that Warner would not be firm enough with Bliss or that strict instructions had to be left in order to secure a copyright in Great Britain that would beat the Canadian pirates. From London he wrote both Warner and Bliss that if they "should change that date [of publication] to telegraph to Routledge; because if Routledge makes a mistake in the publishing day of Bliss it may cost us our copyright." [13]

All of Twain's proofreading was on the English edition. As the Clemens family moved from London, Edinburgh, Glasgow, Chester, and Paris, Mrs. Clemens began to worry about the proof. "There has not one sheet of Mr. Clemens' proof come yet," she wrote home, "and if he goes home before the book is published here he will lose his copyright." He took his family back to the United States in October, returned to England alone in November, and finally in December wrote Livy about proofreading.[14] But by then Bliss and Warner already had the American edition on sale.

Back in March, when the book was still in the process of being written, Twain came up with a suggestion that would have been especially felicitous if Bliss had followed it:

> Now [Thomas] Nast appears to be doing nothing in particular. I want him, solitary & alone, to illustrate this next book, it being an essentially *American* book, & he will enjoy doing it. Nast only has just one *first-class* talent

(caricature,) & no more—but this book will exercise that talent, I think.[15]

It is probable, too, that the use of a specific illustrator would have minimized the possibility of borrowing engravings from other books, and this may have been part of Twain's intention. After the trouble with *Roughing It,* Twain specified a definite illustrator for each of his American Publishing Company books, but this time he did not have his way. Undoubtedly Bliss was shrewd enough not to borrow too many engravings so soon after the *Roughing It* disagreement. He paid $150 for one illustration—a full-page one, probably, at that price— which would have gone on page 337 of the original edition had he used it,[16] and in one of his advertising squibs for *The Gilded Age* he boasted that the illustrations for the book cost $10,000. It is possible that as many as two or three prospective customers really believed him.

The title of the book was for once no problem; before it was completed the *Tribune* proclaimed, "We are able now to announce its name. It is called 'The Gilded Age'—a name which gives the best promise of the wealth of satire and observation which it is easy to expect from two such authors." [17]

Other delays caused trouble, though. Twain, always over-optimistic about publication dates, first announced that the book would be released "in the end of summer." Next, to the editor of the *Daily Graphic,* he set the publication date as "early in the Fall," and Bliss had the book in plates early in October, since the first prospectuses came from the bindery on October 7. He should have been ready to release the first copies later that month, and this would have been ideal, for as Twain once explained to Howells, a "subscription book issued in the fall has a much larger sale than if issued at any other season of the year." [18] But if English copyright was to be secured, an American book had to be released there before its publication in the United States, and the English edition was nowhere near ready in October—and would not be ready until

June, 1874. Apparently exasperated at seeing the market slip away, Bliss ignored Twain's instructions about copyright and called for the binding of *The Gilded Age* to begin in time to capitalize on the Christmas season. On December 11 the first 480 cloth copies arrived, and by the end of the year 12,446 copies were bound and being delivered to customers.

Then, on January 20, 1874, Escol Sellers made his appearance. He had been communicating with Warner (Twain was still in England) since December, and a week before the January 20 meeting in Bliss's office, Warner had written Sellers, "We have stopped the press and struck out from the stereotype plates the name of 'Eschol' whenever it appeared, and substituted another name in its place." At the meeting, Bliss and Warner had also agreed to recall the "2,000 or 3,000" copies not delivered to customers and to send Sellers a copy of the corrected book. But months later Sellers still could not buy a copy of the corrected version—in Cincinnati, Memphis, and Philadelphia, *The Gilded Age* was still being sold with "Eschol" instead of "Beriah" for Colonel Sellers' given name. Sellers was ready to clear the matter up with a suit against the *Evansville* (Indiana) *Courier*, which had printed a story identifying Escol as the central character in the novel, and to call Warner, Twain, and Bliss—"not a man to inspire confidence"—to the stand.

Ultimately, Escol Sellers was mollified, but the facts suggest that he actually caused not a minute's delay because of the changing of plates—which Bliss took his own good time to accomplish—and also that Twain's versions of the incident represent both an embroidering of fact and a too ardent protestation of innocence for the Illinois Sellers not to have played some part in the creation of the Colonel.[19] Bliss was too interested in sales to stop printing during the first flush months to make changes in the plates.

Following up his belief that initial publicity set the tone for the later reception of a book and that *Roughing It* had suffered because of the lack of advance notoriety, Twain (and Warner) wrote Whitelaw Reid in April, 1873, requesting from the *Tribune* what Twain called "either exceedingly complimentary additions, or pitiless abuse accompanied with profanity." After a lukewarm review (*Tribune*, April 19, 1873, p. 6), apparently by John Hay, Mark Twain explained further just what he wanted: "I want the Tribune to say it *right* and say it powerful—and then I will answer for the consequences. The consequence will be that all other papers will *follow suit*—which you know as well as I do. And then our game is made and our venture launched with a fair wind instead of a baffling one." He acted more pleased with a second review (April 23, p. 4): "Now, *that* notice is bully! If any man is deceived by that he will be deceived in the happy direction, at any rate—and that is what we want." [20] That sounds as if Twain were delighted at the squib, but he harbored resentment against Reid for refusing to allow E. H. House to write a *third* notice of the book for the *Tribune*.[21] Later, the misunderstanding was ironed out, but in 1873 the humorist was outraged. In May he left instructions for Warner:

> Ask House to tell you about Whitelaw Reid. He is a contemptible cur, and I want nothing more to do with him. I don't want the Tribune to have the book at all. Please tell Bliss *not to send a copy there under any circumstances.* If you feel at any time like explaining, you may tell Reid or anyone that I desired this.[22]

And even in 1880 he told Howells, "I am justified in being afraid of the general press, because it killed the 'Gilded Age' before you had a chance to point out that there were merits in that book." [23]

If notoriety was what he wanted, it is surprising that Clemens resented the treatment he remembered receiving from the New York *Daily Graphic*. In his *Autobiography* Twain recollected that

the editor of the *Daily Graphic* persuaded me to let him
have an advance copy, he giving me his word of honor
that no notice of it should appear in his paper until after
the *Atlantic Monthly* notice should have appeared. This
reptile published a review of the book within three days
afterward. . . . It was charged that I had used my
reputation to play a swindle upon the public—that Mr.
Warner had written as much as half of the book, and that
I had used my name to float it . . . and that this conduct
of mine was a grave fraud upon the people.[24]

Twain must have given the review copy to the editor when he
took his family home from England in the fall of 1873, and the
review appeared on December 23. As reviews go, it was
perceptive in pointing out the defects in the novel. "It is simply
a series of incoherent sketches," the reviewer said, "with
fragmentary characterization and chaotic plot." "We are inclined to think that Mark Twain originally intended that the
story should be made as . . . a capital burlesque," the review
went on, but it theorized that each author had so altered the
other's work that "we look almost in vain for the traces of
either's pen." [25] This was valid literary criticism, and it nowhere
suggested that Mark Twain had not written his fair share of
the book.

Balancing with the *Graphic* condemnation, however, were a
number of more important—for Twain's market, anyway—
newspaper reviews from Bridgeport, Cincinnati, Hartford,
Philadelphia, Boston, New York, Rochester, Springfield, Syracuse, Utica, Waterbury, and Worcester. These reviews, which
generally summarized the plot, quoted long extracts from the
book, and reprinted Bliss's advertising copy, were almost
unanimously favorable, though not notably sophisticated.
They praised the satire, the humor, the literary skill of the
authors—even the illustrations.[26] Nevertheless, reviews in the
respectable literary journals followed the *Graphic*'s lead and
panned *The Gilded Age* with relish. The *Literary World*, for
example, noted, "The book has a strong savor of lucre; it was

evidently written to sell, and in the hope of gaining a liberal heap of that money, whose worship it purports to ridicule." [27] The *Chicago Tribune* was even more unfavorable: "They have willfully degraded their craft, abused the people's trust, and provoked a strong condemnation," it said. "As for identifying the hand of the two authors, that is impossible when both are performing work too inferior for recognition." But far from denying Twain's fair share of the work, the *Tribune* on November 27, 1875, even declared that Warner's "share in 'The Gilded Age' is now understood to be the weak part of the book." [28] Unjustified though it was, however, Twain did feel deep animosity toward the *Daily Graphic* and told Charles Webster a decade later that review copies of books should never go to the paper.[29]

The use of a "fake" title page of *The Gilded Age* was most likely a part of Bliss's sales technique for the book, and if it was, it traces back to the old subscription practice of "dumping." Openly, subscription publishers made a big point of the fact that their books were unobtainable in bookstores. Since the various agents and general agencies received from 50 to 60 per cent of the retail price of the volume, it was necessary for the subscription publisher to declare his fervent loyalty to the peddlers and to insist that their volumes were not going to bookstores. If the publishers sold to the regular trade stores at the same price they sold to agents, and then the bookstores offered the books at a slight markup, no one would purchase from the agents. Undersold and out of business, the agent would desert to another house. Now, publishers did "dump" books regularly, but in order not to alienate agents they waited until the subscription market was exhausted and then released to the stores. Split-second skill was necessary in order to know just when the subscription market was exhausted and the regular trade would still be interested in offering a subscription volume. In the case of *Huck Finn* Twain was vehement when Estes & Lauriat listed the book in their catalog, *before publication,* at fifty cents less than the subscription cost; but he advised Osgood to dump *The Prince and the Pauper* on February 12, 1882, a little over a month after publication.[30] More significant, Twain suggested to Webster that it would be good business to publish *Huck Finn* on December 15, 1884, "& 'dump' books the same day & catch the holiday trade." [31] This is apparently just the temptation Bliss could not resist. In order to escape his general agents' detection, he manufactured a phony title page which did not identify the general agent for whom the book was published, tipped it into the book, and flooded the Christmas, 1873, market. Unfortunately, Bliss made the mistake of inserting the "fake" title page before the pages were cut and gilded, and if contemporary agents did not notice the incriminating evidence, a recent literary sleuth, Denis Woodfield, has.[32]

In the prospectus Bliss advertised his book as "a literary curiosity," as "unique and original in all things, and while ostensibly a novel, will differ from books generally known as such. . . . Its satire, although directed against prominent persons and things, will not be found to be misplaced." [33] *The Gilded Age* was, the prospectus boasted, a tour de force in which everyone would find something to his taste: "The superficial reader will find abundant entertainment in this volume, the careful, studious one an ample supply of material for afterthought, while the scholar will discover something upon which to exercise his ingenuity." Trumbull's chapter headings, to which the "scholar" was apparently supposed to direct his attention, backfired though. They were not accepted as philological puzzles as Bliss had intended. One of the reviewers thought them a great joke: "The work is given a consistently burlesque air [the *Galaxy* noted] by quotations from non-existent languages at the beginnings of chapters." And *Old and New* commented, "Nor must the grotesque parody on the motto business, at the chapter heads, be overlooked." [34] Twain was very sensitive when one of his jokes fell flat—remember his burlesque review of *Innocents Abroad,* at which he raged and fumed. I suspect that he was badly smitten by the lack of success of his chapter headings, and that this diatribe from *A Tramp Abroad* can be explained only in the contexts of *The Gilded Age:* "A man who writes a book for the general public to read is not justified in disfiguring his pages with untranslated foreign expressions. It is an insolence to the majority of the purchasers, for it is a very frank and impudent way of saying, 'Get the translation made yourself if you want them, this book is not written for the ignorant classes'" (Chapter XXX). It also says some things, incidentally, about his sensitivity to his popular audience.

Even though he insisted on the universal appeal of the book, Bliss was extremely selective about the material included in the salesmen's sample. Almost the entire prospectus was chosen from the first hundred and ten pages, the Twain chapters with the description of Obedstown, the steamboat race and explosion, and Colonel Sellers and the turnip dinner. Only four of the fifty sample pages were of Warner's material. None of the satire on Washington politics, none of the murder trial, none of the pages exposing speculation and corruption were there. Bliss, Warner, or whoever made the selection and decided to base almost the entire sampling on Twain's first eleven chapters, made a wise choice, for DeVoto has suggested that "when the second paragraph introduces Obedstown, East Tennessee, we are on a higher level of realism than American literature had ever before attained." [35]

It may be that this material was chosen because it was the first part of the manuscript and therefore the most readily available. But since the entire manuscript was turned over to Bliss at once and certainly all was available in type by the October date of the prospectus, there is also the alternative to consider that Bliss was an amazingly shrewd critic, perceptive to the tastes of his book buyers and to the qualities in Mark Twain that constituted his peculiar genius. Bliss exploited the irreverence of *Innocents,* the historical value of *Roughing It,* the realism of *The Gilded Age,* and as we shall see, the appeal of *Tom Sawyer* to an adult, not juvenile, audience.

Interestingly, Bliss did not take advantage of the topical material in *The Gilded Age* when he wrote his advertisements, except for the one veiled reference in the prospectus to "prominent persons and things." Nothing in it or in the other advertisements called attention to the Pomeroy scandal or to the Laura Fair trial which were creating sensations in 1873 and were adapted to the plot of the novel. At first thought it would seem that Bliss was missing a fine sales point. On the other hand, Bliss knew his customers, knew that public interest is ephemeral, and perhaps believed that emphasis on the topical parts of the book would work to its detriment after a short time. If he was worried, he had every reason to be. He did use the pages of *The American Monthly* to advertise for canvassers for the book. In September he announced *The Gilded Age* as one of the "new Fall books now in the press of the American Publishing Co." He also took the opportunity here to exploit the curiosity of the novel:

> This novelty in the way of books, will draw the attention of the public more than anything printed for years. The great popularity of the authors, and the desire to see how two so different in style can write upon the same subject upon the same pages, will make its sale sure and easy. This book will be fully illustrated and will, we are sure add to the fame of its authors, and put money in the pockets of agents.[36]

But, as the sales statistics show, this was whistling in the dark.

After the 12,466 copies which had been bound between December 11 and the end of 1873 came from the bindery, the sales remained brisk for two more months: in January the total rose to 26,821; in February, to 35,745. These sales were worth celebrating. Neither of the earlier American Publishing Company books had sold so well in the first two and a half months. But in March, 1874, sales dropped to only 1,000 copies, and at the end of its first full year *The Gilded Age* had sold only 50,325 copies, 15,000 less than *Roughing It* and almost 20,000 less than *Innocents* in their first years. Twain had optimistically told Dr. John Brown immediately after the book came out that he saw the sale of 100,000 copies as the ultimate saturation point,[37] but even at the end of 1879 the total was only 56,484 volumes: 41,233 cloth copies, 505 gilt, 14,005 Leather Library, 683 half-morocco, and 58 full-morocco. Only 1,362 prospectuses had been needed. These sales were prophetic; commercially, Mark Twain was entering a serious decline which would last for the rest of the decade and would result in a period of what Walter Blair has called Mark Twain's "frenzied finance." For the next literary project, Twain resuscitated his plan for a book of sketches.

Mark Twain had been unhappy from the very first with Charles H. Webb's job of publishing *The Jumping Frog*. The typesetting was poor, many of the sketches were aimed at a local Western audience, and on occasion even "The Jumping Frog" seemed a fragile anecdote upon which a humorist's reputation should rest. So, as soon as the humorist cemented his "partnership" with Bliss, he began to think of ways to issue a new volume of collected sketch material which would be more satisfactory to his own improving taste and would also wrestle from Webb the copyright on the earlier material.

Early in 1870 Twain suggested to Bliss, "I am prosecuting Webb in the N. Y. Courts—think the result will be that he will yield up the copyright & plates of the Jumping Frog, if I let him off from paying me money. Then I shall break up those plates and prepare a new volume of Sketches, but on a different and more 'taking' model."[38] Later in 1870 he told Bliss of the *Galaxy*'s offer of a column, which included the publication of his magazine sketches, and in October he decided that he was ready to accept the *Galaxy* offer and publish a "Mark Twain's Annual—1871" provided, he tantalized Bliss, "they will pay me about 25 per cent. That is what they offered once, I believe. I believe a Christmas volume will outpay Josh Billings' Allminax. What do you think? Write me at once—& don't discourage me." [39] Bliss, who Clemens knew wanted to prevent his star author from " 'whoring after strange gods,' which is Scripture for deserting to other publishers," immediately made a contract for a book "to be made up in part of old articles written by sd. Clemens herebefore, but to be altered in such a manner that a new copyright will hold upon them—other parts of the book to be of new matter." [40] It is just possible that Bliss used coercion to get the contract for *Sketches New and Old.* The *Roughing It* contract had forbidden the publication of another book until the Western volume was released, and a letter Twain wrote Webb suggests that Bliss called the point to the humorist's attention. "I could not consent to a new edition of the J. F. anytime within two or three years without vitiating my contracts with my present publishers & creating dissatisfaction. I would have issued the Galaxy (they belong wholly to me) & other sketches, in a couple of volumes, before this, but for the reason abovementioned," [41] he explained to Webb.

He was enthusiastic about the book at first. Even before the contract was signed he told Bliss, "You'd better go to canvassing for the vol. of sketches *now*, hadn't you? You must illustrate it—& mind you, the man to do the choicest of the pictures is Mullins." Bliss agreed to Mullins and suggested, "Dont you think Jumping Frog would be a big thing in the sketch book? Seems to me it will do you as much good there as anywhere & pay you best." [42] Twain thought, though, that the Frog would do better by itself: "I want you to issue Jumping Frog *illustrated,* along with 2 other sketches for the *holidays* next year. I've paid high for the Frog & I want him to get his price back by himself." [43] (It had taken $1,400 to get his rights in the book back from Webb.) [44]

In January, 1871, he worked on the book of sketches rather than on *Roughing It* and had grandiose plans for the volume. "Name the Sketchbook 'Mark Twain's Sketches' and go on canvassing like mad," he told Bliss. "In the course of a week I can have most of the matter ready for you I think, Am working like sin on it." [45] Bliss had his contract now, however, and became reluctant to rush the actual publication of the sketches. Later in January Twain wrote Bliss about a shift in plans that Bliss himself had suggested:

> Orion says you hardly know whether it is good judgment to throw the Sketch Book on the market & interfere with the Innocents. . . . So if you like the idea, suppose we defer the Sketch Book till the *last*. That is, get out the big California & Plains book first of August, then the Diamond book first March or April 1872—& *then* the Sketch book the following fall. . . . By that time I can write a great many brand new sketches & they'll make the book sell handsomely—& by that time, too, some of the best of the *old* sketches will be forgotten & will read like new matter. [46]

The book of sketches was shoved into the background for over a year.

Then in 1872 James R. Osgood wrote Twain about the possibility of a book of sketch material, and again the humorist had to decline because of his contract with Bliss: "Indeed I *would* like to publish a volume of sketches through your house," he explained, "but unfortunately my contracts with my present publisher tie my hands & prevent me." [47] He *was* at work on a volume for Routledge, though, and renewed his idea of doing the book for Bliss. He wrote Elisha about the idea:

> At last I have sat down in earnest & looked the new book through—& my verdict is, better a long sight *leave the*

Jumping Frog out. There is too much fun in the book as
it is. For Heaven's sake let us not add to it.—Don't hesitate about it but just *take the Frog out.*[48]

The book was apparently either *Mark Twain's Celebrated
Jumping Frog of Calaveras County, and Other Sketches. With
the Burlesque Autobiography and First Romance* or *Mark
Twain's Sketches . . . Selected and Revised by the Author,*
both of which Routledge published in 1872, and which Twain
must have intended to be used for the American version as
well. This persistent and pessimistic verdict of "The Jumping
Frog" may have been prompted by his wish to keep the
copyright on the tale out of Bliss's hands or by a desire to get
a sketch book published without further delay. At any rate, it
was not until the following year that Twain decided to include
"The Jumping Frog" in his book.

In August, just as he was preparing to leave for England,
Twain wrote Bliss to "hurry up your figuring on the volume of
sketches, for I leave for England in 10 or 12 days to be gone
several months." [49] Whatever figuring Bliss may have been
doing, there was certainly no need to hurry. *Sketches New and
Old* was still three years from publication, and by the time the
book finally did issue, the author was a lot less interested in
pushing it.

The next spring, Twain found Thérèse Bentzon's article,
"Les Humoristes Américains," and was jubilant over her
translation of his "Jumping Frog." "Got a French version of the
Jumping Frog," he wrote back to Livy,

> fun is no name for it. I am going to translate it *literally,*
> French construction & all (apologizing in parenthesis
> where a word is too many for me) & publish it in the
> Atlantic as the grave effort of a man who does not know
> but what he is as good a French scholar as there is—& sign
> my name to it, without another word. It will be toothsome
> reading.[50]

Howells, if he got a chance at the story for the *Atlantic,*
apparently did not consider it as "toothsome" as Twain did.

More probably, though, Howells never got a chance at the new version. Twain's triple telling as it appears in *Sketches* bears the date, "Hartford, March, 1875," at the end, which suggests that he was delayed quite a while—until just at the time he turned the entire manuscript over to Bliss—before he completed writing up his idea.

The next year Twain again returned to the book of sketches, as he explained to Mrs. Fairbanks. "I am preparing several volumes of my sketches for publication, & am writing new sketches to add to them." [51] The two volumes were presumably *Sketches Number One* (published by the American News Company in 1874) and *Sketches New and Old*. It was probably during this burst of enthusiasm that he composed "A True Story" and "A Fable for Good Old Boys and Girls" which he submitted to Howells that September for consideration by the *Atlantic*. Howells refused the "Fable," and Twain probably revised it before including it in the book.[52]

Osgood returned on the scene in 1875, and by that time Twain had either forgotten his earlier contract with Bliss or had decided that he would follow Orion's suggestion about ignoring the American Publishing Company contracts after the *Roughing It* fiasco. He actually began negotiating with Osgood for a book the material for which, he suggested, was already complete: "I reckon I can get the sketches ready in time, though publishing books don't pay for the trouble of writing them—only this one don't *have* to be written." [53] But Bliss was not to be denied, and Twain had to report back to Osgood a conversation that had taken place in Bliss's office:

> Concerning that sketch-book. I went to Bliss yesterday & told him I had got all my old sketches culled & put together & a whole lot of new ones added, & that I had about made up my mind to put them in your hands. Whereupon he went to his safe & brought back a contract *four years old* to give him all my old sketches, with a lot of new ones added!—royalty 7½ percent!
> I had totally forgotten the existence of such a con-

tract—totally. He said, "It wouldn't be *like* you to refuse
to first fulfill this contract."

I said, "You flatter me, & moreover you have *got* me.
But I won't fulfill it at 7½ per cent."

"We never have shown a disposition to be mean with
you—state your terms," said Bliss.[54]

Twain's terms were that his royalty be raised to 10 per cent as
soon as 50,000 copies of the book were sold, the 10 per cent to
apply on the first 50,000 copies, too. Bliss, perhaps self-
assured that over 50,000 copies of a sketchbook would never
sell, agreed cheerfully. The addendum (now at Yale) was
signed the same day, February 12, and Twain turned over the
manuscript at about the same time.

The material included in the book was mostly reprint stuff.
Only seven of the sixty-three sketches were new, even though
Twain claimed in the preface that he had "scattered through
this volume a mass of matter which has never been in print
before." Among these seven, three were probably written and
consigned to the volume of sketches when Twain was at work
on his book on England in 1872 or in 1873, both periods when
he at least contemplated *Sketches New and Old*. " 'Party Cries'
in Ireland," "Speech at the Scottish Banquet," reprinted,
according to its first paragraph, from the London *Observer* in
1872, and "The Blind Letter Department, London P. O." are all
concerned with the material of his English trips during those
years. "The Jumping Frog Restored to the English Tongue
after Martyrdom in the French," "A True Story," and "Some
Learned Fables . . ." have already been mentioned as belong-
ing to 1874 and 1875. "Petition Concerning Copyright" was
certainly a late entry in the book, for Twain's interest in the
problem began to become vocal in 1875. Only "Experience of
the McWilliamses with Membranous Croup" remains a mystery.[55]

Twain did the very minimum necessary to comply with the
stipulation to revise the older sketches "in such a manner that a

new copyright will hold upon them." Most of the revising was involved with clearing the material of Western allusions and of bits of coarseness. He added no new material but merely read the sketches, excised short portions, and divided lengthy paragraphs. From the sketch, "An Item Which the Editor Himself Could Not Understand," for example, he removed a reference to the office of *The Californian*. From "The Launch of the Steamer Capital" he removed all the introductory topical matter, leaving only the story of the Scriptural panoramist. In " 'After' Jenkins" he toned down some of the more grisly parodies of fashion items that he had allowed to stand in *The Jumping Frog*. He eliminated references to the breath of Mrs. L. R. who "was attractively attired in her new and beautiful false teeth," to Mrs. T. who wore only hoops and "showed to good advantage," and to Mrs. X's anatomical structure—"all one would have to do would be to pull out her key-pin and she would go to pieces like a Chinese puzzle." It was dreary work resurrecting and examining these skeletons from his journalistic past. He was embarrassed about it—"I destroyed a mass of sketches, & now heartily wish I had destroyed some more of them," [56] he told Howells about the book—and aware that there was no reason to expect it to do well on the market.

The contract for *Sketches New and Old* called for the book "to be published in the early spring of /71 if possible." That it was not possible is less surprising than that when he *did* get the manuscript, Bliss conscientiously saw it through the process of publishing in what was relatively rapid order. He appointed True Williams, an illustrator who was to provide grounds for disagreement between Twain and Bliss in 1876, to work on the engravings, and Bliss was able to deposit a title page with the Library of Congress on July 25, 1875. He forgot to send along two copies of the book, though, to complete copyright, and twenty years later Twain still nourished a grievance over the neglect.[57] By September the book was in press and, by Clemens' standards, exceedingly "handsome." [58]

Nevertheless, he showed unusual disregard for seeing *Sketches New and Old* through the press. In part he was too busy with other projects, all of which have bearing on the American Publishing Company (and in part, too, he may simply have been indifferent). There are no indications that he read proof, but since most of the material was set in type from earlier writings, he may have allowed someone in Bliss's offices to do the irritating proofreading.

At any rate, 1875 was a bad year for proofreading. Twain was involved with his "Old Times on the Mississippi" articles, which he told Howells "has been uncovering itself by degrees, until it has exposed such a huge hoard to my view that a whole book will be required to contain it if I use it. So I have agreed to write the book for Bliss." Later the same year he was talking to Bliss about having "a bigger book [than *Tom Sawyer*] ready" in the fall of 1876, presumably the Mississippi volume. Not until the summer of 1876, when he told Mrs. Fairbanks, "My pet book . . . lies at home one-third done & never more to be touched, I judge," [59] did he give up work on what was to become *Life on the Mississippi* seven years later. There was also *Tom Sawyer* to be done and a batch of literary projects of friends that he needed to intercede with Bliss about. Most important, William Wright (Dan DeQuille of the *Enterprise* days), was at work on *The Big Bonanza* and staying with the Clemenses. Twain helped—until he got bored with the process. He also suggested Joaquin Miller to Bliss, who published Miller's *Unwritten History* in 1874. He was trying to persuade Aldrich and Howells to give Bliss books, and he got Bliss, to his later regret, to publish Harte's *Gabriel Conroy*. Bliss may have been less than joyously thankful; *The Big Bonanza* sold only 2,173 copies in its first five months, and *Gabriel Conroy* reached only 3,354 in its first year.

Summer was always the slack period in subscription book selling. In May, June, July, and August, 1875, for example,

Bliss sold only 816 copies of all Mark Twain's books. And 1875 was a bad year, anyway, especially for humor. As the *New York Tribune* put it on September 21, "At the two extremes of science and humor there is equally little. Mark Twain's collected sketches and the 'Alminaxes' represent the latter. The humorists had their say last year." [60] And Twain told Charles Webb in 1875, "It is a mighty tough year for books. But I think that the next 3 months will show a different state of things. Therefore I am venturing to bring out a new book—a thing I could not have been hired to do during any part of the past 12 months, for it would have been a sort of deliberate literary suicide." [61] Other conditions did not presage well for the new volume. It contained old reprinted material almost entirely and had only 320 pages, just about half as many as a regular subscription book. It was almost doomed, in other words, to be commercially unsuccessful in comparison with the humorist's earlier books, and when the first copies came from the bindery on September 25, Mark Twain had already persuaded himself that he had no cause to celebrate.

In his preface to an English edition of *Mark Twain's Sketches*, printed incongruously in *Mark Twain's Speeches* (1910), Twain acknowledged that a reader could not read the book at a single sitting but needed to attempt only a page or two at a time:

> If I were to sell the reader a barrel of molasses, and he, instead of sweetening his substantial dinner with the same at judicious intervals, should eat the entire barrel at one sitting, and then abuse me for making him sick, I would say that he deserved to be made sick for not knowing any better how to utilize the blessings this world affords. And if I sell to the reader this volume of nonsense, and he, instead of seasoning his graver reading with a chapter of it now and then, when his mind demands such relaxation, unwisely overdoses himself with several chapters of it at a single sitting, he will deserve to be nauseated, and he will have nobody to

blame but himself if he is. There is no more sin in publishing an entire volume of nonsense than there is in keeping a candy-store with no hardware in it. It lies wholly with the customer whether he will injure himself by means of either, or will derive from them the benefits which they will afford him if he uses their possibilities judiciously.

When he agreed to the delay of the sketch book in January, 1871, it was because some of the older material "will be forgotten & will read like new matter." Whether the idea would have worked is impossible to determine, since at least twelve volumes of various sketches, including English and pirated editions, were published between 1871 and 1875. There was simply no chance for the older work to be forgotten.

By the time the book of sketches appeared, their author was persuaded that the idea of printing disconnected sketches at all was foolish. To Dan DeQuille, who was considering the publication of a volume of sketches from the *Enterprise* in addition to the historical account of *The Big Bonanza*, Twain wrote, "The winning card is to nail a man's interest with *Chapter I*, & not let up on him till you get him to the word 'finis.' That can't be done with detached sketches." [62] It is a revealing statement, suggesting that Twain was by this time working toward a solution of the problem of subscription publication that he found in the amalgamation of fictional sketches into the texture of a longer narrative—consciously and deliberately working out a formula that many Twain critics have insisted was nothing more than a combination of his informal temperament and his background in oral technique.

It also constitutes an implied dismissal of *Sketches New and Old*. Economic factors and Twain's indifference to "plugging" the volume as he had *Innocents* and *Roughing It* made prospects dim enough, but the *coup de grâce* was delivered by the newspapers and journals, who ignored the volume com-

pletely. Twain was ecstatic over Howells' review in the
Atlantic (and so was Livy). That Mrs. Clemens was grateful
for Howells' pointing out that Twain showed "a growing
seriousness of meaning" is not surprising, but that the humorist,
too, thanked Howells for critical evaluation is unusual. Just
three years earlier he had told Reid that he did not care
whether the first announcement of *The Gilded Age* praised or
damned the novel as long as it was notorious, sensational,
eye-catching, and likely by implication of creating free publicity. With *Sketches*, though, Twain was pleased that Howells,
"the recognized critical Court of Last Resort in this country,"
had been able to find some praiseworthy things in the book. If
Twain was becoming sensitive to the opinions of literary
critics, he was doing so at the sacrifice of the media that would
assist and assure big sales; to value Howells' pronouncements
over the newspaper squibs that were reprinted as "floating
articles" all over the country and to resent being "persistently
glorified as a mere buffoon" was indicative of a shift in attitude
which, even if it suggested a growing concern for "literary"
rather than "popular" acceptance, was at least in small part
responsible for the dismal failure of *Sketches*.

Only the *New York Tribune* carried an announcement of the
book; on September 21, it noted,

> "Mark Twain" is to be honored by a complete edition of
> his sketches, new and old. It will be issued in a subscrip-
> tion volume of the usual size, but with more noteworthy
> illustrations and better typography than in the common
> subscription volumes. The American Publishing Com-
> pany, of Hartford, announce the volume as "the 'Big
> Bonanza' of the literary world." "The Jumping Frog," the
> erudite papers on "Political Economy" and "Cannibal-
> ism," and the other productions by which Mr. Clemens
> has become famous in the scientific world, will be
> included in the volume.

This was exactly the sort of announcement that would have
sold the book, had it been picked up and copied extensively,

but the newspapers were not interested in it any more than the magazines were in reviewing *Sketches*. *Appleton's Journal,* the *Galaxy, Harper's Monthly* and *Weekly, Lippincott's, Literary World, The Nation,* and *Scribner's* all maintained a silence toward the volume. In this case, Howells was not only the court of last resort; he was the only court before which *Sketches* was tried.

In advertising the book as a "Big Bonanza," Bliss was indulging in some skullduggery at the expense of DeQuille's *The Big Bonanza,* which was released on July 31, 1876. Customers in the Far West were looking for Dan's book with eager anticipation—Twain had suggested including flattering references to the notables so that they would all buy copies of the book—and in the spring of 1876 canvassers for *Sketches* appeared in Virginia City. As DeQuille told Twain,

> Your agents have captured a few of my subscribers. The advertisement of your book was headed:
>
> "The Big Bonanza"
>
> of
>
> Wit and Humor," etc.,
> and several of my friends went for it as soon as they read the top line.[63]

Had DeQuille's book been a hit, Twain would have reaped some profit from the scheme (and presumably everybody who suddenly discovered himself an owner of *Sketches New and Old* but really wanted *The Big Bonanza* would order the other book), but Dan was doing no better than Mark.

In the prospectus Bliss accented the excellence of Twain's shorter work and of True Williams' illustrations. "Unlike its predecessors," the prospectus explained,

> this is not a connected story, yet has all the peculiar features which have so characterized his former works; and is made up of the very best of all that has emanated from the pen of its popular author. Nowhere does his

ready wit and keen satire more forcibly display itself than in his sketch writings; in fact, his richest vein of humor seems to empty itself into these.[64]

Williams' macabre illustrations were a big selling point. Bliss advertised, "Artist has vied with Author in the preparation of this book, and the result is a volume of rare beauty; THE MOST ARTISTIC ILLUSTRATIONS are profusely scattered over its pages, and the reader will often hesitate which first to enjoy—the sparkling humor of the Pen or Pencil." Williams was known around Hartford as a lush who climbed lightpoles in his soberer moments,[65] and anyone familiar with his illustrations can only conclude that he worked on them when he was unable to navigate the lamp posts. Grisly, poorly executed, heavy with ink, Williams' engravings have little to recommend them except their vastness; most of the pages of *Sketches* contained a large illustration and very little text,[66] and, to Bliss's credit, he included many of these pages as samples in the agents' dummy.

Although there were sixty-four sample pages, Bliss showed ingenuity in choosing his prospectus material.[67] Portions of twenty-eight different stories were available for the prospective customer's perusal, but not a single one was complete except "A Fashion Item" and "A Fine Old Man," both of which were only one page long. Since the other selections were printed with a page or two missing, the prospectus tantalized the customer but did not satisfy his curiosity. Only the purchase of the book could do that.

For obvious reasons the American Publishing Company did not care about advertising the number of pages in the book, for, unlike *Innocents Abroad*, *Roughing It*, and *A Tramp Abroad*, it was not large enough for size to be a selling point. The *Tribune* squib had passed over size as "usual," and concentrated on the "noteworthy illustrations and better typography" of *Sketches*, and since the *Tribune* undoubtedly got the facts from Bliss, its notice suggested the sales pitch that the

American Publishing Company would take toward the book. Bliss emphasized *Sketches'* "rare beauty," its "super-calendered, delicate tinted paper," its "dainty blue cover so tastefully adorned with fanciful designs" of black and gilt stampings, its "artistic" illustrations, and its "large, open, honest pages." Deceitfully shrewd as Bliss's techniques were, they did not succeed in selling the book.

Perhaps, as DeLancey Ferguson has suggested, Bliss looked on *Sketches New and Old* as merely a stopgap while he waited for *Tom Sawyer;* more likely, he was overwhelmed with his vast publishing plans for 1876 (see p. 114). At any rate, the volume sold—insofar as it sold at all—"mainly on the strength of the author's reputation," and at a rate that was decidedly inferior to the three earlier books.

For a short while after the first copies came from the bindery on September 25, 1875, sales were relatively brisk. By the end of November 12,985 copies had been bound, and at the end of the year the figure had reached 22,871. After January, 1876, though, sales dropped disastrously to less than 400 a month, and at the end of its first year *Sketches New and Old* had sold just barely over 27,000 copies. From then, September, 1876, to the end of December, 1879, the book sold only 3,776 copies, or less than 100 a month. At the end of 1879, 23,556 cloth copies, 1,889 gilt, 5,145 Leather Library, 298 half-morocco, 6 full-morocco, and 1,369 prospectuses had been bound.

Because of that extra 2½ per cent he was to receive on all copies of *Sketches* as soon as sales passed 50,000, Mark Twain kept his eye on the book's sales long after he left the American Publishing Company. In July, 1882, the humorist estimated that 40,000 copies had been sold and cautioned Webster to

> find out exactly how many of each of my books have been sold, if possible. And especially how many *Sketches*—for when they have sold 50,000 Sketches they will owe me a rebate of 2½ percent on each copy of the whole 50,000. It

is a three-dollar book—so the rebate coming to me will be $3,750.[68]

In spite of a *Hartford Courant* review of *The Stolen White Elephant* (June 7, 1882), which reported sales of *Sketches* as over 100,000,[69] they had not risen even to the magical 50,000—as Twain's letter beginning, "Damnation," to Webster later in July attests. Even by February, 1893, the book had not reached the 50,000 mark. Frank Bliss wrote Twain suggesting a one-dollar edition of *Sketches* to supply the cheap market before the copyright ran out, but that 2½ per cent clause made problems.

> In event of our publishing a lower priced book and paying you 10% royalty on it, instead of 7½% as on present book, you will release us from that "50,000 copies" part of the contract, which, if present yearly rate of sales continues, it will take nearly 30 years yet for us to fulfill.

Twain agreed to the dollar edition and the cancellation of the troublesome clause.[70] But the transaction could only serve to remind an author whose first three books had sold 50,000 copies in the first dozen months or less that *Sketches* had not reached that level in almost two decades. And, ironically, it was while *Sketches New and Old* was undergoing the mechanics of publication that Twain was enthusiastically at work on an even more dismally disappointing financial failure—*The Adventures of Tom Sawyer.*

Antecedents for *Tom Sawyer* trace all the way back to the mid-1860's. Walter Blair has noted a number of the scenes and episodes that appeared in Twain's earlier writing:

> The title of the cat and the pain-killer incident (chap. xii) and details about boyish cures for warts (chap. vi) were mentioned in a notebook of 1866, when Clemens was in the Sandwich Islands. The story of Tom and the Temperance Society (chap. xxii) was part of an *Alta*

California newsletter of 1867. The yarn about the school-
room game with the tick (chap. vii) was used in a speech
delivered at a Congressional dinner in Washington in
1868. The account of Robin Hood games on Holliday's
Hill (chap. viii) first took up a few lines in a reminiscent
letter of 1870. And details of the Sunday School scene
(chap. iv) were part of a letter to Annie Taylor in 1856,
of a letter to Olivia Clemens in 1870, and of *The Gilded
Age* in 1873.[71]

Though he used some of these isolated episodes earlier,
Twain's first extensive exploration of his boyhood adventures
occurred when he answered a letter from Will Bowen on
February 6, 1870. The letter was little more than a catalog of
memories which were to reappear in *Tom Sawyer* and *Huckleberry Finn*, but the first jump was to the "Boy's Manuscript," [72]
written in the same year as the letter to Bowen.

"Boy's Manuscript" was not only the prototype for *Tom
Sawyer;* it was also the humorist's first attempt at sustained
fiction. As such, it provides a gauge of how far Twain was to
advance with the method of fiction in the five short years
between 1870 and 1875. Mawkish, "romantic," full of unbeliev-
able pieties ("I prayed the good God not to let the apple make
her sick, and to bless her every way for the sake of Christ the
Lord"), and strained word play ("I had the branch dammed
up beautiful for water-mills, but I dont care for water mills
when you are away so I traded the dam to Jo Whipple for a
squirt gun though if you was here I wouldnt give a dam for a
squirt gun"), "Boy's Manuscript" is almost the antecedent that
Twain burlesqued in *Tom Sawyer*. It suggests in its hesitancy
and uncertainty just why Mark Twain would consider "fiction"
an "experiment." To a mind that linked public acceptance
with literary approval, *The Gilded Age*, *Tom Sawyer*, and
Huckleberry Finn were experimental in ways that "Boy's
Manuscript," *The Prince and the Pauper*, and *Joan of Arc* were
not. Twain certainly burlesqued Sunday-school fiction in *Tom*,
but to facets of his mind "Boy's Manuscript" represented

something more closely allied to the proper modes of fiction.

Even if "Boy's Manuscript" is, in DeVoto's felicitous phrasing, "*Tom Sawyer* untouched by greatness," [73] there is no evidence that its author was anything less than completely sincere in writing it. There can be little doubt that at one point he even referred back to the inchoate version when he wrote *Tom Sawyer*. Both Billy Rogers and Tom empty their pockets during the course of their adventures, and the inventory for both includes marbles, a jew's-harp, a spool cannon, chalk, a broken bottle stopper, a toy soldier, a doorknob, a knife, and a dead animal—a frog for Billy, a rat for Tom.

Twain worked on the manuscript next during his trip to England in 1873. He recalled in his *Autobiography* relating the whitewashing scene to Irving and Wills at Bateman's; DeVoto assumed that the reference was to his first trip in 1872, but since Twain did not meet Wills until the summer of 1873, the second trip is more probable. The long reference to the ice storm of January 9, 1873, in the margin of the whitewashing scene, also supports the later dating. [74] At any rate, he retained the first-person form for the scene and even included one page of the earlier version in his manuscript for *Tom Sawyer*: page 37, originally numbered 6, with the *I*'s changed to *he*'s is in the original of the manuscript in the Georgetown University Library, Washington, D. C.

Exactly when he began work on *Tom Sawyer* is uncertain. In April, 1874, he complained, "I am going to work when we get on the hill—till then I've got to lie fallow, albeit against my will." [75] Unless he changed his mind, then, he did not get started until the summer of 1874. Originally, he contemplated a full subscription-length book, one that would take his hero up to his late thirties or early forties, have him wander far away from St. Petersburg, and then return there at the conclusion of the novel. Such a form would take at least double the ultimate manuscript that *Tom Sawyer* contained and, more significantly, would make it definitely a book for adults, not children. To assist himself, he wrote an outline of his plot for the book on the first manuscript page, suggesting a volume in four parts (of which *Tom Sawyer* is no more than half):

> 1, Boyhood & youth; 2 y & early manh; 3 the Battle of Life in many lands; 4 (age 37 to 40 [?],) return & meet grown babies & toothless old drivelers who were the grandees of his boyhood. The Adored Unknown a [illegible] faded old maid & full of rasping, puritanical vinegar piety.

Bearing in mind that The Adored Unknown was a name Twain used for Becky Thatcher (in Chapter III) before he actually christened her, one can date the outline as an early plan for the novel. It was a plot that fascinated Mark Twain, for he contemplated its use on several later occasions. But *The Adventures of Tom Sawyer* turned out, because he met formidable structural problems and ultimately persuaded himself that it was a children's book, to be something else again.

In later years Twain described to Brander Matthews the way he went about composing *Tom Sawyer,* and Matthews recorded the report:

> He began the composition of "Tom Sawyer" with certain of his boyish recollections in mind, writing on and on until he had utilized them all, whereupon he put his manuscript aside and ceased to think about it, except in so far as he might recall from time to time, and more or less unconsciously, other recollections of those early days. Sooner or later he would return to his work and make use of memories he had recaptured in the interval.[76]

As he wrote through the first half of the book he made just the sort of recollections Matthews described, and used the margins of his manuscript to preserve them. On several occasions, the notes bore fruition immediately: on page 15 he wrote "coppers" and on page 19 the passage in which the "new boy" throws two pennies to Tom by way of challenge. Alongside the Sunday-school superintendent's speech in Chapter IV he noted, "City of Hartford." Evidently his first thought was to utilize an anecdote from his May, 1870, "Memoranda" column for the speech:

> "Just about the close of that long, hard winter," said the Sunday-school superintendent, "as I was wending toward my duties one brilliant Sabbath morning, I glanced down toward the levee, and there lay the City of Hartford!—no mistake about it, there she was, puffing and panting, after her long pilgrimage through the ice. . . . I should have to instruct empty benches, sure; the youngsters would all be off welcoming the first steamboat of the season. You can imagine how surprised I was when I opened the door and saw half the benches full! My gratitude was free, large, and sincere. I resolved that they should not find me unappreciative. I said: 'Boys, you cannot think how proud it makes me to see you here, nor what renewed assurance it gives me of your affection. I confess that I said to myself, as I came along and saw that the City of Hartford was in——'
>
> "'No! But is she, though!'
>
> "And as quick as any flash of lightning I stood in the presence of empty benches! I had brought them the news myself." [77]

In the margin of page 161 the author reminded himself, "burnt up the old sot." This reference to his own boyhood experience of having given matches to a vagrant drunk who proceeded to burn up the jail and himself was not incorporated directly into *Tom Sawyer*. The man corresponding to the tramp was Muff Potter, and his death in jail would have made it necessary to omit the dramatic courtroom scene in Chapter XXIII. But like Sam Clemens, Tom did smuggle "small comforts" to the man in jail and suffered agonies of conscience to the point of talking in his sleep.

On manuscript page 210, Twain wrote, "Learning to smoke. The dead cigar man. Rolling the rock. Burying pet bird or cat." The first note he amplified in Chapter XVI, where Huck instructs Tom and Joe Harper in the art of smoking; the second

I have not identified; the third, referring to the Holliday's Hill episode used in *Innocents Abroad,* was rejected; and the fourth received brief mention in Chapter XXII ("He drifted listlessly down the street and found Jim Hollis acting as Judge in a juvenile court that was trying a cat for murder, in the presence of her victim, a bird"). In the margin of page 213 he mentioned a "candy-pull," apparently toying with the idea of introducing "Jim Wolfe and the Cats" into *Tom Sawyer.*

In another hand, probably Mrs. Clemens', there were two notes which Twain used in his novel. Written possibly from Twain's dictation while the couple went over the manuscript in the winter of 1874, they suggest, "Take of[f] his wig with a cat," and "Tom licked for Becky." Twain reiterated both suggestions in notes in his own handwriting much later in the course of composition: on page 464 he noted, "T takes B's whipping," and on page 573, "(Dropping cat)."

Again, at the edge of manuscript page 209, where he was writing about Tom's daydream of becoming a pirate with a "crimson sash," and remembered that the red sash was his enticement for joining the Cadets of Temperance, he wrote "Cadets of Temp." in the margin. In his early *Alta* letter, Mark Twain had described the episode in a brief paragraph:

> And they started militia companies, and Sons of Temperance and Cadets of Temperance. Hannibal always had a weakness for the Temperance cause. I joined the Cadets myself, although they didn't allow a boy to smoke, or drink or swear, but I thought I never could be truly happy till I wore one of those stunning red scarfs and walked in procession when a distinguished citizen died. I stood it four months, but never an infernal distinguished citizen died during the whole time; and when they finally pronounced old Dr. Norton convalescent (a man I had been depending on for seven or eight weeks,) I just drew out. I drew out in disgust, and pretty much all the distinguished citizens in the camp died within the next three weeks.

In *Tom Sawyer* there were significant alterations that accented the process of maturation the outline note suggested:

> Tom joined the new order of Cadets of Temperance, being attracted by the showy character of their "regalia." He promised to abstain from smoking, chewing, and profanity as long as he remained a member. Now he found out a new thing—namely, that to promise not to do a thing is the surest way in the world to make a body want to go and do that very thing. Tom soon found himself tormented with a desire to drink and swear; the desire grew to be so intense that nothing but the hope of a chance to display himself in his red sash kept him from withdrawing from the order. Fourth of July was coming but he soon gave that up—gave it up before he had worn his shackles over forty eight hours—and fixed his hopes upon old Judge Frazer, justice of the peace, who was apparently on his deathbed and would have a big public funeral, since he was so high an official. During three days Tom was deeply concerned about the Judge's condition and hungry for news of it. Sometimes his hopes ran high—so high that he would venture to get out his regalia and practise before the looking-glass. But the Judge had a most discouraging way of fluctuating. At last he was pronounced upon the mend—and then convalescent. Tom was disgusted; and felt a sense of injury, too. He handed in his resignation at once—and that night the Judge suffered a relapse and died. Tom resolved that he would never trust a man like that again.

Twain shortened the membership from four months to less than a week, omitted the unrealistic "drinking" from the pledge, and emphasized Tom's irresoluteness and immaturity by motivating him with overwhelming desires to violate the rules. At the same time, notice that Tom is learning; he "found out a new thing" about human nature in realizing that "to promise not to do a thing is the surest way in the world to make a body want to go and do that very thing." But the process is erratic, for he also learns not to trust a man like Judge Frazer, a humorous bit of resolution that undercuts and burlesques the earlier bit of knowledge by its illogical reasoning, which suggests that even though Tom may be maturing, he still has a long process ahead of him.

For a while, work went smoothly "on the hill" in Elmira; on September 4 he boasted that he had been writing fifty pages of manuscript a day (though he was also at work on "A True Story," "A Fable for Good Old Boys and Girls," and some of the dramatization of *The Gilded Age*), but by then he "had worked myself out, pumped myself dry." [78] So about then he put the manuscript aside and many years later recollected the hiatus in the composition:

> At page 400 of my manuscript the story made a sudden and determined halt and refused to proceed another step. Day after day it still refused. I was disappointed, distressed and immeasurably astonished, for I knew quite well that the tale was not finished and I could not understand why I was not able to go on with it. The reason was very simple—my tank had run dry; it was empty; the stock of materials in it was exhausted; the story could not go on without materials; it could not be wrought out of nothing.[79]

So he put the manuscript aside and worked on the "Old Times" articles instead. Incidentally, those critics who point to Twain's analogy of the well running dry as proof of his amateurishness in matters of composition would do well to re-read Henry James's preface to *The American,* in which an author against whom that charge could certainly never be lodged points out that the germ of his novel "had so much to give" that he "dropped it for the time into the deep well of unconscious cerebration: not without the hope, doubtless, that it might eventually emerge from that reservoir, as one had already known the buried treasure to come to light, with a firm iridescent surface and a notable increase of weight." [80]

Twain's inability to continue the plot of *Tom Sawyer* was the result of uncertainty over the marginal outline for the original structure of the novel and the notion that perhaps he was writing a children's adventure story rather than a novel for grownups. Even when he returned to the novel the following spring, he was not sure which course to take, and the picaresque nature of the novel could allow him to continue into Tom's mature years or to stop with boyhood without too much difficulty either way. So, even as late as June, 1875, he told Howells, "I am going to take into serious consideration all you have said, & then make up my mind by & by. Since there is no plot to the thing, it is likely to follow its own drift, & so is as likely to drift into manhood as anywhere." A couple of weeks later he told Howells further, "I have finished the story & didn't take the chap beyond boyhood. . . . See if you don't really decide that I am right in closing with him as a boy." [81] The point at which the manuscript broke down, nevertheless, was one that required Twain at least to consider the drift of his novel in 1874.

Page 403 of the manuscript, where the work halted in September, 1874, appears toward the end of Chapter XV. Tom, Joe Harper, and Huck have run away to Jackson's Island to become pirates, but Joe and Huck have become homesick and are all too ready to return to St. Petersburg. Tom, who does not share their wish to go back to civilization, withers them with derision. The cannons on the boat have boomed in an attempt to bring up the boys' bodies. Just as in *Huckleberry Finn,* Twain has managed his plot, set the stage, and prepared the devices for an imminent departure. After the other boys go to sleep, Tom scrawls a note for Joe Harper on a piece of sycamore bark and leaves it, along with his "school-boy treasures of almost inestimable value"—a leave-taking that sounds much more permanent and serious than would be necessary merely for Tom to deliver another note to Aunt Polly. He writes her a note, too, and at page 403 is standing over his sleeping aunt. Twain had thus made ready for Tom to begin his "Battle of Life in many lands," to leave St. Petersburg and his comrades who were about to return there. But the manuscript shows that the author, uncertain of the wisdom of the move, pondered which course to take. Indecisively, he wrote out alternatives: in the top margin, "Sid is to find and steal that scroll" and "He is to show the scroll in proof of his intent"; in the left margin, two lines canceled so as to be illegible; across the page itself, "No, he leaves the bark there, & Sid gets it" and "He forgets to leave the bark."

Now, if the note was merely to contain the message, "We ain't dead—we are only off playing pirates," Twain's ruminations about its ultimate outcome were all out of proportion to its significance. If Tom left Jackson's Island merely to deliver this message and then return, the bequest of his proudest possessions to Joe Harper was absurd. If, as one of the notes suggested, he was to forget to leave the scroll after swimming part of the river and sneaking under Aunt Polly's bed, his actions would be preposterous. But if the bark was to contain a farewell message for Aunt Polly and was to be stolen by Sid, this scene might prepare for Tom's return at age thirty-seven to St. Petersburg.

Though it is admittedly conjecture, it seems plausible to suggest a court trial or some other identification scene in which the stolen bark would be the crucial evidence, since Twain was especially fond of sensational trial scenes in the 1870's. In addition to the one in *Tom Sawyer,* there were others in *The Gilded Age,* "Ah Sin," and "Simon Wheeler, the Amateur Detective." Almost literally, the piece of bark with a scrawled message separated the reader from something very similar to *Adventures of Huckleberry Finn;* the scroll of sycamore bark became the key to the further progress of *Tom Sawyer* that the resurrected raft would be in Twain's masterpiece. Used in one way, as a farewell message, the plot would continue in the direction Twain envisioned in his original outline; used in another—the way he finally chose—the direction would change.

Twain decided not to have Tom start his travels. The boy

returns the scroll to his jacket pocket, where Aunt Polly discovers it a few chapters later. Then Twain turned back to page 401 and inserted a paragraph that set the stage for the boys' return to their own funeral: "This was Wednesday night. If the OVER [then on the back of the page] bodies continued missing until Sunday, all hope would be given over, & the funeral would be preached on that morning. Tom shuddered." The plot changed its direction, but the theme of Tom's maturation remained.

The rest of the manuscript, the part composed in the spring of 1875, gave Twain some problems. In several places he reminded himself marginally to insert Aunt Polly's discovery of the message in Tom's pocket: on page 409, he jotted down, "The piece of bark at Aunt Polly's," and on 464, "Aunt P's bark." But he never explained satisfactorily Tom's similar message to Joe or his strange bequest of his "treasures" to his friend.

Twain also had some difficulties in arranging the various chapters in the latter part of the book. Basically, he juggled his material extensively in order (1) to insert the material on the graduation ceremony (Chapter XXI) and on the Cadets of Temperance (Chapter XXII), which were written later and then placed in their present positions, (2) to exploit the climactic outcome of the picnic, which ends with Tom and Becky trapped in the cave, and (3) to adjust material so that the last chapters of the novel would be ones in which Tom, still maturing even though he did not leave St. Petersburg, could act most adult and manly in a fashion which would suggest that *Tom Sawyer* "could not go much further without becoming the history of a *man*." In the same way, Twain's delaying his use of the suggestions to have Tom take Becky's whipping accents both Tom's development and Twain's conscious manipulation of his material to serve the ends of a theme of maturation.[82] And Brander Matthews described this method of composition accurately:

> When at last he became convinced that he had made his
> profit out of every possible reminiscence, he went over
> what he had written with great care, adjusting the several
> instalments one to the other, sometimes transposing a
> chapter or two and sometimes writing into the earlier
> chapters the necessary preparation for adventures in the
> later chapters unforeseen when he was engaged on the
> beginnings of the book.[83]

At the same time, Twain continued to use the opportunistic
method of marginal notation in the second half of his book, but
to a much lesser degree than in the 1874 section. On page 409
he wrote "storm," and then began describing the storm on
Jackson's Island on 432. On 322 he wrote the inexplicable
"Silver moons," and on 464 two notes he decided not to use:
"Becky had measles" and "Joe drowned." He found Mrs.
Mary Ann Harris Gay's *The Pastor's Story and Other Pieces*
and could not resist using her orations and declamations for
the graduation ceremonies.[84] He had a plot for the removal of
Injun Joe that involved a character named Ezra Ward, "an old
back-country farmer . . . who had been a schoolmate of Aunt
Polly's so many . . ." The page (manuscript page 600, Chapter
XXIV, just before the final sentence of the published book)
ended, and whatever Ezra was supposed to do to lift "a boy's
burden when it begins to get too heavy for him" must have
been on manuscript consigned to the wastebasket.

The book was a combination, then, of reminiscence of
boyhood memories, of associational development, and of
haphazard recollection, but all shaped and formed, selected
and rearranged, in a fashion suggesting that Twain was
conquering the bugaboo of "fiction" and coming to grips with
problems of form, theme, and structure consciously for the first
time.

After Twain signaled Howells that the novel was finished on
July 5, 1875, there was still some revising to do. Some of the
work was the fault of a foggy memory: Twain changed
"Bessie" to "Becky" and "Fletcher" to "Thatcher," and canceled

a passage DeVoto has suggested began a burlesque section. He left a good bit of the chore of revising up to Howells, though. First he asked him to go over the material, adding emphatically that the book was composed for grown-up readers, not children, aware that the point was significant. Howells agreed, but Twain "realized all of the atrocity" of saddling Howells with proofreading and called in a theatrical agent to take the manuscript and the temptation away, to have a copy made. Later in the year, though, after Bliss had the original copy for the American Publishing Company's typesetters, Howells read the amanuensis copy and made suggestions. In addition to proposing the removal of the final chapter, which presumably became the first of *Adventures of Huckleberry Finn*, Howells revised with an eye to his belief that Twain "ought to treat it explicitly *as* a boy's story. Grown-ups will enjoy it just as much if you do; and if you should put it forth as a study of boy character from the grown-up point of view, you'd give the wrong key to it." Exactly how much material concerning Huck's life at the widow's was removed cannot be definitely stated. Twain had told Howells earlier that his manuscript ran to 900 pages,[85] and the final manuscript page is numbered "876." Occasionally, though, Twain wrote on the reverse of a page, and once he skipped ten pages in his pagination (333 should have been 323). But a total of 875 pages is roughly correct, which means that perhaps he sacrificed twenty-five pages at the end; but his figures were chronically incorrect.

Not until January, 1876, after four weeks of illness, did Twain get down to the task—"the dreary & hateful task"—of reading the amanuensis copy Howells had annotated. Persuaded by both Howells and Livy "that the book should issue as a book for boys, pure & simple,"[86] he agreed to the taming of "various obscenities." Both DeVoto and Ferguson[87] have examined Howells' revisions at length and correctly minimized their influence, especially in light of Twain's own change of mind about a juvenile audience. But they nevertheless suggest the kinds of things Twain thought appropriate for an adult reader that were forbidden to the youthful one. At Howells' suggestion, Twain eliminated most of the Sunday-school superintendent's speech from Chapter IV, because children would be unable to comprehend its satire. The censored portions (MS. p. 89) went like this:

> Instead of playing with dolls on the Sabbath day or robbing the poor little birds of their little ones—for birds have feelings just like us, and it grieves them just as it would us to take away our little ones. Think how your dear parents would feel if some great ogre came and took you away and destroyed you? Would they not mourn, and perhaps even die of sorrow? Now always remember, when you find a bird's nest, stop and think how the mother will feel. We all love the Sunday-school, don't we? (Enthusiastic nods and smiles of assent.) That is right. Let us try to keep loving it.

Since Howells recommended the removal of the passage in the "dog and the pinchbug" episode which described the pup "with his tail shut down like a hasp," he was probably also instrumental in the removal of a passage immediately following which described the dog as "fiercely expressing at one end the woe that was torturing the other." Another which, even if Howells did not suggest it, would have had his approval to be removed, occurred in Chapter IV, where Tom was learning his Bible chapters. Originally Tom has chosen the Sermon on the Mount, "though he was strongly attracted to another chapter that had one verse which he strongly coveted: 'Jesus wept'—the shortest verse in the Testament." [88]

Bliss had some of the original manuscript of *Tom* in November, 1875, when Twain told him, "You may let Williams have all of Tom Sawyer that you have received. He can of course make the pictures all the more understandingly after reading the whole story."[89] Apparently Williams used the manuscript, and then Bliss returned it to Twain for the corrections that Howells had suggested. By January, at any rate, Williams had "made about 200 rattling pictures for it—some of them very dainty. . . . He takes a book of mine, & without suggestion from anybody builds no end of pictures just from his reading of it." [90] Bliss went through the manuscript, too, marking out the spots at which Williams' illustrations were to be placed, and on April 3 Twain made the enigmatic critical pronouncement that the illustrations were "considerably above the American average, in conception if not in execution." [91] But storm clouds were gathering which would ultimately persuade Twain to seek a new publisher after *Tom Sawyer* issued.

Bliss set the book up in galley proof early in 1876, for Howells acknowledged a set on March 20, 1876, which he used to write the untimely review that appeared in the May *Atlantic.* But Twain threw a sizable monkey wrench into the publishing plans. On April 11, 1876, Frank Bliss wrote the expectant author:

> Father says that he had an estimate all ready for the electros of "Tom Sawyer", but as you changed the size it involves making a new estimate all through, & he is fearful that reducing the size so much, of many of the cuts, will interfere with their printing nicely, he is making inquiries about it however will report the result in about two days.[92]

It is possible—indeed, probable—that Bliss had used a number of Williams' illustrations in full-page or near full-page size in an attempt to use up space and make *Tom Sawyer* appear a larger, more acceptable subscription volume. Then it was necessary to reset the book, and proofreading had to begin anew. Twain, who had originally wanted to release *Tom* for "the early spring market" and then expected Bliss "to do your canvassing and issue 'Tom' the middle of April" [93] or at the latest the middle of May, saw Howells' review appear without any sign of the book's release. He wrote a letter that reflects his own sense of frustration:

> Bliss made a failure in the matter of getting Tom Sawyer
> ready on time—the engravers assisting, as usual. I went
> down to see how *much* of a delay there was going to be,
> & found that the man had not even put a canvasser on or
> issued an advertisement yet—in fact that the *electrotypes*
> would not all be done for a month! [94]

As he waited for the book to issue, he forgot his own
contribution to the delay in changing the size of the illustrations and found a partially justifiable reason for heaping the
blame on Bliss.

The humorist discovered that summer that Bliss was seeing
so many other books through the presses that he had little or
no time for *Tom Sawyer*. In addition to Twain's novel, the
American Publishing Company issued Harte's *Gabriel Conroy*,
DeQuille's *The Big Bonanza*, Warner's *Moslems and Mummies*,
Henry C. Fish's *Bible Lands Illustrated*, William H. Daniels'
D. L. Moody and His Work, A. B. Meachum's *Wi-ne-ma*,
R. H. Phelps's *The Newgate of Connecticut*, J. H. Trumbull's
The True Blue Laws of Connecticut, and a centennial edition
*Fac-simile of Gen'l Washington's Account with the United
States from 1775 to 1783*. When he found out about it, Twain,
who by now believed himself to be an authority on subscription
selling, exploded. On June 24 he delivered a kind of ultimatum
to Bliss:

> I have been thinking and have arrived at the conclusion
> that if the Company will sell out two thirds of its
> copyrights & electrotypes & also its printing office &
> presses by auction, & move back into cheap quarters
> again & publish about one or two books at a time, it can
> declare some more dividends. . . . I think the present
> extended business is a considerable detriment to my
> pocket. I think we publish books so fast that canvassers
> are likely merely to skim the cream of a district & then
> "lay" for the next new book.

Though Bliss did not realize it, this was more than idle
suggestion; it was the terms of a peace treaty. Of course, the

suggestions were made with major concern for the publishing of *Tom*. As Twain put it to Bliss, "I shall be mighty sorry to see Tom Sawyer issue when any other book of the firm is being canvassed or within six months of being canvassed." [95]

Bliss replied, as usual, by turning the argument against Twain; but for once the technique would not work. On July 18 Bliss answered Twain's letter, first explaining that the delay of proofs which he had promised Twain early in May, had been caused by his "indisposition." "I send you by mail to night 2 chapters proofs & original copy, which please return as soon as convenient. . . . Shall send 2 chapters more tomorrow, & so on & put it through rapidly." But Twain's suggestions required more space to answer:

> And now as respects the company business you mention. I would say, I should certainly offer no personal objection or use any personal influence to prevent the adoption of any plan deemed proper by the other directors. I do not know as you are aware of the condition of the Co. or not, you have never been present at any of the meetings and have never asked for information of me. I am not ashamed to show my business up, for the past 10 or the past single year. . . . I am sorry you found it necessary to talk against my management outside our board as I have several times heard you have. Even the poor drunken Williams comes and boastingly taunts me with what you tell him—while another of my help gets letters from N. Y. stating what he says you told there. For myself I care nothing, but it seems poor policy to injure the stock this way, and our stock is too valuable to be made to suffer. . . . The business can be cut down, & with a cheaper man at the helm, expenses can be made low, & possibly larger profits made. The experiment can be made & I will most cheerfully assist with all my might. [96]

It was a neat combination of the old excuse about damaging the commercial value of the American Publishing Company, of which Twain had been a director since 1873, and an offer of self-sacrificing nobility. But it didn't work.

Twain replied on July 22, adamant about his theories on the way to sell *Tom Sawyer*:

> The business seems to be a great unpaying thing, whereas the reverse would be the case if it were shrunk up, perhaps. . . . There is a matter in which I am strongly interested. You told me, several times that a subscription house could not run two books at once & do justice to either of them. I saw no reason to disbelieve that, & I never have disbelieved it. Therefore, I am solicitous about Tom Sawyer—more so than I would be about another book, because this is an experiment. I want it run by itself, if possible, & pushed like everything. Can this be done?—& when? Give me your ideas about it. What do you think of canvassing in September & October & issuing 1st Nov? Shall you be canvassing any new book then? [97]

When Twain wrote Bliss on August 8, returning proof for Chapter X or XI and congratulating his publisher on their quality, he agreed to an alternate date: "I like the idea of issuing Nov 1st—or *Dec* 15th, whichever seems best." [98] Perhaps there was to be another attempt to capitalize on the Christmas market.

When Bliss sent proofs and manuscript for Chapter XVI, he wrote a note on the back of manuscript page 432:

> *Wms* [apparently one of the three compositors] seems to have run all this into one chapter, whether by your directions or not I don't know; but I find it so and it can't [illegible] be altered, as the chapter *Headings* will all be disarrayed.
> It is not very long as it is and dont seem to be disconnected in subject.

Originally the four paragraphs beginning, "About midnight Joe awoke and called the boys," and ending, "there was not a dry spot to sleep on, anywhere around," were marked as part of Chapter XVII. Apparently in order to assist in the problem of chapter headings, Twain wrote the four final paragraphs of

Chapter XVI, manuscript pages 447A to 447D. He had finished up all the proofreading by September 14 when he sent Bliss a hurried note reminding him to dedicate the book "to my wife." [99] Finally, a year and a half after its completion, *Tom Sawyer* was ready to issue, but there was no reason to celebrate.

The book was doomed commercially even before Bliss received the first copies on December 8. The English edition had been published back in June, and from it, Canadian pirates flooded this country with a seventy-five cent paperback and a dollar cloth version that had gone to a third edition by October, 1876. [100] In other words, as Twain watched helplessly, but with what one can imagine was stirring profanity, the Canadian publisher, Belford Brothers, was selling a tremendous number of copies to Bliss's customers. Then there was the problem of Howells' review, which Twain hoped would "modify or shut up the unfriendly." Since it appeared in May, it reached the public seven months before the American Publishing Company edition of the book. The *Boston Transcript* quoted some passages from Howells' review as early as April 28, and, ironically, the Canadian pirated edition excerpted a few sentences of the review. In the same way, Moncure Conway's review appeared in the *Chicago Tribune* on July 3, much too early to assist the American sales. Conway, incidentally, had been in charge of the arrangements for the English edition: On January 5, 1876, Twain asked Conway "to take my new book to England, & have it published there by some one (according to your plan) before it is issued here." [101] Conway's plan, as he explained in a letter to his wife two weeks later, was to "pay for the manufacture of his own book and pay the publisher for each copy sold." [102] Twain still had fantastic confidence in the value of the pronouncement of the future "Dean of American Letters," and insisted that Bliss quote Howells' review in "the prospectus & in the slips that go to editors, & a line or two of it in your advertisements, for I think it will have a good effect." [103] But it was pretty shopworn by the time it might have helped the sales of Bliss's edition.

As the year dwindled to a close, Twain used the slack business conditions to alibi the book's delay. He told Howells back in April that after looking at the sales of his earlier books that first quarter he informed Bliss, "*This* ain't no time to be publishing books; therefore, let Tom lay still till autumn, Mr. Bliss, & make a holiday book of him to beguile the young people withal." Again in September, he told Stoddard, "I haven't issued Tom Sawyer here yet. Am waiting for a livelier market. Shall issue right after the presidential election." In October Warner, whose *Moslems and Mummies* was also on Bliss's publishing schedule, told C. H. Webb, "In a flush time Bliss is more difficult to open than an Egyptian tomb, and there is no treasure in him when he is opened. . . . Mark's Tom Sawyer is also waiting for the fall rise. I fear we shall none of us get rich out of it." [104]

In his prospectus Bliss quoted reviews that the English edition of *Tom Sawyer* had received, in addition to the Howells notice, reviews from the London *Examiner,* the *Athenaeum,* and, incongruously, the *Cincinnati Daily Enquirer.* He also made a significant sales pitch to adult readers, and not to children at all. If Livy, Twain, and Howells believed that *Tom Sawyer* was a children's book, Bliss did not: "In announcing this volume," he explained, "the publishers have no hesitation in declaring it to be one of the most original, unique, piquant and entertaining of all Mark Twain's works."

> The genius requisite to render the written adventures of a boy overwhelmingly fascinating to grown up readers, is possessed by but few, and challenges the deepest admiration. That Mr. Clemens has this, is evident from the burst of enthusiastic praise with which the publication of "Tom Sawyer" in England, has been received. No words have seemed too strong to express the pleasure felt at this fresh exhibition of the author's powers, exerted in a direction least expected. . . . From beginning to end, the pages of

"Tom Sawyer" are replete with lively sallies, humorous ideas, and scathing hits.[105]

The selections, from widely scattered portions throughout the book, included most of the "dog and the pinchbug" episode, the graveyard scene, Muff Potter's confession, "the cat and the pain-killer" complete, most of the boys' return to their own funeral, several pages of the graduation ceremony, all of Muff Potter's trial, and those pages of Tom and Becky in the cave which contained the largest and most terrifying of True Williams' illustrations. The agents' dummy thus combined the comic, sensational, and the morbid in a skillful but hardly juvenile blend.

Tom Sawyer was sent to the major journals and magazines for review, but the results were almost negligible. The *New York Times* reviewed the novel, the Philadelphia *Sunday Republic* printed the whitewashing scene, and the *Boston Transcript* spread selections from the book—but from the English edition—over three days in June and July, 1876.[106] So far as this was free advertising, it appeared too early to help. Bliss also mailed out circulars to customers, mail-order fashion, the first page of the text on one side and the advertisement from the prospectus on the other. To this he pasted a small announcement:

> We will send to your address, either by mail or express, free of expense, the book you name, on receipt of the price for the style in which you wish it bound; for the different styles of binding and prices, refer to the accompanying circular.[107]

No matter what Bliss tried, however, the public just was not buying.

Poor business conditions, the enormous list of other new books Bliss was peddling, the small bulk of *Tom Sawyer* with its 275 pages—less than half the regular subscription book—all were factors contributing to its failure. One lady agent in the San Francisco Bay area reported that she was embarrassed at delivering so small a volume to her customers and that they were universally dissatisfied with the book for that reason.[108] In 1877 Bliss switched to heavier paper in an attempt to increase the book's thickness, but even so, *Tom Sawyer* was the least successful of all Twain's first six major books; it sold even more poorly than *Sketches New and Old.*

The first fifty prospectuses were delivered to Bliss on November 14, and the first hundred cloth copies of the book on December 8. Sales never had the benefit of an early rush; after the first month, when 9,378 copies were bound, the demand was so sluggish that only about 2,000 a month were bound. In March, 1877, when Bliss was searching for canvassers and bragging that 30,000 copies of *Tom Sawyer* had been sold in two months, he had actually sold only 13,319.[109] At the end of its first year *Tom* had sold 23,638 copies, and in the twenty-four months to the end of the decade only 5,000 more volumes were required. At the end of 1879 the bindery had sent Bliss 24,241 cloth copies, 798 gilt, 3,620 Leather Library, 300 half-morocco copies, 3 in sheets, and 890 prospectuses. In 1885 sales had climbed to only 35,000 copies, an increase of 6,000 more.

The cliché that *Tom Sawyer* was an immediate best seller is a particularly dangerous one. Twain's decision to go to a new publisher occurred, not after the publication of *A Tramp Abroad,* but as a result of the failure of *Tom Sawyer.* Actually, *Tom, Sketches New and Old,* and *The Gilded Age,* or Twain's portion of it, were similar in several ways. Less than suitable length and unique among subscription books because they were fiction, they marked a steady decline in sales and income. Committed to writing—book-writing—as a career and profession and "over-extended" financially as a result of the success of *Innocents Abroad* and *Roughing It,* Twain was in desperate straits because of the unimpressive income from these three books. By almost anyone else's standards, an aggregate sale of 100,000 copies would be impressive; but because the *Sketch*

book and *Tom Sawyer* were smaller books and because Twain
got only half the authors' royalty on *The Gilded Age,* the
income was not up to par. In a house that cost, by present
standards, somewhere between $350,000 and $400,000 and that
was a perpetual "open house," requiring a staff of six whose
salaries ran to $1,650 annually, Twain had reason to be
perplexed over his dwindling popularity. The dramatizations
of *The Gilded Age* and "Ah Sin," the fiddling with his
Self-Pasting Scrap Book, lecture tours, plans for a round-
robin "blindfold" novel all cut with a double edge. They took
considerable time away from more important writing, and they
uniformly failed to bring in the money that the three literary
disappointments were not securing. Comparative figures are
not worth much, because the books had varying times in which
to sell, but *Innocents Abroad* and *Roughing It* paid Mark
Twain a total of more than $58,000 through the end of 1879,
and *Sketches* and *Tom Sawyer* combined brought him only
$15,000.[110]

Twain was also aiming at the rupture with Bliss when he
flirted with other publishers in the mid-1870's. There were the
Nast Almanacs, *Sketches Number One,* Osgood's *A True Story
and the Recent Carnival of Crime,* and Slote, Woodman's
Punch, Brothers, Punch! and Other Sketches, all of which
appeared before Twain made his contract with Osgood for
The Prince and the Pauper and even before the publication of
A Tramp Abroad. They were all "trade" books, though, and
Twain's argument was not with subscription technique but
only with Bliss's methods of managing the American Publishing
Company. "By Subscription" was still the only way to sell a
book, but Mark Twain, with five subscription volumes to his
credit, was under the dubious impression that he knew better
than Bliss how to run a subscription house. He apparently
discussed the matter of changing publishers with Dan Slote,
crony of the *Quaker City* trip and publisher of the *Scrapbook,*
and unburdened himself of the injustices Bliss had heaped

upon his back. In 1878, at any rate, Slote wrote Twain a letter that strongly suggests Twain had considered Slote, Woodman as his future publishers. "Should the Amer Publishing Co ever let go their grip," Dan soothed Twain, "we can get 'good and even' on your future writings." [111]

It was only by a quirk of circumstance that the American Publishing Company got *A Tramp Abroad*, and before Twain would agree to let them do the volume, he included clauses in the contract that would insure against repetition of the wrongs that had accompanied the publication of *Roughing It* and *Tom Sawyer*. But firmly convinced that the American Publishing Company's business was too extensive to sell his own books properly, Twain needed only the further revelation of Bliss's cheating on his royalties to confirm his plans to leave the company.

CHAPTER IV

BLISS IS DEAD

*A*MONG THOSE abortive manuscripts Twain piled up in the years between 1876 and 1879 were "Cap'n Simon Wheeler, the Amateur Detective" and the narrative version, *Simon Wheeler, Detective, Ah Sin,* the "Autobiography of a Damned Fool," which was as much a continuation of the *Tom Sawyer* outline as the beginnings of *Huck Finn* were, contributions to *The Atlantic Monthly* like "Some Rambling Notes of an Idle Excursion"—all decidedly substandard by any criterion. As Twain went to Washington to supervise the production of *Ah Sin,* to Bermuda with Twichell, became embroiled in the Hayes-Tilden election, and began, singlehandedly almost, to pick out Hayes's diplomatic corps for Howells' edification, he veered away from concern for literary matters of consequence. It was not the compulsive sort of impotence that characterized the last decade of his literary life and that left such a multitude of unfinished stories and tales as a testament, but it was true that Mark Twain had a problem.

He was convinced that the American Publishing Company, which he could rightly claim he had elevated to its position at the top of the subscription publishing industry, was ungrateful. He had bought $5,000 of stock in the company and was a member of the board of directors from 1873 to 1881; he had received a 10 per cent dividend in 1873, but from then until he sold out his shares in 1881, Bliss never declared another.[1] Instead, the company used its money to expand tremendously and to the detriment of Twain's own books. Now, as is obvious, by 1876, Twain believed that he knew at least as much as Bliss did about the running of a subscription house. As director, though, he was never advised in time of the company's meetings and never attended one. There was in Twain's mind a strong suspicion that Bliss was not marketing his books as they should be sold, and there was still the smoldering doubt that Orion had kindled about the royalty on *Roughing It* coming far short of the half-profits Twain believed he deserved. These financial aspects of the problem were not insignificant, either. When *The Gilded Age, Sketches,* and *Tom Sawyer* all returned relatively insignificant royalties to the man whose decision to become a writer of books was based in large part on the flush income from *Innocents Abroad* and *Roughing It,* major problems developed. As Twain told Howells in 1878, "You know that for two years we have been coming to want, every little while, & have straightway gone to economising." [2] He had stopped feeling poor, he explained, but it must have galled him to know that it was because of the Langdon coal company annual report and not because of the royalty statements.

More significant than the financial part of the problem, though, was the literary facet. Twain was too sensitive about his own reputation not to be aware that the animosity of the regular trade was as strong toward a subscription book author as it was toward the book itself. In the 1880's Twain was to receive several personal attacks on this score: The *Chicago Tribune* pointed out that *The Stolen White Elephant* had been "placed in the hands of a respectable publisher instead of offering booksellers a premium on dishonesty in order to obtain for their shelves copies of a book 'sold only by subscription' "; when he made fun of the banning of *Huck Finn* by the Concord Public Library, the *Boston Advertiser* archly questioned whether "his impudent intimation that a larger sale and larger profits are a satisfactory recompense to him for the unfavorable judgment of honest critics, is a true indication of the standard by which he measures success in literature";[3] and in 1886 John Wanamaker printed an advertisement in the Philadelphia *Press* commenting on his sale of Grant's *Memoirs*. The "unfortunate manner of publication," Wanamaker claimed, had made the family of Grant, the book-buying public, and the bookstores all losers. "And who are the gainers? Book-pedlers and book-pedler publishers; nobody else."[4] Even earlier, though, Twain could not have ignored the subscription book versus trade book war of the 1870's and 1880's (described in Chapter I), and he certainly could not have failed to notice that Howells, his literary court of last resort, had turned down the idea of publishing his Hayes campaign biography with Bliss.[5] As he depended more and more on Howells' pronouncements about him in the *Atlantic* book reviews, Twain obviously developed a mote in his eye: he wanted the critical approval of those "honest critics."

But the earnings of the four books published in the late 70's in the regular trade were dismal in comparison even with those of *Tom Sawyer*. So though Twain could announce significantly in 1877 that "Osgood was the best publisher who ever breathed, and that [Osgood] could have everything he owned," he also told Howells in 1879, after a half-dozen years of what to him were failures, "I want to make a book which people will *read*."[6] It was not simply the problem of income, either; Twain was aware of two distinct audiences, one of whom he had not reached even with Howells' help, and the other which he reached all too well by painting himself striped and turning cartwheels. But he craved and yearned for that audience's approval just as much as he did for the "honest critics'." The familiar letter to Andrew Lang which the English reception of *The Connecticut Yankee* prompted was foreshadowed by a whole decade of self-doubt expressed when he wrote Howells about the audience reaction to *Ah Sin,* "Nearly every time the audience roared, I knew it was over something that would be condemned in the morning (justly, too) but must be left in—for low comedies are written for the drawing-room, the kitchen & the stable, & if you cut out the kitchen & the stable the drawing-room can't support the play by itself."[7] Even though Osgood might be the best publisher in the country, he did not sell books by the fifty thousands and he did not sell books for the kitchen and the stable.

Two other factors, conjectural indeed, may have contributed to Twain's solution of his dilemma. First, there were serious problems connected with Twain's writing for the *Atlantic.* As soon as the *Atlantic* appeared, Canadian, English, and other journals picked up his material and printed it. This involved complications both about copyright and about royalties, so in the late 1870's the correspondence between Twain and Howells included voluminous directions about "simultaning" with other journals; that is, sending proof sheets to a foreign periodical so that it could print material and secure a foreign copyright the same month it was released in the *Atlantic.* Between 1877 and 1879 Twain tried to "simultane" with *Belgravia, Temple Bar,* the *Canadian Monthly,* the San Francisco *Argonaut,* and the Melbourne *Victorian Review.*[8] It would have operated only minimally, and the complications were various and time-consuming and not completely satisfactory; they may have had some small effect on Twain's interest in writing for the *Atlantic.*

The other factor was the Whittier Birthday Dinner speech which Twain delivered before the assembled arbiters of taste in America on December 17, 1877. Contemporary readers of the speech appreciate the hilarious spoofing of Emerson, Holmes, and Longfellow, and realize that Twain, with the overly fastidious encouragement of Howells, exaggerated the incident out of all proportion. But it is with Twain's own reaction rather than with public reception that it is necessary to deal; the humorist was mortified at the *faux pas* he believed he had committed. He must have felt as if the door to respectability had been opened only for him to stumble and kick it shut before he had a chance to enter. He insisted that he would have to stay out of the pages of the *Atlantic* in order not to injure it and asked Howells to suppress "The Loves of Alonzo Fitz Clarence and Rosannah Ethelton" from the magazine. Whatever may have been the public attitude toward the "hideous mistake," it is obvious that Twain viewed his speech as a serious error that alienated him from the literary hierarchy of his day.

His solution was to continue to publish by subscription, but not with the American Publishing Company—in 1881, he would finally be able to combine the services of the best publisher, Osgood, with the subscription method. For the present, though, he decided to work with Frank Bliss, Elisha's son, who had resigned as the treasurer of the American Publishing Company in order to open a subscription house of his own and to publish just one book, *The Life of the Hon. William F. Cody, Known as Buffalo Bill, the Famous Hunter, Scout and Guide. An Autobiography,* during the short happy life of Francis E. Bliss Company. Twain signed the contract, which stipulated that "Bliss agrees that if at the end of the first year one half of said gross profits exceeds the amount of said royalty for said year, then said Bliss will pay to said Clemens the amount of such excess in addition to said royalty," [9] just one month before he left for Europe and less than three months after the Whittier Birthday Dinner fiasco.

There was considerable secrecy involved with *A Tramp Abroad,* in part because Twain and Frank Bliss kept the news

of the contract from Elisha, in part because Twain no doubt
preferred not to have competing subscription publishers issue
European travel volumes in the wake of his new book, and in
part simply because Twain enjoyed the grandstanding of
intrigue and suspense.

Elisha did his best to get the new book for the American
Publishing Company as soon as news of it began circulating
around Hartford in 1879. He reported to Twain, without a hint
of a suspicion that Frank had a contract for the book, that his
son "is not with the Co. and is doing nothing, except organizing
for future business, corresponding with agts, making General
Agencies etc. and getting his machinery in shape for work."
Elisha, blithefully unaware that Frank was now competition,
allowed his son to use illustrations from *Roughing It, The Big
Bonanza,* and *Tom Sawyer* in Buffalo Bill's *Autobiography* and
pressed Twain for the volume that was to become *A Tramp
Abroad.*

In the same letter telling Twain of Frank's doings, Elisha
made a three-pronged attempt to get the book. First, he
cajoled Twain: "Your new book is looked for with eager
interest by the public—it will be likely to have an enormous
sale & I think you will yourself be surprised at the extent of its
circulation." Implicit here is the suggestion that the American
Publishing Company could logically "push" a Twain book
better than another publisher and that only if published by
subscription would *A Tramp Abroad* have an enormous sale.
Next, Bliss tantalized Twain with the offer of the plates of his
old books. For two decades after the break with Bliss, Twain
was to yearn to have the copyrights of his American Publishing
Company books in his own hands and was to invent elaborate
schemes for pressing the company to release them. Bliss
couched his offer in terms that had the obvious ring of Artemus
Ward's "you scratch my back and I'll scratch yours." "Would
you like to buy up the plates of your books?" he asked. "I
expect to leave the Co. by & by & I have thought that perhaps

the Co. would sell any of their plates. I do not know surely that they would sell your books, but perhaps they would *to you.*" Just to be sure, though, Bliss used the same technique that had worked with *Sketches New and Old;* he went to his safe and pulled out a book contract that had been lying there for a half-dozen years and tried using it to coerce Twain into making an agreement for the new volume.

Back in December, 1870, Twain had been inspired to exploit the South African diamond fields through the use of a proxy, his friend James H. Riley. After quite a bit of letter-writing between Twain, Bliss, and Riley, the humorist worked out an elaborate arrangement whereby Twain would pay Riley's passage to Africa and back, would allow Riley to keep the first $5,000 of diamonds he found lying around (they would share everything over $5,000), and would make Riley so popular that he could earn $10,000 on the lecture circuit. Riley was to keep voluminous notes of his trip and on his return to the United States transmit his information to Twain—who would write it all up as if he had been in Africa.[10] Riley would make nothing out of the profits from the book itself, but he would be able to make $100,000 from lecturing and from raking in diamonds. On February 1, 1872, Twain figured, 500,000 copies of the diamond mine book would be released to a breathlessly waiting world.

On December 6 Bliss sent Twain a contract stipulating an 8½ per cent royalty for the author, who on his part agreed to furnish a book "upon some other subject which shall be mutually agreed upon [,] the manuscript for the same to be of same quantity and ready at time arranged for"[11] if the diamond mine book did not reach fruition. The American Publishing Company advanced $2,000 to Twain for Riley's passage. Riley made the trip, but he contracted blood poisoning on the return voyage. Before Riley died, Bliss protected himself with another contract (dated June 22, 1872): "In case the health of sd Riley should be such as to render it utterly

impossible for the said Clemens to write the book on the
Diamond Fields at all," it read, "then he shall be freed from his
agreement to write a book on that subject but shall proceed to
prepare the other book at once—viz the one upon which he is
to appear as author and on which he is to receive 10%
copyright." [12] From 1872 to 1879 this contract was unfulfilled
and the $2,000 unrepaid. In his letter to Twain, Bliss brought it
up as a final attempt to obtain the contract for the new
book.

> The point is the old African enterprise—embracing the
> advance by the Co of $2000—& your contract to write for
> them a book in lieu of the *Riley book;* and of the
> copyright on the same the $2000 was to be paid back to
> the Co.
>   You have never intimated to me that you considered
> "Gilded Age" The Sketches, or Tom Sawyer, as being the
> book to take the place of the Riley book, consequently
> the $2000 has never been deducted from the copyright
> but has stood against you. . . . It seemed to me the best
> way is for you to pay up the $2000—now & cancel all
> papers relating to the matter & end it & then if you
> prepare to write another book for the Co. that it be on
> a new basis & under a new contract; one free from all
> connection with other matters.[13]

Bliss knew that Twain could not pay the $2,000 out of royalties
due him; his quarterly checks from Bliss were averaging about
$600 during 1877 and 1878 ($510.73 on November 9, 1876;
$625.76 on January 24, 1877; $599.55 on October 1, 1877; and
$868.42 on January 23, 1878, for example). He also undoubt-
edly knew that the trip to Europe was in part an economizing
effort. So his suggestion that Twain simply pay back the $2,000
was probably not so generous as it appeared to be on the
surface.

At any rate, it persuaded Twain that Elisha would have to
have the first book that he wrote, and in the front page of a
notebook that carries entries from February 26 to September 8,

1879, he wrote a reminder to himself: "REMEMBER," he jotted down and then canceled later, "the present book is to satisfy the Riley contract. Frank Bliss must wait for the next one." [14] He also told Mrs. Fairbanks that if her son Charles wanted to offer some illustrations for the travel book, he should send them to Elisha Bliss rather than to Frank; but in May he realized he had stirred up a "hornet's nest in Hartford" by having the illustrations sent there. "*Privately.* . . ," he explained, "I'm in the midst of a quarrel with the American Publishing Company, & Charley's sending those pictures there was an awful mistake." [15] The situation was further complicated because, as Frank reported to Twain in March,

> It is beginning to get noised about that I am to publish your book; the rumor naturally excites a little anxiety on the part of some of the Company & folks are asking me how it is. I tell them all that I shall try to get your book as it is my priviledge to do. Should you say anything in your letters to any one here respecting the publication of the book please don't mention that our contract is not of recent date, as, while it is no ones business, it may perhaps *keep things* smoother all around. [16]

Twain replied that he had "never mentioned your contract & mine to anybody unless it was Twichell, & I don't think I mentioned it to him," [17] and expressed concern about Elisha's suggestion that he was going to be leaving the company soon. If that was true, Twain was more worried about his two hundred shares of stock than he was his copyrights and wanted to sell them. Elisha re-entered the picture with his letter of April 1 which suggested that

> this Co. is emerging strongly from the shock it received by the . . . hard times. . . . It will some day resume its old time dividends, I have no doubt. It exists to publish books for you in the future—& is ready to do so at any time. Are you not ready now to make a contract for a book with us? We trust you will not forget us although dividends have been few & far between lately. [18]

(Elisha also mentioned the Riley contract and the $2,000 again, too.) On May 29, after Twain presumably explained the trouble to Frank, the younger Bliss suggested that *Tom Sawyer,* for which the American Publishing Company and Twain had never signed a contract, be allowed to fulfill the Riley agreement, and Twain relented: "All right," he wrote Frank, "have just written Perkins that Tom Sawyer fills the Riley contract, & instructing him to have the Co. endorse all my contracts as completed, & deduct $2,000 from copyrights now due, in satisfaction of the Riley debt." [19]

Elisha gave up trying to get *A Tramp Abroad* for the American Publishing Company—he even gave Frank suggestions about the illustrations for the book. But another member of the American Publishing Company, one for whom Twain had a healthy dislike, was pestering the humorist, too. Sidney Drake, the same director who had taken Twain for a buggy ride back in 1869 and had attempted to persuade him to withdraw *Innocents Abroad* from publication, wrote Twain a letter in May "inquiring somewhat particularly into my affairs,—on the behalf of the company I suppose,—but I suppose he can wait for an answer as long as I have waited for one to the letter I wrote the company on the same subject 3 years ago." After the Hartford papers had definitely announced Frank's contract, the younger Bliss wrote to Twain that the story "will set things buzzing again around here and Mr. Drake among the rest." And finally, on June 27, Frank mentioned that "Mr. Drake was inquiring the other day how long it took for a letter to go to Paris and an answer to get back, he is getting anxious I guess." [20] By 1883 Twain would deny having ever heard of Sidney Drake. [21]

These complicated technical tempests both arose and abated after Twain was already hard at work on his book. His original intention had been to "fly to some little corner of Europe and budge no more until I shall have completed one of the half dozen books that lie begun, up stairs," [22] books which might have included the Mississippi volume, Orion's biography, or *Huckleberry Finn*. Not for some time after arriving in Europe did he abandon that plan in favor of a new travel book. To Howells he wrote in May:

> We left Hartford before the end of March, & I have been idle ever since. I have waited for a "call" to go to work—I knew it would come. Well, it began to come a week ago; my note-book comes out more & more frequently every day since; 3 days ago I concluded to move my manu-scripts over to my den. *Now* the call is loud & decided, at last.[23]

The moving of manuscripts suggests that he was still at work on those half-dozen books he had brought over with him. By July, though, he sounded in a report to Frank Bliss as if he had determined to write about Europe:

> I have written 400 pages of MS—that is to say about 45 or 50,000 words, or one-fourth of a book, but it is in disconnected form & cannot be used until joined together by the writing of at least a dozen intermediate chapters. These intermediate chapters cannot be rightly written until we are settled down for the fall & winter in Munich. I have been gathering a lot of excellent matter here during the past ten days (stuff which has never been in a book) & shall finish gathering it in a week more.[24]

Here there is both the suggestion of the European content of the material and, more important, a hint of a formula for the construction of the book that will be discussed later.

Then after Twichell arrived and started on the walking tour with Twain, the humorist came up with a new plan for the volume. "Since Twichell has been with me," he wrote Frank,

> I have invented a new & better plan for the book. Therefore I shall tear up a great deal of my present batch of MS. and start fresh. . . . I have instructed Twichell to keep the title & plan of the book a secret. I will disclose them to you by letter, presently, or through Twichell—but I do not want them to get into print *until the book is*

nearly ready to issue from the press—They are in themselves a joke—& a joke which the public are already
prepared for is no joke at all.[25]

Throughout the autumn and winter of 1878–1879 Twain
worked away at the book, grandiosely believing that the idea
of a burlesque tramp in which no walking was done would be
fine fare for his audience. He was too busy even to write Frank
Bliss,[26] but he reported in November, 1878, that he had written
"two or three chapters about Wagner's operas" [27] (IX and X in
the finished book). The next January he told his mother-
in-law he had written nine hundred pages of manuscript and
told Twichell that in addition to the nine hundred he had torn
up four hundred more.[28] He informed Howells the book was
half finished and let him in on the secret: "In my book I allow
it to appear,—casually & without stress,—that I am over here to
make the tour of Europe *on foot*. I am in pedestrian costume,
as a general thing, & *start* on pedestrian tours, but mount the
first conveyance that offers, making but slight explanation or
excuse, & endeavoring to seem unconscious that this is not
legitimate pedestrianizing." [29]

Then he lost his Swiss notebook and decided to propose
some other book to Bliss; the notebook turned up, though, and
he "went solidly to work." [30] In January he hit upon the plan
which would provide structural unity up to Chapter XIX, the
raft trip on the Neckar: "I shall fetch them [the two charac-
ters]," he told Twichell, "home on a raft; and if other people
shall perceive that that was no pedestrian excursion, they
themselves shall not be conscious of it." [31] In a letter to Howells
at the end of January, 1879, Twain outlined the progress of his
material so far: "In yesterday's chapter we have started back to
Heidelberg on a raft, & are having a good time. The raft is
mine, since I have chartered it, & I shall pick up useful
passengers here & there to tell me the legends of the ruined
castles, & other things—perhaps the Captain who brought the
news of the Pitcairn revolution. I have invented quite a nice

little legend for Dilsberg Castle." He had also "exposed the German language in two or three chapters, & I have shown what I consider to be the needed improvements in it. I mean to describe a German newspaper, but not satirically—simply in a plain matter of fact way." [32] Thus Mark Twain had completed the manuscript only to Chapter XIV, but he had written "Appendix D—The Awful German Language," a version of "Appendix F—The Journals of Germany," and "The Legend of Dilsberg Castle" for Chapter XIX. He had also on hand for use in the book "The Stolen White Elephant," "The Invalid's Tale," "Ritter's Tale," and presumably "The Legend of Sagenfeld," "Concerning the American Language," and "Mental Telegraphy." [33]

The process of reconstruction is extremely important here because it provides a glimpse into Twain's method of composing the book. The material on German student duels, Chapters V, VI, and VII, was probably written quite early: his notebook, upon which the chapters are based, records the facts on May 17, 1878. [34] The French duel scene which followed was a later addition, written in November and printed separately in the *Atlantic* in February, 1879. [35] When one compares the amount of anecdotal, discrete manuscript with what Professor Franklin Rogers has called "the narrative plank," [36] a vital fact becomes obvious. Twain had spent his time until the idea of a burlesque walking tour came to him writing sketches, tales, short stories, and anecdotes. The German duel scene was composed months before the French scene which complemented it. "The Great Revolution in Pitcairn" was to be introduced into the story, as an afterthought, by a captain who would board the raft. "The Man Who Put up at Gadsby's" was reworked and expanded from a *Territorial Enterprise* letter which Twain wrote from Washington, D. C., on February 8, 1868.

What Twain had meant when he told Frank Bliss in July, 1878, that he had written 45,000 to 50,000 words "in disconnected form" which needed "at least a dozen intermediate chapters," was that he had reversed the process he had used in writing *Innocents Abroad*. In the earlier book he had a "narrative plank" ready for use in the *Alta* letters, and he peppered the narrative with anecdotes. Now, though, the digressive tale actually became the unit of composition, with the unifying principle of a burlesque walking tour added later. When he found out that the "Pitcairn" and "French Duel" manuscripts were not lost in the mails as he had feared, he expressed his relief to Howells in terms that reinforce this theory concerning his method of writing. "Ordinarily," he said,

> I should trouble myself but little about the loss of 2 articles . . . but when a body is yoked down to the grinding out of a 600-page 8-vo. book, to lose a chapter is like losing a child. I was not at all sure that I should use both of those chapters in my book, but to *have them around,* in case of need, would give that added comfort which comes of having a life-preserver handy in a ship which *might* go down.[37]

In addition to the enormous amount of anecdotal material mentioned above, there were "Paris Notes" (written in the summer of 1879 and included in *The Stolen White Elephant*), "The Professor's Yarn" and Lem Hackett's story which turned up in *Life on the Mississippi*, the Blue Jay yarn, the other Rhine legends, the Nicodemus Dodge story, and a number of suggestions—"several hasty plot outlines for what appear to be separate stories," [38] Albert Stone has described them—in the Notebooks for the period. A letter to Twichell in which Twain boasted that he had spent a year removing material that "hindered the flow of my narrative" and that "the yarn swims along without hitch or halt" [39] suggests that Twain was far from being disturbed with the method, that, quite the contrary, he believed he had perfected a formula for writing a travel book that made the sketches an integral part. The source of the technique was not the oral tradition described by DeVoto:

He took the humorous anecdote, combined it with autobiographical reminiscence, and so achieved the narrative form best adapted to his mind. . . . The mode of creation that expressed him was a loosely flowing narrative, actually or fictitiously autobiographical—a current interrupted for the presentation of episodes, for, merely, the telling of stories.[40]

There is some strong evidence to suggest that the method was one with origins in the requirements of voluminous size of the subscription book and in the special understanding Twain had of his audience.

Writing the episodic material beforehand had advantages which Twain realized before he began work on *A Tramp Abroad*. When Dan DeQuille was preparing to write *The Big Bonanza*, he thought about publishing two books, one a straightforward history of the Comstock and the other a collection of his humorous newspaper sketches, but Twain advised him to do no such thing:

Dan, there is more than one way of writing a book; & your way is *not* the right one. You see, the winning card is to nail a man's interest with *Chapter I*, & not let up on him till you get him to the word "finis." That can't be done with detached sketches; but I'll show you how to make a man read every one of those sketches, under the stupid impression that they are mere accidental incidents that have dropped in on you unawares in the course of your narrative.[41]

So even if the technique had its origin in the oral narrative and the newspaper apprentice work, it was the subscription travel book which forced Twain to adapt the method to book-length compositions. DeVoto has suggested the kind of development that took place:

[*Innocents Abroad*'s] steady progress is accomplished by means of stories. Some of them are brief, unelaborated anecdotes, in no way different from the type out of which

they proceed, but others already show Mark's perception
that this form can be utilized for more intricate
effects. . . .

This same framework produces "Roughing It," "A
Tramp Abroad," "Life on the Mississippi," and "Following the Equator." The narrative interlude is organically
developed in these later books; possibilities are more
thoroughly realized. . . . Sometimes the intent is a mere
mechanical joke . . . sometimes . . . it is a means for
presenting in silhouette a lifetime or a civilization.[42]

Improvement in the discrete anecdote was obviously erratic:
the "Skeleton of a Black Forest Novel" and some of the Rhine
legends in A Tramp Abroad are much inferior to most of the
anecdotal material in Roughing It. But nothing in Innocents
Abroad equals some half-dozen yarns in Roughing It; and
Twain never wrote better sketches than the "Blue Jay Yarn"
and "Nicodemus Dodge." His craftsmanship in handling episodic material reached its highest point when he called upon
reminiscences from his own youth and Western years, but his
refinement of the technique went beyond the increased exploitation of autobiographical material.

Formal arrangement in each of the first three travel books
was largely dictated by the material available to Twain
beforehand. In Innocents Abroad, with a sustaining narrative
available from start to finish, the stress of adding to the original
material is least evident. In Roughing It, in which travel
narrative dwindles into a "rather aimless sequence of events in
his actual experience," [43] and in A Tramp Abroad, for which he
wrote a mass of anecdotal material before thinking of a
structural pattern, the rigors of composition are in one sense
more apparent. In order, Roughing It, A Tramp Abroad, and
Life on the Mississippi (after the "Old Times" segment) are
looser, more autobiographical, less unified than Innocents
Abroad simply because they depend less and less on a
preconceived "narrative plank." But at the same time, the
anecdotal material becomes more and more successfully inte-

grated into the narrative movement, at least through *A Tramp Abroad*. In *Innocents,* most of the anecdotes are on the associational level, tied onto the narrative thread by only the most mechanical means. Thus Twain introduced the account of himself in his father's office with the corpse by the sentence, "It is hard to forget repulsive things. I remember yet. . . ." The "Benton House" passage follows the statement, "We are stopping at Shepherd's Hotel, which is the worst on earth except the one I stopped at once in a small town in the United States." The story of the avalanche on Holliday's Hill proceeds from a description of the Great Pyramid to a description of a bluff on the Mississippi above Selma, Missouri, to the sentence, "In still earlier years, than those I have been recalling, Holliday's Hill, in our town, was to me the noblest work of God." In a large share of *Roughing It,* as Henry Nash Smith has shown, most of the anecdotes relate in some way to the narrative pattern describing "the process by which the tender-foot narrator is transformed into the old timer, the vernacular character." Only the story of the camel who ate the manuscript in Syria is purely "associational." And in *A Tramp Abroad,* too, most of the "separatable stuff" [44] which was retained in the book contributes to the burlesque. Even the "Blue Jay Yarn" and "Nicodemus Dodge" exploit the distinction between appearance and reality that underscores the spoofing of a "walking tour" by two inspired idiots incapable of realizing that they were not walking at all. *A Tramp Abroad* would have been a much better book if Twain had only written more anecdotes, had possessed a larger stock of "chapters" to thread onto the plank. The process was a slow one though, and, typically, he ran out—his tank went dry—in the middle of 1879. He had raw material of the first rank available, but the pressure of completing the book made it necessary to ignore the suggestions in his notebooks.

After January, 1879, he continued to make progress: he told Mother Fairbanks that he had been experiencing difficulties with his "confounded" book. It was heartbreaking, too, to discover that his nine hundred pages was not half a book, but only a third. So at the end of February he "buckled in & wrote 400 pages in . . . 8 days & so brought my work close up to half-way." [45] His work moved so rapidly from March to May that he told Frank Bliss, "I am making good progress and hope to have the book done before the end of July." [46]

He had hit upon the idea that had worked in *Innocents,* where he burlesques Prime. On April 25 he asked Chatto & Windus to mail him Edward Whymper's *Scrambles Amongst the Alps,* and on May 15 he was beginning a chapter which would "burlesque Mr. Whymper & the other fantastic Alps-climbers." [47] (These are Chapters XXXVII, XXXVIII, and XXXIX.) Material based upon Whymper, Baedeker, and d'Arve, though second-rate writing, was of enormous value, for in ten days, from May 15 to May 25, he proceeded from XXXVII through XLV: he told Aldrich that he was at manuscript page 1959, and "600 or 700 more will finish the book (Say six weeks.)." [48] In the next four days he wrote eighty-two more pages of manuscript, to 2041,[49] but with the coming of summer the Clemens family began a trip through Belgium, The Netherlands, and finally, England, so that work on the book progressed very little. The family left Liverpool on August 23 and arrived in New York on September 3.

The New York papers interviewed the returning author, and he gave out some enlightening information. He announced, "I have been writing a new book and have it nearly finished, all but the last two or three chapters," but it was, unhappily, an exaggerated prediction. He also suggested that he was about half through with the process of revision.

> The first half of it, I guess, is finished, but the last half has not been revised yet; and when I get at it I will do a good deal of rewriting, and a great deal of tearing up. I may tear up the first part of it, too, and rewrite that. . . .

Finally, the *New York Times* reported Twain as commenting that *A Tramp Abroad* was to be issued "by the same company that brought out my other books," [50] so by then the American Publishing Company had finally succeeded in getting the contract.

During the spring of 1879 Twain had begun to take an interest in the illustrating of his book; at first he expected engravings to be done in the United States by artists who would "roost in Hartford where they can have access to the MS." [51] Then in May he concocted the idea of having some of the illustrations done in Europe. To Frank Bliss he suggested that he could get fifty-eight cuts for $1,325 or $1,350, which would compare favorably with the $7,000 Elisha had spent on *Innocents Abroad*. "If you will send me Eleven hundred dollars, gold, to Paris," Twain offered,

> you shall receive in return for it.

10 full-page plates	@	$18	....	$180.00
25 half-page do	@	9	....	225.00
75 quarter-page do	@	4.50	....	337.50
100 sixth-page do	@	3.50	....	300.00
210 plates		Totals		1042.50

"*In addition*," he proposed "to give several pages of space to my own pictures." [52] Frank insisted that the illustrating could be done more cheaply in Hartford and pointed out that some of the engravings had already been completed—he was also hard pressed financially and asked for delays in forwarding money to Europe for the work done there. As usual when Twain had an inspiration, it was almost impossible to dissuade him, and on June 10 he sent thirty-five drawings by Brown and a couple of his own, noting, "Yes, will leave space for some pictures to be drawn at home, as you suggest." [53] Having seen some of the illustrations (probably Twain's own), Frank wrote with apprehension:

> I've just been talking with Father about the drawings & looking over them again. [H]e suggests that I call your

> attention to one point . . . in the A. P. Co we always
> tried to avoid, in the illustrations, the making of a funny
> picture by a monstrosity. . . . Max Adeler, Billings &
> those writers you know get deformities for funny pictures.
> I like to avoid them don't you? [54]

Actually, though, whatever the critical appraisals Frank and
Elisha made about the expensive European engravings, the
important consideration was that Frank's fledgling publishing
house was in serious financial difficulty. Not only had Frank
met problems in the costs of illustrating, but there was
obviously reason to worry whether the new company could
market a Mark Twain volume with the speed, skill, and
efficiency of the vast American Publishing Company's appara-
tus.

At any rate, by the time he returned in September Twain
was willing to relent. Elisha's health had begun to fail, and
Frank felt an obligation to the American Publishing Company.
On September 8 Twain wrote Frank outlining the terms of his
capitulation:

> A stranger writes me that the A. P. Co. have had a new
> book of his under consideration for some time. Now if we
> publish my new book through the A. P. Co. let us have a
> written agreement with them that they shall not canvas
> *any* book *but mine* between this present date & a date 9
> *months after the actual publication & issue* of my
> forthcoming book.
>   They put off Innocents a whole year in direct violation
> of contract in order to run in two new books—but no
> matter about that, my object in having them was to have
> *an entirely* unencumbered field—& if I return to them, I
> don't want *any* books (new or old) canvassed but mine
> until my new book shall have had its full run. [55]

In a couple of months the problems the indignant author
caused with his ultimatum had apparently been ironed out, for
on November 1 Elisha wrote an addendum to the contract for
Clemens' signature:

> I hereby agree to the transfer by F. E. Bliss of the
> contract for a book now existing between him and myself,
> to the American Publishing Co., in case he makes
> satisfactory arrangements with sd Co. for such transfer,
> provided sd Co. agree with him not to publish any other
> new book within 9 months from the time of the publica-
> tion of my book.[56]

Even before he signed the agreement, however, he had turned
over to the American Publishing Company all the manuscript
he had finished—all but the last five chapters.

The kind of revising Twain did on the book can be examined
in approximately two hundred pages of the manuscript (in
CWB). Chapter XXVI, for example, was first labeled "Chap
37," then "Chap 25," and, finally, "Chap 26." Likewise XLV
was originally marked "Chap 56," and XXXI was intended first
as "42" and then "28." The page numbers for these chapters
have all been canceled, and another, from two hundred to
three hundred pages lower, has been inserted. Thus, somewhere prior to Chapter XXIV Twain either removed eleven
chapters and about three hundred pages of manuscript or
shifted them to follow Chapter XLV. Chapter XIV was one of
the most wayward of all: it began as "14," became "16,"
dropped down to "13," and wound up as "14" again.

The manuscript of "The Invalid's Tale" was written as a
"separate" chapter, paginated 1 to 21. Four introductory pages,
100 to 103, replaced pages 1 and 2, and pages 3 to 21 were
renumbered 104 to 122 in order to fit the material into *A Tramp
Abroad*. The four introductory pages also provide a glimpse at
the book as it might have been written had the burlesque
"tramp" idea not occurred to Twain; the numbering of the
pages, 100–122, suggests a very early attempt to introduce the
story into the European material. The book would have been a
diary apparently: page 100 begins, "*May 11*—Stumbled upon
that man Douglas again. . . ." And on 102 Twain introduces
the invalid's story with

> The above is all that my diary has to say about "that man Douglas." But as its language suggests, I had met him before. It was a year & a half or two years ago, when I was coming up from the Bermuda Islands in a steamer. He was a great invalid & one day he told us his story. . . .[57]

If this bit of material is representative, Twain had no more satisfactory formal conception than a diary strewn with desultory anecdotes. And the juggling that the chapter numbering suggests affirms Twain's frenetic tearing up, discarding, and rewriting that he reported all through 1879. The last five chapters were to proceed no better than the rest.

He told Howells that he hoped to finish the manuscript in Elmira by the middle of October, but a little later he reported to Twichell:

> I am revising my MS. I did not expect to like it, but I do. I have been knocking out early chapters for more than a year now, not because they had not merit, but merely because they hindered the flow of the narrative. . . . Day before yesterday my shovel fetched up three more chapters and laid them, reeking, on the festering shore-pile of their predecessors, and now I think the yarn swims right along, without hitch or halt.[58]

Back in Hartford in November, though, he still had not finished the last chapters, and worse yet, Bliss had begun sending along the proof for the bulk of the manuscript which Twain gave him just after returning to this country:

> [My] object is . . . to wail over the fact that my proofsheets have begun to pile in on me at last, & *that* means, the dozen closing chapters of my book have got to be tackled now & stuck to without interruption till they are all written & completed.[59]

Throughout December he pegged away at the book, and finally, on January 7, 1880, in desperation, he took Bliss 288 pages of manuscript, the final batch of the 2,600 pages from which he had culled another 1,400.[60]

After spending a year and a half on the tasks of writing and revising, Twain went through the proofs in rapid order. No doubt he did some work on them in November and December and sent copies along to Howells (who suggested the softening of at least one "yarn"). After Twain and Livy packed off for a month in January, though, the humorist expected to be "head over heels with proof-reading in Elmira, but I had rather do that than be the slave I have so long been in *writing* the book." [61] It was a task that did not take long, either, because by February 26 he was "grinding away now, with all my might, & with an interest which amounts to intemperance, at the 'Prince & the Pauper.'" [62] "The Old Man of the Sea," as Twain had christened the book, was finally done.

As the earlier travel volumes had, *A Tramp Abroad* fell back upon the quotation from other authors as Twain became exasperated with the inordinate length of manuscript he was trying to pile up. Among the materials he snatched up to fill space, in addition to Whymper, were his Baedeker, F. J. Keifer, *Legends of the Rhine from Basle to Rotterdam*, Stephen d'Arve, *Histoire du Mont Blanc*, and Thomas W. Hinchliff, *Summer Months Among the Alps*. The material he based on these volumes, without exception, is dull, uninspired, straightforward exposition: a description of a near-fatal fall from the Matterhorn to contrast the author's burlesque ascent of the Riffleberg (Chapter XXXVII); descriptions of glaciers (XL); a history of the conquest of the Matterhorn (XLI). But he worked too rapidly. Practically all the guidebook material was written in the last two weeks of May, 1879, and the amalgamation reflects the haste. Except for providing a contrast with his own burlesque ascent, the quotations add nothing more to *A Tramp Abroad* than a few pages of narrative or description. Twain did not manipulate them for use in scathing satire, as had been the case with Prime in *Innocents,* or into the contexts of a humorous situation, as he had with Dimsdale in *Roughing It.*

But the material he completed after his return to the United States, the last five chapters which he turned over to Bliss in January, 1880, is even more chaotic. The narrative thread, slender enough to begin with, unravels into pointless statistics on comparative death rates and burlesque European recipes. From his notebook Twain grasped the story of the thief in St. Mark's (XLIX); from an incident which purportedly occurred on the *Quaker City* excursion he took the story of his robbing a beggar woman in Odessa; [63] and from *Innocents Abroad* he borrowed the technique of ridiculing the Old Masters with burlesque illustrations.

For once, the mechanics of publishing did not cause a long delay in bringing out the volume. When Twain predicted the book would be ready for fall publication, and then for November (1879) publication, it was his own delay that made the dates unrealistic. Things moved surprisingly smoothly with *A Tramp Abroad;* the title was presumably chosen way back in 1878, when Twain said it was a part of the secret joke. Illustrations had been a matter of concern all along, so there was no delay over them. Finally, since the electrotyping had begun almost as soon as Mark Twain returned from Europe, Bliss was able to have a prospectus bound and ready for agents on November 19, 1879. By the end of 1879 the American Publishing Company had received 869 copies of the prospectus which provides clues to exactly what material was being set up and printed before the manuscript was complete. That it represented an inchoate manuscript is obvious from its mispagination and lack of pagination. Occasionally it presented on one page material that was divided into two pages in the book. Also, it used illustrations that were changed before the printing of *A Tramp Abroad.* The collation works out as follows:

1879 Pros.	A Tramp Abroad	1879 Pros.	A Tramp Abroad
17	17	24	32
22	27	377	113
23	28	n.p.	121
23	31	64	126
25	35	25	39
24	38	580	331
26	40	470	504–5
34	43	515	184
35	44	n.p.	186
36	45	317	186–87
37	46	318	188
38	47	n.p.	196
39	48	n.p.	197
41	52	n.p.	329–30
20	23	n.p.	296
21	24	n.p.	299
50	100	n.p.	496
51	101	n.p.	305
52	102	n.p.	306
53	103	n.p.	307
60	122	n.p.	355
61	123	n.p.	356
62	124	n.p.	434
63	125	319	191
66	128	320	192
67	129	469	193
68	130	n.p.	340
510	182	n.p.	341
120	97	n.p.	342–43
121	98	n.p.	104
375	111	n.p.	150
376	112	n.p.	151
43	54	n.p.	152
31	64	n.p.	448
40	49	n.p.	449
571	399–400	490	391–92
240	301	n.p.	419–20
241	302	n.p.	304
242	303	42	53
506	167	n.p.	519

This pagination suggests, certainly, that the American Publishing Company had the bulk of the manuscript before November 19. Portions were possibly added to the early parts of the manuscript at a later date (the confusion in pagination suggests this), but Twain had definitely written to page 519 of the book, regardless of what he added later. Therefore the material he wrote in the winter of 1879–1880 consisted of Chapter XLV to the end of the book, Chapter L. Even though the appendixes were written earlier, Twain apparently did not give them to the company until after the 1879 prospectus was issued, since none of them appear in it.[64]

In addition to this rudimentary prospectus, the company distributed advance sheets of the book to several newspapers which announced the book. Among the reviews of A *Tramp Abroad* which appeared early enough to be included in the 1879 prospectus were those from the Cleveland *Herald, Plain Dealer,* and *Leader,* the Scranton *Free Press,* and the *Tolland County Leader.*

Though this very early electrotyping of the book served a function in selling A *Tramp Abroad,* it was probably not intended for that purpose. It seems more likely that this early agents' dummy was an attempt by the company to evade the spirit of the codicil to the A *Tramp Abroad* contract which specified that no other book should be published for nine months after its appearance. Perhaps the company intended to claim that "publication" had occurred in November, 1879, when the prospectus issued, rather than in March, 1880, so that canvassing of other volumes could begin again in August or September, 1880, in time for the autumn season, rather than on December 13, 1880. Unfortunately, the Berg Collection's Stock Ledger of American Publishing Company Books ends with 1879, but there is one bit of supporting evidence for the theory. Sometime in 1880—since trade journals were very lax in noting subscription publications, the date cannot be narrowed down—the American Publishing Company issued Marietta

Holley's *My Wayward Pardner* and her *Lament of a Mormon Wife*.

Clemens told the interviewer for the *New York Times* on September 3 that he expected his book to be published in two months, in November. Actually, it appeared just two months after he gave the company the final batch of manuscript, remarkably speedy processing for Bliss. And it is possible that, as with *The Gilded Age*, *A Tramp Abroad* was delayed somewhat in order to allow Chatto & Windus to get the English edition ready. But Frank Bliss, like his father, got impatient or thought the delay too costly and issued his edition before the English one was released. On May 3 Chatto & Windus wrote Clemens that Bliss had "emperiled" his English copyright by publishing too early, and in the margin Twain wrote Frank, "I *must* blame you for not telling me, in time, that you had not informed Chatto what date you meant to issue on." [65] It may be that the younger Bliss felt his advance orders, which were somewhere between 25,000 and 48,000 copies, warranted releasing the book no matter what the detriment to the English edition and British copyright. [66]

Mark Twain was originally dubious about the prospects for *A Tramp Abroad*. While in Europe he thought he was writing a volume "which few would read & everybody execrate." [67] Once he saw the volume on March 20, 1880, he brightened and told Frank,

> I like the book exceedingly well; it is handsomely gotten up (barring the old type), & I believe it is going to take. Roughing and Gilded Age sold nearly double as many copies in this length of time, so I imagine the Canadians have been working us heavy harm. [68]

Even though Twain cautioned Frank Bliss (Elisha had presumably retired from the business by May, 1880, when Twain told Orion that the elder Bliss had heart disease so seriously that it would probably be fatal) [69] to prevent any newspaper exploitation of the book, [70] the journals gave *A Tramp Abroad*

much free publicity. Before it was known that Frank had the
contract for the book, the Hartford papers buzzed with
rumors, and when reporters interviewed Twain at his return,
the talk naturally centered on the new book. The notices of *A
Tramp Abroad* which appeared in papers in time to be
included in the 1879 prospectus called attention to the method
of ordering the volume. The *Tolland County Leader* explained,

> Mark Twain's new book, "A Tramp Abroad," is being
> canvassed for in this place by R. W. Perkins. . . . You
> may have been bored and talked to death by book agents,
> but when this work is brought to your door you should at
> least look at it, and if the agent doesn't call, send for
> him.

Once the American Publishing Company had the complete
manuscript and set *A Tramp Abroad* in type, it corrected
irregularities of the 1879 prospectus (in FCW, there is an
intermediate version, dated 1880, but containing the pagination
of the 1879 version). The later prospectus reproduced pages
39–54, 173–88, 223–38, 259–96, and 299–308 of the book.[71]
Again, as with *Roughing It* and *The Gilded Age,* someone
exercised fairly acute critical judgment and chose to exclude
from the dummy the later strained, uninteresting chapters of
the book. Also as with *Roughing It,* the book was advertised as
a "companion volume to Innocents Abroad." Though the
publisher advertised the humor of the volume, he played
prominently on those features which he believed were responsible for Twain's first success as the author of a subscription
book—iconoclasm, irreverence, and skepticism concerning European culture:

> With his eyes and notebook open, he tramped along;
> mingled with other tourists, learned how they "do Eu-
> rope," and then struck out new paths for his own
> footsteps. The guide-books pass under his inspection,
> and are subjected to his tests, and put on the defensive;

scores of masked errors, heretofore universally accepted
as truths, are fearlessly questioned and exposed.

Only one of the selections from the book, the encounter with
the "specimen tourist" in Chapter XXVII, fortifies this claim.
The others include the Blue Jay yarn, the Nicodemus Dodge
story, the Dilsberg Castle legend, and Alpine description. If
the prospectus selections were an indication, then, the publisher believed that Twain's anecdotes were better selling
points than his exposure of "masked errors."

After the publication of the book, selections appeared in
newspapers and magazines throughout the country, giving
gratuitous advertising. The *Boston Transcript* reproduced the
Blue Jay yarn and an excerpt on "Mark Twain as a German
Scholar" on May 5 and 7. The *Literary World* reproduced the
"Tale of a Fishwife" and a selection from the burlesque ascent
of the Riffleberg, but as one of the most vitriolic critics of
subscription publications, it archly cited its selections as from
the London, Chatto & Windus, edition. The *Chicago Tribune*
printed "Characteristic Passages from *A Tramp Abroad*" on
July 17. This widespread printing of sample selections worked
in the same way the prospectus was supposed to; it could not
help but assist sales, no matter what Mark Twain's own
opinion about its value was.

The volume was receiving, in other words, the kind of
"push" that Twain's books, and all subscription volumes,
required and that *Sketches New and Old* and *Tom Sawyer* had
so significantly lacked. So far as sales went, Mark Twain was
back on the right track. He reported on April 23, "It has sold
35,000 copies & all the steam presses & binderies in Hartford
are still hard at work on it, night and day. This is almost
assurance that the first quarter's sale is to be as great as that of
any previous book of mine." [72] And the same week he told his
English printers, "No book of mine has made so much talk here
since Innocents Abroad—& to my definite delight, it is strongly
complimentary talk. Howells's 'Atlantic' notice has just arrived,

& pleases me exceedingly." [73] By July 1, according to one of Frank Bliss's statements, it had sold 47,563 copies. By September Frank had "got off close onto 55,000 up to the present time and we have the 60th thousand on the press." [74] By March, 1881, its first anniversary, *A Tramp Abroad* had sold 62,000 copies, but by then a much more important event had occurred. Elisha Bliss was dead.

Shortly after Elisha died on September 28, 1880, a meeting of the board of directors was called to appoint his successor, who was G. W. Root. The directors also went into business matters, and Twain learned, even though the year stipulated in his contract had not passed, that his 10 per cent royalty was not the equivalent of half-profits. He wrote a long letter to Orion summarizing the situation and admitting that Orion had been correct in his suspicions back in 1872. If Perkins, Twain's lawyer, had listened to him and sued the American Publishing Company, Bliss would have been scared into making a settlement:

> I felt sure of that, at the time, but Perkins was loath to go for a man with no better weapon than to use a "scare"—& Bliss went into the accounts & details & satisfied Perkins & his expert that 7½ per cent *did* represent half profits up to 50,000, & that after that the publisher had a mere trifling advantage of the author. . . .
> I did a lot of ciphering, & struck for 10 per cent on the next book [*The Gilded Age*]. Bliss stood the raise, but "proved". . . that 10 represented more than half profits.
> I never bothered about the next 2 books [*Sketches New and Old* and *Tom Sawyer*]—I cared nothing about them . . . but *this* time, . . . I did take an interest. I told the directors I wouldn't publish with them at any figure, because their business was too much spread out; [Frank] Bliss had resigned; so I gave him the contract, at ½ profits. Then he was ashamed to leave the company to perish; so he asked my permission to transfer the book to them; & I said I was more than willing, since they would

be obliged to publish only *my* book during the first 9
months. Well, as a consideration for the book, he required
them to allow him one-half of the *company's* entire profits
for 3 years!—& they were exceedingly glad to comply. For
it saved the company's life & set them high on their pins &
free of debt. Frank has taken his father's place, & the
business goes on.[75]

He calculated that he had lost sixty thousand dollars on his
books since *Roughing It* and announced, "I shall probably go
to a new publisher 6 or 8 months hence." Actually, in less than
a month he was writing Osgood about the idea of issuing
subscription books:

> You just look into one of the big libraries, and you'll find
> all those books; If I should order Frank Bliss to send
> them to you he would think he smelt a rat, and I'm not
> ready for him to begin to smell a rat yet. Most of your
> book-sellers keep my books under their counters, too—you
> just borrow them, won't you?

By November 27 he had made his contract with Osgood for
The Prince and the Pauper.[76]

The fact that Twain was embittered by his realization that
he had been swindled by Bliss is common enough knowledge,
but almost pathetically, the humorist was intensely aware of
his own loss in leaving the company. In May, 1881, he sold his
200 shares of American Publishing Company stock, certain, he
told Webster, that the company would be "getting mighty
feeble" because of his departure; he warned Joel Chandler
Harris that he "couldn't recommend my former publishers to
anybody except an enemy." [77] His bitterness included not only
Elisha, but the entire organization, and in July he lashed out at
Frank:

> The 1*st* of July I shall expect to be paid half the profits
> accruing upon Tramp Abroad up to that time. I don't
> know whether that is the letter of the contract or not, but
> it is the spirit of it. It having now been demonstrated that
> 10 per cent represents less than half the profits, there can

be no reasonable use in the company's retaining a part of my money 9 months in order to demonstrate it again.[78]

A couple of months later Twain decided that he wanted all his copyrights returned to him from the company, and he asked Daniel Whitford, a lawyer, to examine his contracts. Whitford's report was not encouraging: for *Innocents Abroad, Roughing It,* and *Tom Sawyer,* there was little hope:

> By their terms Mr. Clemens sells the manuscript and copyright of his books to the Publishing Company and the title rests in them. . . . There is no provision made as to what shall be done in case of insolvency or failure or inability to perform. Mr. Clemens therefore would be compelled to fall back upon his legal rights which he has guarded very carelessly in these contracts.

For *The Gilded Age:*

> The title to the book seems to remain in the authors and the exclusive license given by them to the Publishing Company to publish the work is to expire on the failure to fulfill their part of the contract.

And for *A Tramp Abroad:*

> This agreement leaves the title to the book in Mr. Clemens and in case the contract is broken by Mr. Bliss in addition to giving Mr. Clemens a right of action against him he would probably forfeit his rights under the contract.[79]

Twain contemplated the lawsuit that would somehow intimidate Bliss into relinquishing the contracts and even threatened the company; in 1884, when pirates were encroaching again, he wrote, "Unless you bring suit at once to enjoin these pirates, I must sue for the annulling of my contracts with you, upon the ground that you make no sufficient efforts to protect my copyrights from infringement." [80]

He concluded that there was skulduggery on the *A Tramp Abroad* contract, too, and figured his loss on that book as from

$5,000 to $18,000, though he ultimately decided that "there was no default on Tramp Abroad."[81]

At the same time, Twain was aware of the enormous potential for selling books that the American Publishing Company represented. He marveled that Frank was selling his old books at as high a rate as Osgood was selling the new ones, and he told Cable with obvious envy, "They do know how to push a book."[82] He even planned to give *Huckleberry Finn* and the Grant *Memoirs* to Frank Bliss at first, but he asked for a 60 per cent cut of the profits on *Huck*, and Frank declined.[83] About the only satisfaction Twain got out of the company was the thought that he had lost them a voluminous amount of business by refusing to give them Grant's book. In an autobiographical dictation he mused over the matter:

> There was a sort of dignity about my adventures with Elisha Bliss, Jr., of the American Publishing Company, in 1872. . . . Bliss, in beguiling me into the belief that in changing the agreed wording of the contract for "Roughing It" from "half profit over and above cost of manufacture" to a specified royalty was setting a trap for me, whereby he expected to rob me of about $30,000, a trick which succeeded, as I have already explained. There was a sort of dignity about that, for the reason that $30,000 was a great sum of money to that poor little publishing company, and worth the sinful trouble which Bliss took to acquire it. . . . Bliss captured my $30,000, but I made it cost him a quarter of a million thirteen years afterward.[84]

Perhaps the greatest compliment Twain paid to Elisha Bliss, though, was to quote him as authority to Webster when conflicts about the marketing of Charles L. Webster Company books arose.[85]

In his *Autobiography* Mark Twain summed up the situation as it existed in the first months after the release of *A Tramp Abroad* (though with errors in dating attributable to the distance between 1881 and the dictating of the material):

> When the book had been out three months [actually, a year] there was an annual meeting of the stockholders of the company and I was present. . . . A statement of the company's business was read, and to me it was a revelation. Sixty-four thousand copies of the book had been sold, and my half of the profits was thirty-two thousand dollars. In 1872 Bliss had made out to me that seven and a half per cent royalty, some trifle over twenty cents a copy, represented one-half of the profits, whereas at that earlier day it hardly represented a sixth of the profits. Times were not so good now, yet it took all of fifty cents a copy to represent half.[86]

The question of how much money Clemens actually "lost" because of his contracts is highly technical: exact costs of paper, printing, binding, and illustrating are not extant, and they varied from volume to volume. The size of a book could cause a difference in profit—mailing costs, additional engravings, the extra plates and paper could all cut significantly into the profits with just fifty extra pages if the retail price did not rise. *Innocents Abroad* and *Roughing It* both sold for $3.50 in cloth, even though the earlier book contained 651 pages and the latter 591. Also, the various higher priced bindings, sheep, morocco, even turkey, would bring in a larger profit. It is possible to approximate the various costs and the profit; I have argued elsewhere, using the figures that are available for the printing of *A Tramp Abroad,* that roughly a 15 per cent royalty would have equaled the half-profits that Twain expected. Briefly, the first annual sales report for *A Tramp Abroad* recorded that the book had sold 62,000 copies, that the American Publishing Company had received $106,000, and that their profit was $64,000. Twain received half of this, $32,000. This means that the general agents received just over 50 per cent of the retail price, since the book sold for $3.50 and the company made only $1.70 a volume. The manufacturing costs of *A Tramp Abroad* averaged sixty-seven cents a copy, and the book therefore realized a profit of just over a dollar a volume. Twain's half of this was fifty-one cents, or just a fraction under 15 per cent of the retail price.[87] If that 15 per cent applied to all of his books, more or less, then it is possible to make an intelligent guess at how seriously Bliss really cheated Twain. From the date of publication to the end of 1879, I figure Twain's "losses" as follows:

Roughing It, 96,083 copies, $22,000
The Gilded Age, 65,484 copies, $16,000
Sketches New and Old, 30,894 copies, $7,100
Adventures of Tom Sawyer, 28,962 copies, $4,000

In other words, if Twain expected half-profits just on *Roughing It,* he had lost $22,000; if he considered half-profits a part of the understanding for all four contracts, he lost $49,000, more or less.

It is only just to reiterate that it was not the contract of *Roughing It* that Bliss violated, but the verbal understanding which a lawyer told Twain in 1872 was tenuous legal footing. But Twain, forewarned by Orion, continued to give his manuscripts to Bliss, almost in defiance of good business sense. Twain knew how Howells' books sold, and there can be little doubt that he realized he was doing much better than any of his friends publishing in the "trade." Between 1869 and the end of 1879 Bliss sold 337,902 volumes of Twain's books and gave the author about $73,000 in royalties, a sum that was certain to impress the humorist.

By the end of the 70's, circumstances had led Mark Twain to the brink of the catastrophic financial involvements of the 80's. Committed by temperament and training to subscription publication and isolated by temper from the American Publishing Company, Mark Twain was well on the way to the era of the Midas touch of the mid-1880's, when his own subscription house prospered and his other financial schemes always seemed on the verge of repaying his investments. When that world collapsed in the 1890's, Twain returned—significantly, I

think—to the American Publishing Company that had lifted
him up out of the journalistic trade. It would overburden the
event to suggest that Twain's return to Frank Bliss for the
publication of *Pudd'nhead Wilson* and *Following the Equator*
represented atonement or symbolized an attempt to negate the
fourteen-year hiatus. It does, though, suggest that Twain never
forgot how successfully the company could "push" a book.

It is tempting to speculate what would have happened if
Twain had stayed with Frank and had been more reasonable
about the contracts for *Huckleberry Finn* and the Grant
volumes. Would the murky despair reflected in *The Mysterious
Stranger, What Is Man?* and the other later works have been
any the less if financial collapse had not combined with
personal tragedy in the last years of the century? Charles L.
Webster Company's bankruptcy was only one of the monetary
problems, one fairly overshadowed by the fortunes of the
Paige typesetting machine. And Frank, like Cousin Charley
Webster, was a younger man than Twain, partly overawed by
him and partly uncertain how to handle him. Elisha Bliss never
surrendered to Mark Twain, always stood his ground, fulmi-
nated, attacked, threatened, cajoled, and intimidated the
humorist in a fashion that would probably have been as
foreign to Frank as it was to Webster. Twain's overwhelming,
and occasionally overbearing, personality was a juggernaut
under which Webster threw himself for eight years, and Frank
was just as quietly patient, docile, and self-effacing as Webster—definitely not the combination of character traits that
Elisha had used to keep Twain writing for the American
Publishing Company. Without the personality of "the Old
Fox," the American Publishing Company would probably have
found Twain as much a nuisance as Webster must have. It was
Elisha's death rather than his cheating that was crucial to
Twain's further career, for Bliss *père* could certainly have
juggled his figures and statistics one more time, fired back a
letter or two just as caustic as need be, and probably have

herded Twain back into the fold, had he just had the chance.

Whatever Mark Twain's opinion of Elisha Bliss and the American Publishing Company may have been, there can be little doubt that his decade under Bliss's tutelage wrought enormous changes on the humorist. What Twain might have become if he had not accepted Bliss's offer back in 1867 and become embroiled in the subscription method has been suggested in part by Leon Dickinson. Comparing *Innocents Abroad* with James DeMille's *The Dodge Club, or Italy in 1859,* Dickinson suggests that the latter book "remained obscure, partly, it would seem, because it did not enjoy the wide distribution provided by subscription books." [88] Since for Twain writing was a business as well as an art, marketing of his books was an extremely significant factor. Indeed, it seems quite probable that if *Innocents* and *Roughing It* had flopped, Twain would have turned back to the journalistic trade for which his apprentice training had prepared him and from which he could expect reliable profit.

At an even more significant level, though, Twain adapted his writing to fit the requirements of subscription publication. I have tried to suggest the ways the travel books forced him to alter his tendency to write episodes into a technique which would help produce 600-page books. Length, in other words, was a factor. He not only reached his quantitative goal in nonfiction, but as he placed one anecdote after another, especially in the overland trip in *Roughing It,* he created a form that DeLancey Ferguson has pointed out was "nearer to picaresque fiction than to history." [89] The transfer of the episode to sustained fiction, in part at least a carry-over from the travel narratives, produced *The Prince and the Pauper, Adventures of Huckleberry Finn,* and *A Connecticut Yankee in King Arthur's Court.*

Additional facts suggest that Twain not only adapted his craft to the requirement of subscription length, but that he also modeled his books to appeal to the special subscription audience. Twain was himself much like his audience, fitted the pattern that might describe the qualities of the "typical" subscription book buyer. He was Midwestern, basically preferred history and biography to fiction, and retained no small quantity of his Calvinistic upbringing. He struck a responsive note in his audience, then, without contrivance. As the *Syracuse Daily Standard* put it, "The eyes with which he sees are our eyes as well as his. . . . And thus the book [*The Innocents Abroad*] becomes a transcript of our own sentiments." [90] He could, no doubt, have appealed to his audience, as Scott Fitzgerald once insisted he did, simply by recording his own reactions.

The audience, to repeat, expected—in lieu of fancy "literary" frills—information and entertainment. They were not likely to make a pleasure jaunt to Europe, so the statistics and the descriptive material in the travel volumes satisfied their curiosity. They got the thrill vicariously of looking down from the cathedral at Milan, of contemplating the Sphinx, or of climbing the Matterhorn. These were experiences outside the realm of the popular reader, and by skillfully alternating description and statistics with humorous passages, Twain gave them information in doses small enough to satisfy without becoming as boring as the standard guide book. As Twain suggested to DeQuille in 1876, "Bring along *lots* of *dry statistics*—it's the very best sauce a humorous book can have. Ingeniously used, they just make a reader smack his chops in gratitude. We must have *all* the Bonanza statistics you can rake & scrape." [91]

Bliss and the newspapers that reviewed Twain's books all called attention to the unique juxtaposition of information and entertainment. *Roughing It* was advertised as "Designed to Amuse and Instruct." A squib for *Innocents Abroad* announced that "While running over with wit and humor, . . . it still teems with glowing descriptions, and with elegant and classical allusions." *A Tramp Abroad,* a copywriter claimed, "will be found not only exceedingly amusing, but like its predecessors, brimfull of valuable information." Of *Innocents* the *New York Express* noted, "Truth is told to us in such winsome form, that we cannot but listen to it with agreeable sensations," and the Trenton *True American* summed it up with, "The work abounds in historical facts, descriptions of different countries and important personages, scenes and incidents, so bound together by wit, pleasantry and flashes of grotesque humor, as to make it one of the most readable and amusing books of the period." [92] The Scranton *Free Press* said of *A Tramp Abroad*, "People do not like to read a volume of travels because it is dry and prosy, but when all this knowledge is combined with sparkling wit the reading becomes a pleasure instead of a task," and the *Tolland County Leader* claimed that factual material "which if given by other writers would be dry and uninteresting is here fairly 'sugar-coated,' as none but Clemens knows how to do." [93]

Not only did Twain's injunction to DeQuille imply a contrived formula for the shuffling together of anecdotal and statistical material; as these reviews attest, readers did indeed smack their chops in gratitude. The anecdotes, in which Bliss claimed "no where does his ready wit and keen satire more forcibly display itself than in his sketch writing," struck a note familiar to the audience and gave the travel books an aura of informality, balancing the impersonal statistics. Twain suggested his awareness of this technique of apposition of information and anecdote when, referring to the German and French duel chapters of *A Tramp Abroad*, he explained to Mrs. Fairbanks that the contrast between the German duel—"a description which simply *describes* the terrific spectacle, with no jests interlarded & no comments added"—and the French duel "will be the silent but eloquent comment." [94]

Twain was also intensely aware of the appeal of novelty and topicality in his works to be sold by subscription. He was embittered when the American Publishing Company resusci-

tated their biography of Grant in order to make some profit
from the Webster volume, and he once told Webster not to ask
the company for permission to use material from one of their
books in his *Library of Humor* until a week before the date of
issue because otherwise "they'll rush out a rival book ahead of
us." [95] But if he did not care to be imitated, Twain did keep a
keen eye on public interest when he chose a topic for a
subscription book during his decade with Bliss. Remember,
one of his chief reasons for resenting Bliss's delays in publishing
Innocents Abroad was that the book needed to issue while
public interest in the *Quaker City* excursion was keenest.
Twain conceived the idea of writing *Roughing It* "because he
believed his experience of the mining boom provided him with
a subject that would interest his readers," but he soon discovered that the avalanche of Western material made his own
book "hackneyed." [96] In addition to Bret Harte, John Hay,
Clarence King, and Joaquin Miller, subscription volumes like
Richardson's *Beyond the Mississippi* (1869), Mrs. Francis
Victor's *The River of the West* (1871), Mrs. Fanny Kelly's
Narrative of My Captivity Among the Sioux Indians (1872),
and Stephen Powers' *Afoot and Alone* (1872) exploited the
topic.

This same desire for topicality influenced the humorist's
fiction. In his utilization of graft and political corruption in
The Gilded Age, he was making an attempt, according to
Albert Kitzhaber, "to get a good sale by capitalizing on current
news." [97] The Pomeroy scandal had been good newspaper
copy—the *New York Times Index* lists twelve articles on
Pomeroy between January 29 and March 5, 1873. Tweed was
convicted in November, the Crédit Mobilier scandal broke,
and the failure of Jay Cooke and Company precipitated the
Panic of 1873. The authors obviously expected their readers to
be aware of the political and financial situation when they
wrote the ironic introduction. Though *The Gilded Age* and,
years later, *Democracy* were the only major fictional treatments

of the corruption of the era, it was a familiar enough topic to the average reader through the hundreds of books, articles, pamphlets, and newspaper editorials—Charles Francis and Henry Adams' *Chapters of Erie,* W. S. Robinson's *The Salary Grab,* J. D. McCabe's *Behind the Scenes in Washington,* and Tilden's *The Tweed Ring* all come to mind—which took political corruption as their topic. On a more literary level, *Democratic Vistas* and Lowell's "Ode for the Fourth of July, 1876" reiterated the public distress over chicanery and political malfeasance.

Tom Sawyer was written in the wake of a number of books by such writers as Thomas Bailey Aldrich, C. B. Lewis, James M. Bailey, and Robert Burdette, who had as their aim the "satirizing [of] some of the excesses of Sunday School fiction." [98] *Tom,* "Old Times," and the first chapters of *Huck* were all begun during a period in the mid-70's when the "new" South and a bloody-shirt campaign provided material for magazines and journals.[99] Consistently, then, Twain in the decade of the 1870's was aware of and adapted to his purposes themes and topics that, although they were not of literary interest to most of the major writers of his generation, had captured the popular imagination.

Novelty, on the other hand, was also a selling point. The ingenious, the unique, the bizarre were qualities at which the subscription book aimed, and Twain exploited this idea, too. In the Preface to *Roughing It* he explicitly noted that the book contained information "about which no books have been written by persons who were on the ground in person, and saw the happenings of the time with their own eyes." While composing *A Tramp Abroad* he thought it important to tell Frank Bliss that he had accumulated "stuff which has never been in a book"; and even as late as the publication of *Pudd'nhead Wilson* he was boasting that the material on fingerprinting was "absolutely *fresh,* and mighty curious and interesting to everybody." [100]

Twain's point of view, undoubtedly his most natural and uncontrived base of appeal to a subscription audience, was nevertheless one that varied somewhat from rigid fact. The Mark Twain persona measured by completely American standards, preferred Tahoe to Como, chromos to the Old Masters, and rural American food to European cuisine. It was exactly the standard of values the subscription book reader recognized and shared, and Twain was well aware that the resulting "irreverence" was an enormous sales factor. His slatings against sentimentality, European cultural and moral standards, and those Americans who showered their adulation upon anything European were most likely what Twain had in mind when he explained in his autobiography:

> Humor must not professedly teach, and it must not professedly preach, but it must do both if it would live forever. By forever, I mean thirty years. . . .
> I have always preached. That is the reason that I have lasted thirty years. If the humor came of its own accord and uninvited, I have allowed it a place in my sermon, but I was not writing the sermon for the sake of the humor. I should have written the sermon just the same, whether any humor applied for admission or not.[101]

Only rarely did these "sermons" attack the mores of the popular audience. As Willard Thorp has pointed out, he satirized those pilgrims who were determined "to find a Presbyterian or Baptist Palestine" in *Innocents Abroad,* and in *Tom Sawyer* he ridiculed the conventional Good Boy–Bad Boy stereotype. More frequently, he criticized those "high-brow" attitudes which the popular reader would be likely to resent, "those things," according to Carl Van Doren, "which to the general public seemed obstacles to the victorious progress of an average democracy." However congenial it was to Twain's own beliefs—and there are some suggestions that he was aware he adopted a pose for the benefit of his audience—his blatant, bourgeois provincialism was important to his readers because, as Dixon Wecter has phrased it, it "helped to belittle our romantic allegiance to Europe, feeding our emergent nationalism." [102]

Finally, there is that curious mixture of sensationalism and piety (if not prudery) which is so singularly typical of Mark Twain's work. The use of death, mutilation, and putrefaction, the grisly, the macabre, and the grotesque was an almost irresistible compulsion of Mark Twain's, while on the other hand such sanctimonious moral piety as the outburst against Titian's "Venus," in the last pages of *A Tramp Abroad,* or the deification of Joan of Arc were almost as compelling. It was true, whatever the underlying reasons for Twain's combination of the two apparently irreconcilable subjects, that the public, and especially the subscription book reader, liked sensationalism. It even made best sellers of many sensational and sensual books that were wise enough to point a moral at the conclusion. The formula allowed the writer for a popular audience to include the morbid and even the lascivious in his writing as long as he also insisted on the didactic function of the material.

From the story of the corpse in his father's office and the description of the Capuchin Convent in *Innocents Abroad,* through the tales of Slade in *Roughing It* and the account of the glacier yielding up frozen bits and pieces of the members of an early climbing expedition in *A Tramp Abroad,* to the wholesale slaughter in *The Prince and the Pauper, Huckleberry Finn,* and *The Connecticut Yankee,* to mention only a scattering of samples, Twain manifested that nearly adolescent curiosity for the sensational. Even as late as *Following the Equator* he quoted gory descriptions of natives conducting self-amputation by fire, and his publisher devoted a full-page illustration to a "humorous" depiction of a kangaroo beheading a man. The illustrations and contents chosen to go into the prospectuses reinforce the notion that both Twain and Bliss expected physical violence to appeal to an audience perhaps not too far removed from the one that viewed the death of Boggs in *Huckleberry Finn* by "squirming and scrouging and pushing and shoving to get at the window and have a look." However one might construct a theory to explain the psychological basis of Twain's fascination, the subscription publication of his books could only reinforce the idea that it made good, marketable copy.

It was this audience, though, however much Twain appreciated its purchase of over 300,000 copies of his books during the 70's, for whom he was "turning cartwheels to captivate the groundlings." [103] Or, as Sherwood Anderson once phrased it, "He addressed an audience that gets a big laugh out of the braying of a jackass and without a doubt Mark often brayed at them." But as he acquired more "literary" goals, he rankled at his subservience to the subscription audience. His debates about publishing *The Prince and the Pauper* and *Joan of Arc* anonymously, his and Livy's gratitude for Howells' reviews that pointed out the serious qualities in his writing, his calling his pseudonym "my hated nom de plume (for I do loathe the very sight of it)," [104] all present glimpses of a Mark Twain who "had begun to feel the aspirations of an artist, to crave deeper approval than had come to the cracker-box humorist like Sam Slick or Jack Downing." The defensiveness of his 1889 letter to Lang also suggests less than wholehearted endorsement of the people he claimed he addressed.

To some extent Twain's moralizing appealed to a higher browed audience than the subscription book buyer. Even though he attacked high-brow culture more frequently than "Philistine," he at least separated himself from the "mere" humorists. As Howells noted over and over, the qualities of "common sense, a passionate love of justice, and a generous scorn of what is petty and mean" set Twain off from his contemporary humorists of the literary comedian school. As his champion and apologist with the literary world of New England, Howells crusaded: *Innocents Abroad,* he said, had a "didactic mood," and he cataloged many of the "instructive portions" of the book; *Sketches* contained "a growing seriousness of meaning"; *A Tramp Abroad* showed a Mark Twain who had "often the grimness of a reformer." [105] If Howells' judgment was accurate, and it is impossible not to believe that it was, then the common ground between Mark Twain's books and the literary audience to whom the *Atlantic* reviews were directed was an ethical rather than a humorous one.

This touches another point of Twain's appeal to many more literate readers. In addition to outgrowing the "nose-picking school" of American humor, Twain kept his material intended for publication by subscription well within the limits of Victorian moral bounds. The deletion of the few sexual references in *Tom Sawyer* and the melodramatic, retributive death of Laura in *The Gilded Age*, which was Twain's "improvement" over Warner's proposed "Western retirement," only reaffirmed the prevailing sentiment Mark Twain voiced most explicitly in the final chapter of *A Tramp Abroad:*

> Art is allowed as much indecent license to-day as in earlier times—but the privileges of Literature in this respect have been sharply curtailed within the past eighty or ninety years. Fielding and Smollett could portray the beastliness of their day in the beastliest language; we have plenty of foul subjects to deal with in our day, but we are not allowed to approach them very near, even with nice and guarded forms of speech.

To this curtailment, Wecter has noted, "in the main he gave unstinting assent." [106] The Stomach Club Speech and *1601* were exceptions because they were not intended for proper publication.

Finally, it is probable that Twain's strivings for narrative unity and structure, rudimentary and unsustained though they were, originated in his desire to appeal to literary readers. What form he attained was an element in his books which had little interest to his popular readers, for, as Henry Nash Smith has pointed out, "As a rank amateur in the art of book-construction Mark Twain had done his best with *The Innocents Abroad* and the mounting sales showed that his best was amply good enough for his audience. But the problem of structure remained." [107] And to some extent it remained in all Twain's major books. The last parts of *Roughing It, A Tramp Abroad, Life on the Mississippi,* and *Huckleberry Finn* corroborate Smith's suggestion that the motivation to write unified material sprang "from deeper sources than the author's conscious intention." [108] And his constant references to his fiction as "experiments" underscore his uncertainty and confusion. Even when Twain found ideal structural principles, as in *Roughing It* and *Huckleberry Finn,* habit and the pressures of subscription bulk led him to burlesque, extravaganza, and statistics. Nevertheless, that he attempted a unified narrative at all was probably in part an impulse to satisfy the audience symbolized by the *Atlantic Monthly.* The warning Howells had given about not rushing the writing of *Tom Sawyer* "for the sake of making a book" was undoubtedly a plea for more coherence and less padding, but particularly in the longer travel books it was a suggestion with which Twain lacked the sustaining powers to comply. Thus the narrative threads played out, and, significantly, the fiction was uniformly shorter than the typical subscription book.

These were the two extremes, often contradictory, to which Mark Twain's subscription books aimed. As Carl Van Doren has suggested, "The secret alike of his powers and of his limitations must be looked for in the dual, the never quite completed, nature which allowed him on one side to touch, say, Petroleum V. Nasby and on the other William Dean Howells." [109] Mr. Brown's girlfriend picking her nose with a fork was at one end of the scale, Joan of Arc was at the other, and the subscription book was the battleground upon which Twain tried to reconcile their differences. Mark Twain was probably as complex a person as American literature will ever have to deal with, and his art came from other stirrings in addition to those that the subscription book created. It is impossible to guess what and how he would have written if he had published in the "regular trade," if the wealth and ego-satisfying popularity which accrued from Bliss's fateful letter of November 21, 1867, had not come to him. But once the commercial relationship was cemented, Elisha Bliss and the subscription method exerted on the Lincoln of our literature an influence that shaped not only his popular image and his personality but also the bases of his craft.

HELPFUL HINTS
OR HOW TO BECOME
A SUCCESSFUL AGENT

Quoted complete below is a typical agent's guide (Chicago, no publisher, 1887) with instructions for sure-fire subscription selling. The original is in the possession of Franklin Meine, Chicago. See the *Mark Twain-Howells Letters*, II, 879, for a description of another such pamphlet, one issued by Webster for selling Grant's autobiography.

The Successful Agent

READ THIS CAREFULLY

Knowing How. You have been appointed one of our agents, and we take it for granted that you *intend to succeed*. This is right. But you must also *know how*. We can show you how if you will let us. Will you do this? If so, and you will PRACTICE what you learn, we unhesitatingly promise you success.

Canvassing includes *five progressive steps* taken in the following natural order:
First:—Thorough preparation.
Second:—Securing influence.
Third:—Gaining a hearing.
Fourth:—Creating a desire.
Fifth:—Taking the order.

The First Step. Immediately on receiving your Outfit, begin to prepare yourself for your arduous duties. How many agents have we known fail right here, at the very threshold of their work! Better, infinitely better, had they gone to breaking stones on the highway than taken a Book Agency, and neglected to *prepare themselves* for canvassing! The first thing for you to do is to study this manual. Don't dip into it here and there; don't skim hurriedly over it; don't do *anything else* with it than *study it.*

Something that will Surprise You. You think very highly of your book. Of course you do, or you would not canvass for it. You will be surprised, therefore, to be told that you do not more than *half appreciate it.* Yet the chances are twenty to one that such is the case. And this is no reflection upon either your intelligence or your good faith. It is simply another way of saying that you have not yet *thoroughly studied* your book. *You must be interested yourself, or you cannot interest others; and the way for you to become interested, is to* KNOW *your book* THOROUGHLY.

Command of what You Know. What an array of STRONG POINTS you will discover your book to possess! By "strong points," we mean interesting features, valuable features, features that will help you *sell it.* But can you properly *impress your views on* others? Unless you are an apt salesman, and have experience besides, you *can not.* You have yet to acquire *perfect mastery* of what you know, and this can only come from PRACTICE. Remember that in canvassing you must think rapidly, talk fluently, and show your book to the *best advantage;* and all this, too, without *apparent* effort.

Practicing to Make Perfect. *Begin* practicing at home. "Canvass" some member of your household, or some friend, exactly as if to sell him a book. This will show you on what points you require to rub up. *Rub up,* and canvass him again. Don't make a jest of this *trial-work.* Go at it in earnest, for it is very important to you. Nothing will contribute more to your success than just this *self-training*. This done, a little actual canvassing will enable you to give your whole thought to the MANNER of your descriptions; the MATTER of them will come spontaneously. You will then be, indeed, *master of the situation.*

Influential Names to Head your List. These you *must secure*, cost what effort it may. Right here is the GREAT TURNING POINT OF SUCCESS. Every old Agent understands this perfectly. Do not imagine that you are smart enough, or lucky enough to prove an exception to the invariable rule. *You are not.* Start right. Get a few leading names to head your list, and your success is assured. This is not *theory*. It is a *fact, philosophy*, UNIVERSAL EXPERIENCE. Society everywhere follows its leaders. The great majority of people are afraid to trust their own unaided judgment about buying a book; but show them that Dr. A. and Rev. Mr. B., or Judge C. and Professor D., or Colonel E. and Esquire F.—or better still, all of these—have taken your work, and you will decide them immediately. They will feel really *proud* to be on your list in *such* company.

Keep a Good Heart and be Careful. Do not be discouraged if you should not get the names of *all* those you first selected to head your list. Perhaps you have enough as it is; if not, select others, and secure *them*. But on *no account* permit yourself to begin with *inferior* names; and if, by chance, any such should offer at this stage, have them put down on the *third* or *fourth* page of your order book. If one of the most influential "leaders" happens to be out of town, *reserve* a line for his name at the *head* of the list. When you at last find him, you can turn this to good account, and make of it an extremely neat and *effective* compliment.

Testimonials. Secure all of these that you can, from persons of *influence* at every stage of the canvass, but especially in starting. They carry the *most* weight when written on a separate sheet, but it will sometimes be *easier* to get them by handing your order book to the individual, and letting him write in that what he wishes to say. Testimonials should always be *brief* and *to the point*. Two or three *strong, ringing adjectives*, in characterizing your book, are worth more than a page of *description* of it. Always be ready to suggest the wording of a testimonial yourself, in case you should be called upon, or find it advisable to do this.

How to Carry Your Outfit. Gentlemen should have a large pocket on the inside of the coat, directly under the arm, in which to carry it. This will not only be very convenient, but serve to keep out of sight what might excite prejudice, by telling in advance what your business is, and thus preventing you from obtaining a fair hearing. To make such a pocket, without cutting the garment, make a bag large enough for the book, and put two button-holes near the upper edge; then sew two buttons on the inside of your garment, and button the bag on.

Lady agents should carry their outfit in a satchel under a loose wrap.

The Philosophy of Canvassing. If you have faithfully carried out the directions thus far given, you are now ready to begin the general canvass. Do IT at once. Canvassing is something more than simply going from house to house and offering a book for sale. A person *must* desire your book, or he will not buy; and he never will desire it, *until you have shown him what it is*, and pointed out its *many excellencies*. Bearing these *cardinal truths* in mind, you will see at a glance what a fearful blunder it would be to poke your book at a man, and then say, "Don't you want to subscribe?" *Of course* he does not; it is almost impossible, at this stage, that he should. But show him in the proper manner, what it is, and he *will* want it. Always? No, not always, but in the *large majority* of cases he will.

Keep the Book in Your Own Hands. Possession is power. Surrender the book, and you lose the power of showing it. You will be led, instead of leading. This you must NEVER willingly permit. Strive to "keep the upper hand" all through. As nearly as possible, do all the thinking, talking, deciding, that there is to be done, *yourself*. Aim to make your IN-FLUENCE a *controlling* one.

Economize Time. Your time is precious. Study *brevity* in your descriptions. Don't read long extracts. Don't suffer yourself to be led into long discussions on *any* subject. Don't spend time on any feature after you see your *point* is clearly understood.

Objections. These will come in all sorts of shapes. But there never was an objection raised that could not be answered in *some* way. There never will be. *Expect* objections. They are inseparable from your business. But learn to *meet them*. In a *multitude* of cases you will find them mere bugaboos. If interrupted by a question, or a querulous remark, that you are not ready to consider, let it pass unheeded, or say pleasantly, "We shall come to that in a little while, Mr.————," (or something of that sort,) and in the *same breath* resume your description.

Making the Most of Your Points. Not all your points will tell as you thought they would. But some of them will, and this is all you want. Books are seldom bought for what they are as a whole, but for some *particular feature* or *features* they contain. And tastes differ. Acquire the faculty of judging beforehand what will most *strike* different kinds of customers. Many subscribe because their neighbors have done so. *The array of signatures* brings to your aid the mighty influence of example, and has a kind of mesmeric power. MAKE THE MOST OF YOUR SUBSCRIPTION LIST IN ALL CASES. It will generally do more than all your previous talking.

If He Hesitates. If he hesitates, do not *startle* him into refusing you, by abruptly poking your pencil at him, but continue in a pleasant, off-hand way, "Mr.————, your name makes the twentieth order that I have taken," or "my third order this morning," or something of that kind. "I expect to have a very encouraging report to send in this week. Please write your name *there* on *that* line" (pointing to it). Then, if his *manner* indicates acquiescence, hand him your pencil.

What Binding to Sell. If your book is published in several bindings, always sell one of the *higher priced* ones, if possible. There is no better evidence of *good work* in canvassing, than a large percentage of orders for the finer bindings. These not only *pay the Agent* far the best, but the CUSTOMER is invariably *better satisfied* with his bargain.

How to Leave the Subscriber with a Good Impression. When you have taken a person's name for your book, do not leave abruptly, but remain five minutes or so, provided his time be not too much occupied with other business, and show him more particularly than before what you *know* to be strong points in your book, and its superiority to all others on similar subjects, and speak of the success you are meeting with, etc. What you say now will have its full weight, and he will begin to take a lively interest in seeing you prosper. All the information that you need about families or persons ahead, or other matters, he will gladly communicate, and help you with a good word to his neighbors at every opportunity. You may then bid him good-day, in a business-like, pleasant manner, and go on your way rejoicing.

Your Manner and Address. Much depends upon these— more, perhaps, than upon anything else, or *all* things else combined. Your bearing should be open, frank, and manly, as of one who feels the true nobleness of his calling—never that of crouching servility or testiness, nor yet of overbearing and dogmatism. Show that you believe heartily in your book yourself, and are conscious of being engaged in an honorable and laudable undertaking in aiding its circulation.

The Secret of Large Profits. Canvass closely, thoroughly, *exhaustively.* This is the *great secret* of money-making in the book business. It may require *much longer* to canvass a given territory than you expected. Never mind; *take* the time. Your business is not getting over territory. It is *selling books,* and the more books you can place *in a given area, the more money you will make.* Nearly all beginners in this business work too fast. Guard this point. Do not slight one family, office, store, or shop, because you think yourself hurried. And see that you spend enough time in each to show your book *properly.*

Have a Mind of Your Own. Do not be turned aside from the faithful performance of your duty by what *anybody may say.* You must expect to hear a great many discouraging remarks. People *will* talk. In your case, however, they do not know what they are talking about—at least, most of them do not. This is none the less true, either, because *they* may conscientiously believe otherwise, and imagine they are advising you for your own good. Do *not* mind them. A hundred times have we seen the *determined* agent achieve a fine success in a community where he had been gravely assured he could do nothing.

A Large Territory. Perhaps no mistake is so common among new agents as *greed* for territory. In the more thickly settled parts of the Union, two towns or townships are enough for any agent to *begin* with. *Concentration* of effort is essential to your success, and this, in attempting to cover a large territory, is impossible. *Don't worry about territory.* Bear in mind that if you succeed, your employers will be very sure, for their own interest, to ADD to your field all that you can possibly work.

Do Not Run about from Point to Point in Search of Better Territory. This is a very common mistake of new agents, and a disastrous one, resulting in waste of time, and crude, unsatisfactory, and profitless experimenting, instead of faithful, vigorous *work* by which alone you can make the business a success. Do THE BEST YOU CAN under every circumstance, wherever you happen to be at work, and in the end you will see that in no other way could you have accomplished nearly as much.

After canvassing a town or village, do not fly off at a tangent to some remote portion of your field, but continue working gradually outward, first on one road, and then on another. By this means you will keep constantly where your subscribers are well known, and where the INFLUENCE OF YOUR SUB-SCRIPTION LIST will, therefore, be of the greatest value to you. Show a man the names of half his neighbors upon your book, and you bring to bear a tremendous leverage upon him; but twice as many names from another locality may fail to move him at all.

We must repeat once more, CANVASS THOROUGHLY. It requires but little more time or traveling to sell fifty books in a district than fifteen, and it is self-evident that the former result will prove much the more remunerative to the agent.

The business is always most profitable when the largest number of subscribers are obtained in the smallest space.

Avoid People Away from Home. An agent should avoid as a pestilence men in groups, public gatherings, and people at court. Not only can very little or nothing be effected at such places, but those who are taken up on such occasions with other business and refuse to subscribe are almost sure to refuse when called upon at their homes. Walk up to any group of three or four and one of them is sure to be either a joker or a grumbler; and, if either, a laugh or a whine will be made at your expense, and all hopes of getting subscribers be dissipated. Calling upon a man at his house, or in the field, or at his place of business, he feels himself particularly addressed; his mind is free to act, and the chances of success are much greater; for he is but one, and you, if quick-witted, will soon see how to suit him.

Make the Most of Every Day. Be diligent, improving your time to the utmost. Do not loiter about hotels or public offices, in conversation which has no connection with your *business*. Neither should you suspend operations, an hour before dinner, or in the middle of an afternoon, simply because you have found a pleasant stopping place. Nor should you remain unemployed after ordering books. "Time is money." To no business man can this possibly be more true than to the canvasser. The hours of each day should be reckoned as dollars, and their probable pecuniary value carefully counted, before you consent to idle or fritter *one* of them away.

While an agent may incline to suspend his work during unpleasant and stormy weather, he should know that thereby he would sacrifice even better opportunities than usual for increasing his list, since at such times farmers are about their homes, merchants are less occupied and men of all classes will more readily give you their attention. Let it rain or shine, work faithfully from morning until night, and depend upon it, in the end your efforts will be crowned with success. This is an occupation that requires constant exertion, both mental and bodily. The workers conquer; the drones are beaten.

External Influences. The success of an agent is *mainly* dependent upon himself—upon his proper understanding and thorough appreciation of his book, his courteous and business-like deportment, his patient energy and untiring industry, etc. Yet he must expect to find during weeks and months of canvassing a varied prosperity. The business has been aptly compared to fishing—scarcely a nibble on some days, at other times a good haul.

Avoid Hasty Conclusions of Any Kind. Discouragements to new agents often arise from failure to obtain the signature of many of those whom they had regarded as most likely to appreciate the work—judging their want of success in such cases to be a fair test of the business; whereas they misjudge, both as to the readiness of the person to meet the matter intelligently, and as to the probabilities of future success.

Neither a large success nor the want of it should induce you to relax your diligence, or unduly excite either your hopes or fears. Pursue your work steadily and faithfully, and rest assured that, *in the end,* you will accomplish good and satisfactory results.

ORDERING BOOKS

Do Not Be in a Hurry to Begin Delivering. New agents very frequently want to begin delivering books as soon as they have canvassed three or four days, or a week, and obtained from twenty to thirty subscribers. This is a grand mistake. The way to make the business pay is to do it on a *wholesale* scale, to the utmost possible extent, and not fritter away time and labor by doing everything in a petty way. The saving of expense (in freights, etc.) is only one of the *minor* advantages which you will gain by ordering and delivering in lots as large as possible. The greatest gain, perhaps, will be your *saving of time.* Remember, canvassing is your main business; delivering is an *interruption.* One delivery of a 100 books will yield you a *net profit from two to four times* greater than ten deliveries of 10 books each. Professional canvassers generally work up an entire town or township, before ordering books.

Continue Canvassing until the Books Come. You may depend on our filling your order, as a rule, within one day of its receipt by us. But, though the time will not be long between your ordering books and your receiving them, (unless extraordinary delays occur in transportation) it will be entirely too long for you to spend it in idleness. Improve it diligently in canvassing, or, if need be, even in *re-canvassing*. And see that you order in *good season*, so that if there *should* be three or four days' unusual delay, it will not embarrass you.

DELIVERING BOOKS

The Philosophy of Delivering. This is very simple, viz.: There is a *contract* existing between your subscriber and yourself. You perform your part of this contract by delivering the book. You expect him to fulfill his part by receiving and paying therefor. It is purely a business transaction. Never treat it by word, look or manner, as though it could possibly be anything else. *Never* say, "I have brought your book; I *hope* you are ready to take it;" nor anything of similar import. Never let a customer impose upon your *good nature*, or "back out" from his bargain on *any* pretext, except for reasons the most conclusive, and based on circumstances for which he is in no wise responsible.

Serving the Book. Let your manner be courteous, but thoroughly self-possessed and decided. In a word, be business-like. Never show the least misgiving that the customer will give you trouble. Say that you have brought his book, as per agreement, and he will find it a treasure indeed (or something of that kind). Look him full in the face and hand him the book.

Keep Your Order Book. Check off (thus X) the names of subscribers as they pay you. Unless it be *badly* soiled, use the same canvassing book until quite full. Thus you can make the most of the *powerful influence of your subscription list*, which latter will be of immense service, no matter though your next canvassing be done in another community. For similar reasons, whenever you replace an old canvassing book with a new one, copy from your prospectus from 25 to 50 of the most influential names into your new prospectus or order-book. Then you can show your customer that all these took the book, and many others whose names you did not copy.

HINTS TO AGENTS

Every evening think over your failures during the day; do not sleep till you have thought of a remedy for such cases. This is the way to benefit by your failures.

Do not be too easily put off. "No" is not *always* an answer in canvassing any more than in courting. Remember that some natures are naturally slow to act, and others are timid and self-distrustful. In either case, they need to be "labored with" for their own good.

Don't be afraid or ashamed to talk. This is the way sales are effected in all kinds of business. People *expect* you to talk. You *ought* to talk. You can not do *justice* to yourself, your book, or your publishers, unless you do talk. But talk *to the point.* Entertain and *instruct* your customer, if possible.

Be hopeful in mind, that you may be cheerful in manner. Never despair of securing an order, while the chance is left you of *talking.* And strive to carry *sunshine* with you—enough, indeed, to *warm* the most frigid soul you may be brought into contact with.

Be persevering. An occasional order from one who "never subscribes" will help you immensely from this very circumstance. If one of this class gives you only *half* a chance, make up your mind to get him, and don't leave him *till you do.*

Be courteous always and everywhere. This is just as important for its "reflex influence" on yourself as for its influence on others. You must be *habitually* respectful and polite, or you cannot develop the self-reliance, or even the self-respect, which is absolutely *essential* to success in your calling.

Never leave your book where any one can get at it during your absence. When not using it, keep it under lock and key.

Never leave your prospectus, or sample copy, with any one else, for *him* to show some one else, and secure you an order. No matter how good his intentions, he cannot do you justice; he cannot show your book *properly.* You can, for you have studied it, and know it thoroughly. Have an appointment made, if possible, and at the time designated, go around and show it yourself.

Never attempt to show your book when you are tired out. At such times you cannot do justice to it, to yourself, or your employer.

If you are told (as you will be every day) that the times are very hard and everybody is complaining, bethink yourself whether *your publishers* have not understood this, and gotten up something *suited to the times*.

If you are told that people won't buy anything now-a-days that they can't use, call to mind the *useful* and *valuable* features of your book.

If you are told that *so many* books are being canvassed for in this community, etc., set this down (if true) as an evidence that there is an *interest* in books there. All the better chance for the agent with the best and most useful book. Frequent buyers are the most intelligent buyers.

If you are told that the people won't buy anything, just now, that they can do without, examine the statement a moment, and you will see that it is *not true*. People *could* do without shoes and go barefoot, but they *don't*. They *could* live on two meals a day, but they *don't*. They *could* dispense with a hundred things of comfort, luxury and convenience. But they *don't* and *won't*. What they *desire strongly*, that they will and do buy. Get them to wanting your book, by showing it *cleverly* and *they will do it*. This is the grand and cheering FACT that outweighs all the drawbacks which people may dolefully recount to you.

Your Dealings with the Firm. *Mutual confidence and good will* are the basis of all satisfactory relations in business. Let your dealings with the firm be such as to promote these feelings on both sides. Never lose sight of the fact that your interest and theirs are identical. Consult them freely. Give them credit for *good faith* in what they say and do. If you *cannot* do this, take our advice and quit their service.

Do Not Neglect the Duty of Reporting. This is *important*, though you may not see why; important, most of all, to *you*.

Promptly forward copies of the *best* of the testimonials that you procure for your book. The publishers will often be able to have them printed for you.

If you know any good agents in a neighboring community, send on their names and exact addresses. Your employers will feel *grateful* for little attentions of this kind, and will certainly take an increased interest in you.

Here we close. Remember that a knowledge of your business; intelligence and faithful labor in the manner best adapted thereto, moral courage to overcome the difficulties which you must expect in this as in every other calling under the sun, and perseverance sufficient to accomplish great things, *little by little:* these are the elements which will make your canvassing a great success, beyond all peradventure. Begin heartily and *do your best.* If this is less than you expected, persevere! You will do better by-and-by. Under any and all circumstances, DO YOUR BEST, AND IN THE END YOU WILL BE SATISFIED.

Very Truly Yours,

THE PUBLISHER.

A BIBLIOGRAPHY OF AMERICAN PUBLISHING COMPANY BOOKS

*F*OR SEVERAL REASONS subscription books are among the most elusive to track down. Titles changed, works were advertised which never appeared, and different companies published the identical volume with altered titles. Nevertheless it has been possible, with the aid of book lists in the back of prospectuses, advertisements in the pages of *The American Publisher,* and references in the Berg Collection Stock Ledger of American Publishing Company books, to compile the following list of volumes. Wherever possible, I have used the *Library of Congress Catalog of Printed Cards* to double-check dates of publication, but some of the titles have escaped verification. Others are no doubt "ghosts" of other volumes, and it is strongly probable that additional titles belong on the list.

These titles were all either advertised or published between 1865 and 1884. By the end of the century the American Publishing Company was falling on very difficult times and relied on standard sets in fine bindings, like Twain's and Charles Dudley Warner's, for the bulk of its business.

I. AMERICAN PUBLISHING COMPANY BOOKS (exclusive of Twain):

Among the Daisies ["A book of rare beauty and merit; being a collection of all the poems that have ever been written about the daisy."]

Back from the Mouth of Hell, or The Rescue from Drunkenness. By a Reformed Inebriate.

Berkeley, August. *My Wife's Fool of a Husband,* 1884.

Billings, E. R. *A Book on Tobacco,* 1875.

Browne, Junius H. *The Great Metropolis,* 1869.

————. *Sights and Sensations in Europe,* 1871.

Burdette, Robert J. *The Rise and Fall of the Moustache.*

Capen, Nahum. *History of Democracy,* 1874.

Champlin, J. D. *Scripture Reading Lessons for Family Worship.*

Commercial Precedents.

Daniels, William H. *D. L. Moody and His Work,* 1876.

Fac-simile of Gen'l Washington's Account with the United States, 1876.

Fish, Henry C. *Bible Lands Illustrated,* 1876.

Harte, Bret. *Gabriel Conroy,* 1876.

Headley, Joel Tyler. *The Great Rebellion,* 1866.

Holley, Marietta. *My Opinions and Betsey Bobbet's,* 1873.

————. *Samantha at the Centennial,* 1877.

————. *My Wayward Pardner,* 1880.

————. *Lament of a Mormon Wife,* 1880.

————. *Miss Richards' Boy, and Other Stories.*

Hyde, Alexander. *Agriculture,* 1871.

Kane, Elisha Kent. *Arctic Explorations.*

King, Edward. *The Great South,* 1875.

Knox, Thomas W. *Overland through Asia,* 1870.

Meachum, A. B. *Wi-ne-ma (the Woman Chief),* 1876.

Miller, Joaquin. *Unwritten History,* 1874. [Issued as *Paquita: The Indian Heroine* and *Life Among the Modocs* at other times.]

Newcomb, Raymond L. *Our Lost Explorers.*

Olcott, H. S. *People from Another World,* 1875.

Pebbles and Pearls.

Phelps, R. H. *Newgate of Connecticut,* 1876.
Rambles through Our Country. ["An Instructive Geographical Game."]
Richardson, Albert Deane. *The Secret Service,* 1865.
————. *Beyond the Mississippi,* 1867, 1869.
————. *Personal History of U. S. Grant,* 1868.
Shaw, Henry Wheeler. *Everybody's Friend,* 1874.
Smith, Matthew Hale. *Successful Folks—How They Win,* 1878.
Stebbins, Jane E. *Illustrated History of the Bible,* 1867.
Stone, Julia A. *Illustrated India,* 1877.
Stories About Animals.
Trumbull, J. Hammond. *The True Blue Laws of Connecticut,* 1876.
Warner, Charles Dudley. *My Winter on the Nile, Among the Mummies and Moslems,* 1876.
Webster, Mary C. *The Wonderful Christmas Tree,* 1882.
Wood, John G. *Uncivilized Races, or the Natural History of Man,* 1870.
The World of Wit and Humour.
Wright, William. *The Big Bonanza,* 1876.

II. BELKNAP & BLISS BOOKS:
Blitz, Signor Antonio. *Fifty Years in the Magic Circle,* 1871.
The Exposé, or Mormons and Mormonism.
Gardner, Augustus K. *Our Children.*
Kirwan, D. J. *Palace and Hovel,* 1870.
Lossing, Benson J. *Pictorial Field Book of the Civil War,* 1874.

III. R. W. BLISS BOOKS:
Kane, Elisha K. *Arctic Explorations.*
The Last Journals of David Livingstone, 1875.
Schwartz, Madame Maria. *Little Karin,* 1873.

IV. COLUMBIAN BOOK COMPANY BOOKS:
Conybeare and Howson, *Life of St. Paul.*
Dutcher, George M. *Disenthralled: The Story of My Life,* 1872.
Evans, Albert S. *Our Sister Republic,* 1870.
Hyde, Baldwin, and Gage. *The Frozen Zone and Its Explorers.*
Hyde, Alexander, and Francis C. Bliss. *Stanley in Africa,* 1878.

The Past, Present and Future of Mormonism.
Powers, Stephen. *Afoot and Alone,* 1872.
Richardson, Albert Deane. *Garnered Sheaves,* 1871.
Summerings in the Wilderness.
Tyler, Josiah. *Livingstone's Life Work,* 1874.
Victor, Mrs. Francis. *The River of the West,* 1870.
———. *Eleven Years in the Rocky Mountains,* 1877.
Webb, Charles H. *John Paul's Book,* 1874.

V. MUTUAL PUBLISHING COMPANY BOOKS:

Cox, Palmer. *Squibs of California,* 1874.
Kelly, Mrs. Fanny. *Narrative of My Captivity among the Sioux Indians,* 1872.
Tyler, Josiah. *Africa and Its Explorers, or Livingstone Lost and Found,* 1873.

VI. F. C. BLISS BOOKS:

Kirwan, D. J. *London Illustrated* [perhaps a reprinting of *Palace and Hovel*].
The Political Compend, or Handbook for the Millions.

NOTES

$\mathcal{M}$ATERIALS on the subscription book industry in America are scattered and scanty, in part because of its ephemeral nature. Among the most important primary documents are a stock ledger of books the American Publishing Company received from its binderies from 1867 to 1879, now in The Henry W. and Albert A. Berg Collection of The New York Public Library, a collection of thirty-seven prospectuses in the Coe Library of the University of Wyoming, and the material in the Morse-Frear Collection at the Yale University Library. The Morse-Frear Collection, the Barrett Collection at the University of Virginia, and the Frank C. Willson Collection at the University of Texas have between them most of the prospectuses for Twain's subscription books and assorted flyers, circulars, and advertisements, and I own a "Certificate of Agency and Memorandum of Agreement" between Guy M. Laird of Central City, Colorado, and the Union Book and Bible House for the volume, *Briton and Boer in South Africa*. Further information on the bibliography of the subscription book versus trade book battles of the 1870's and 1880's is listed in my "Mark Twain: Audience and Artistry," *American Quarterly*, XV (Spring, 1963), 25–40.

CHAPTER I

1. *My Dear Bro, A Letter from Samuel Clemens to His Brother Orion*, ed. Frederick Anderson (Berkeley, The Berkeley Albion, 1961), pp. 6–8.

2. *Hartford, Connecticut as a Manufacturing, Business and Commercial Center* (Hartford, The Board of Trade, 1889), p. 134.

188   MARK TWAIN AND ELISHA BLISS

3. "Subscription Books," *The Trade Circular Annual for 1871* (New York, 1871), p. 110.
4. Gerald Carson, "Get the Prospect Seated . . . and Keep Talking," *American Heritage*, IX (August, 1958), 39.
5. "Subscription Books," *New York Herald Tribune*, October 28, 1874, p. 8.
6. Hellmut Lehmann-Haupt, *et al.*, *The Book in America*, 2d ed., rev. (New York, R. R. Bowker Company, 1951), pp. 251–52.
7. George Ade, "Mark Twain and the Old Time Subscription Book," *American Review of Reviews*, XLI (June, 1910), 703–4.
8. S. R. Crocker, "Subscription Books," *Literary World*, V (August, 1874), 40.
9. Philip S. Foner, *Mark Twain: Social Critic* (New York, International Publishers, 1958), p. 42. According to Leon Dickinson, though, *Innocents Abroad* was passed out generously to potential reviewers: "Marketing a Best Seller: Mark Twain's *Innocents Abroad*," *Papers of the Bibliographical Society of America*, XLI (1947), 116. And so was *Huck Finn;* see *Business Man*, p. 300.
10. Arthur L. Vogelback, "The Publication and Reception of *Huckleberry Finn* in America," *American Literature*, XI (November, 1939), 266.
11. F. E. Compton, *Subscription Books* (New York, The New York Public Library, 1939), p. 37.
12. Prospectus in the Coe Library, University of Wyoming.
13. *Chicago Tribune*, June 10, 1882, p. 9, quoted in Vogelback, p. 267.
14. " 'Sold Only by Subscription,' " *Publishers' Weekly*, XIX (May 21, 1881), 548–49.
15. Compton, p. 36.
16. John Todd, "Book Publishing and Book Selling," *The American Publisher*, I (January, 1872), 4.
17. Advertising announcement in the prospectus for *The Gilded Age*, CWB.
18. *New York Herald Tribune*, October 28, 1874, p. 8.
19. "The Gilded Age," *Old and New*, IX (March, 1874), 386.
20. *Letters*, p. 402; *Trade Circular Annual for 1871*, p. 111.
21. "Review of Innocents Abroad," *The Nation*, IX (September 2, 1869), 194–95.
22. "The Subscription Book Trade," *Publishers' Weekly*, II (July 25, 1872), 93–94.
23. Quoted in Merle Johnson, *A Bibliography of the Works of Mark Twain* (New York, Harper and Brothers, 1935), pp. 154–55; *Overland Monthly*, IV (January, 1870), 100.

24. DeLancey Ferguson, *Mark Twain: Man and Legend* (Indianapolis, The Bobbs-Merrill Company, 1943), p. 204.

25. Charles Neider, "Introduction," *The Complete Short Stories of Mark Twain* (Garden City, Hanover House, 1957), p. xx.

26. Julian Hawthorne, "Two Views of Book Canvassing," *Critic*, XXV (July 21, 1894), 44.

27. Ferguson, p. 130. See also James Hart, *The Popular Book* (New York, Oxford University Press, 1950), p. 147.

28. *Hartford Courant*, September 29, 1880, p. 2.

29. *Twain-Howells Letters*, II, 591.

30. Twain to Bliss, Elmira, June 24, 1876, Yale, © Mark Twain Company, 1964.

31. *Eruption*, p. 175.

32. Frank L. Mott, *Golden Multitudes* (New York, The Macmillan Company, 1947), p. 156.

33. *Twain-Howells Letters*, I, 107.

CHAPTER II

No discussion of *Innocents Abroad* can ignore Leon T. Dickinson's significant studies: his doctoral dissertation, "Mark Twain's *Innocents Abroad*: Its Origins, Composition, and Popularity" (University of Chicago, 1945); "Mark Twain's Revisions in Writing *The Innocents Abroad*," *American Literature*, XIX (May, 1947), 139–57; and "Marketing a Best Seller: Mark Twain's *Innocents Abroad*," *Papers of the Bibliographical Society of America*, XLI (1947), 107–22. In this chapter and those following, the "American Publishing Company's Stock Ledger of Books Received from the Bindery, 1867–1879," now in The Henry W. and Albert A. Berg Collection of The New York Public Library, has provided accurate figures for sales of Twain's books during the decade; a capsule version of its statistics is available in my "Mark Twain's Book Sales, 1869–1879," *Bulletin of the New York Public Library*, LXV (June, 1961), 371–89.

1. The editorial is reprinted in Paine, pp. 1610–11.

2. *Letters*, pp. 140–41. Fred Lorch, " 'Doesticks' and *Innocents Abroad*," *American Literature*, XX (January, 1949), 447, suggests that he planned to do a book on the *Quaker City* excursion even before he left on the trip.

3. *Letters*, p. 145. Other letters of the same week contain announcements so elated in their tone that they suggest Twain had not really considered the offer seriously until then. See *Mrs. Fairbanks*, p. 14; *Mark Twain's Letters to Will Bowen*, ed. Theodore Hornberger (Austin, University of Texas Press, 1941), p.

16; and *Mark Twain the Letter Writer*, ed. Cyril Clemens (Boston, Meador Publishing Company, 1932), p. 18.

4. Contract for *Innocents Abroad*, MTP.

5. *Business Man*, p. 98.

6. *Mark Twain's Letters to Will Bowen*, p. 18.

7. *Mrs. Fairbanks*, pp. 17, 22, 23–24.

8. Paine, p. 359.

9. Dickinson, "Mark Twain's *Innocents Abroad*," pp. 54–55.

10. Twain to Charles H. Webb, Buffalo, November 26, 1870, quoted in *Mark Twain and Bret Harte, Ah Sin*, ed. Frederick Anderson (San Francisco, Book Club of California, 1961), p. vii.

11. Frank Baldanza, *Mark Twain, An Introduction and Interpretation* (New York, Barnes & Noble, Inc., 1961), p. 60.

12. *Mrs. Fairbanks*, p. 30.

13. Bliss to Twain, Hartford, July 29, 1868, MTP.

14. Twain to Bliss, Elmira, April 29, 1869, MTP.

15. Twain to Bliss, "April Something," 1869, typescript in MTP.

16. Bliss to Twain, Hartford, February 10, 1869, MTP.

17. Twain to Bliss, Elmira, April 20, 1869, published in *The Twainian*, X (January–February, 1951), 1.

18. *Mrs. Fairbanks*, p. 83.

19. Bliss to Twain, Hartford, April 14, 1869, MTP.

20. *Love Letters*, p. 93.

21. *Mrs. Fairbanks*, p. 98.

22. *Ibid.*, pp. 83–84. As he had told Mrs. Fairbanks back in October, 1868, "We have . . . concluded that it cannot be illustrated profusely enough to get it out in December, and therefore we shall make a spring book of it and issue it the first of March." *Ibid.*, p. 40.

23. Twain to Frank Bliss, Paris, May 10, 1879, MTP.

24. American Travel Letters Series Two, Number 12, *Alta California*, November 22, 1868, as reprinted in *The Twainian*, VIII (March–April, 1949), 5.

25. In the final advertising page of Junius Browne's *The Great Metropolis*, the introduction to which is dated December, 1868.

26. *Mrs. Fairbanks*, pp. 84–85.

27. "Why Its First Publisher Accepted 'Innocents Abroad,'" *New York Evening Mail*, May 10, 1910, in the Morse Collection, Yale.

28. Twain to Bliss, Elmira, March 30, 1869, MTP.

29. Bliss to Twain, Hartford, April 14, 1869, MTP.

30. *The Twainian*, X (January–February, 1951), 1.

31. *Love Letters*, pp. 358, 93.

32. Bliss to Twain, Hartford, February 10, 1869, MTP.

33. Bliss to Twain, Hartford, July 12, 1869, MTP.

34. Twain to Bliss, Elmira, July 22, 1869, Yale, © Mark Twain Company, 1964.

35. Bliss to Twain, July, 1869, MTP.

36. Bliss to Twain, August 4, 1869, MTP.

37. Twain to Bliss, Elmira, August 1, 1869, typescript in MTP, © Mark Twain Company, 1964.

38. Twain to Bliss, Buffalo, August 12, 1869, MTP, © Mark Twain Company, 1964. He explained his irritation as a result of his unsuccessful negotiations to buy into the *Cleveland Herald* (*Mrs. Fairbanks*, p. 102).

39. Twain to Frank Bliss, Elmira, September 8, 1879, typescript in MTP.

40. *Letters*, p. 169.

41. Twain to Bliss, Elmira, August 1, 1869, typescript in MTP.

42. See Dickinson, "Marketing a Best Seller," p. 119.

43. Bliss to Twain, Hartford, November 1, 1869, MTP.

44. Bliss to Twain, July 12, 1869, MTP.

45. Dickinson, "Marketing a Best Seller," pp. 117–19.

46. See *Love Letters*, p. 131.

47. Dickinson, "Marketing a Best Seller," pp. 120–21.

48. Twain to Bliss, March 4, 1873, CWB, © Mark Twain Company, 1964.

49. Twain to Bliss, March 20, [1880], NYPL, © Mark Twain Company, 1964.

50. Twain to Osgood, Hartford, March 26, [1881], typescript in MTP.

51. *The Great Metropolis*, p. 706.

52. Prospectus for *Innocents Abroad* (1872), in my possession.

53. In the Morse Collection, Yale.

54. Review from the Meriden, Connecticut, *Republican*, quoted in 1872 prospectus. Other reviews are analyzed in Henry Nash Smith, *Mark Twain, The Development of a Writer* (Cambridge, Mass., Harvard University Press, 1962), pp. 37–41.

55. Twain to Bliss, January 22, 1870, typescript in MTP, © Mark Twain Company, 1964.

56. *Mrs. Fairbanks*, p. 115.

57. See Dickinson, "Marketing a Best Seller," pp. 121–22.

58. As Twain put it on January 28, 1870: "$4,000 is pretty gorgeous. One don't pick that up often with a book" (Twain to Bliss, Elmira, January 28, 1870, typescript in MTP, © Mark Twain Company, 1964).

59. *Business Man*, p. 117.

60. In NYPL.
61. In MTP.
62. Frank Bliss to Twain, Hartford, April 1, 1872, in "Scrapbook, Business 1872–1878," p. 76a, MTP.
63. *Letters*, p. 162.
64. Paine, p. 420.
65. *Mrs. Fairbanks*, pp. 131, 117–18, 144.
66. *Eruption*, p. 152.
67. *Mrs. Fairbanks*, p. 128.
68. Twain to Bliss, Elmira, May 5, 1870, typescript in MTP.
69. Twain to Bliss, May 20, 1870, typescript in MTP.
70. The contract is reprinted in the *Mark Twain Quarterly*, VI (Summer–Fall, 1944), 5.
71. *Letters*, p. 174.
72. Orion to Twain, Hartford, January 25, 1871, typescript in MTP, © Mark Twain Company, 1964.
73. Twain to Bliss, Elmira, August 2, 1870, typescript in MTP, © Mark Twain Company, 1964. This need to reassure Bliss that he was up to no skulduggery echoes Twain's January 22 letter: "You can have the *first* say (that is plain enough) on that or any other book I may prepare for the press, as long as you deal in a fair, open, and honorable way with *me*." Paine, p. 420.
74. *Letters*, pp. 175–76. He did use the present tense, though, announcing that he was "writing" on the book.
75. *Mrs. Fairbanks*, pp. 137, 138.
76. Twain to Bliss, [January] 24, 1871, typescript in MTP, © Mark Twain Company, 1964.
77. Twain to Bliss, Buffalo, January 27, 1871, MTP, © Mark Twain Company, 1964.
78. Orion to Twain, Hartford, March 11, 1871, MTP, © Mark Twain Company, 1964.
79. Twain to Bliss, Buffalo, March 17, 1871, NYPL, © Mark Twain Company, 1964.
80. *Letters*, p. 186.
81. Franklin Rogers, ed., *The Pattern for Mark Twain's Roughing It, Letters from Nevada by Samuel and Orion Clemens 1861–1862* (Berkeley, University of California Press, 1961), pp. 18–19.
82. See *Letters*, p. 127, and Paine, p. 321.
83. Twain to Bliss, Elmira, September 19, 1870, typescript in MTP; *Letters*, p. 188; *Love Letters*, p. 159.
84. *Innocents* with 2,400 manuscript pages (including at least some *Alta* clippings), *Tom Sawyer* with 1,000, *A Tramp Abroad* with 2,600, and a facsimile manuscript page of *The Gilded Age* in

which 399 pages of manuscript equaled 95 book pages (Paine, p. 475), all roughly confirm the ratio.

85. Conveniently reprinted in Bruce R. McElderry, Jr., ed., *Contributions to the Galaxy, 1868–1871, by Mark Twain* (Gainesville, Florida, Scholars Facsimiles and Reprints, 1961), p. 132. The December, 1870, "Memoranda" had—perhaps significantly—three "items" from Sandwich Islands papers (see McElderry, pp. 102, 108).

86. Twain to Orion, Elmira, July 2, 1871, MTP.

87. *Love Letters*, p. 159.

88. *Business Man*, p. 116.

89. Orion to Twain, Hartford, January 25, 1871, MTP, © Mark Twain Company, 1964.

90. *Letters*, p. 185.

91. Twain to Orion, Buffalo, March 11, 1871, CWB, © Mark Twain Company, 1964; March 13, 1871, typescript in MTP, © Mark Twain Company, 1964.

92. Bliss to Twain, Hartford, March 15, 1871, MTP.

93. Twain to Bliss, Elmira, [March] 20, [1871], MTP, © Mark Twain Company, 1964.

94. Bliss to Twain, Hartford, April 22, 1871, MTP; *Business Man*, p. 118. In addition to the selection on "The Pony Express" (May, 1871), *The American Publisher* printed "My First Lecture" (December, 1871), and "A Nabob's Visit to New York" (January, 1872). Other selections from *Roughing It* appeared in February, March, April, and June, 1872. The first issue of the magazine reprinted *Jumping Frog* material (April, 1871), and three issues used *Innocents Abroad* excerpts (November, 1871, February and June, 1872). My "Mark Twain's 'Brace of Brief Lectures on Science,'" *New England Quarterly*, XXXIV (June, 1961), 228–39, reprints two of the three original items by Twain in the magazine. Orion rejected the Bemis and the Bull story because it was similar to another current one (Twain to Orion, Elmira, April 18, [1871], in MTP). An earlier attempt at *The American Publisher* called *Author's Sketch Book* and described in *The Twainian*, II (May, 1940), 1–2, 4–5, must have been Orion's work and not Mark Twain's.

95. Twain to Orion, Elmira, April 4, [1871], MTP, © Mark Twain Company, 1964.

96. Twain to Orion, Elmira, April 8, [1871], MTP, © Mark Twain Company, 1964.

97. *Mrs. Fairbanks*, p. 153; *Business Man*, p. 119; *Letters*, pp. 187–88.

98. *Mrs. Fairbanks*, p. 154.

194 MARK TWAIN AND ELISHA BLISS

99. *The American Publisher,* I (July, 1871), 4. As early as May 11, 1871, the *Chicago Tribune,* p. 2, announced that "a portion of it has already been written and is now in the hands of the printers."

100. Twain to Orion, Elmira, July 2, 1871, MTP.

101. *Love Letters,* p. 159.

102. Twain to Bliss, Wilkes-Barre, October 19, 1871, typescript in MTP, © Mark Twain Company, 1964.

103. Twain to Greeley, Hartford, [October] 17th [1871], MTP.

104. Orion to Mollie Clemens, Hartford, October 3, 1871, typescript in MTP, © Mark Twain Company, 1964; *Love Letters,* p. 162.

105. Henry Nash Smith, "Introduction," *Roughing It* (New York, 1959), p. xiii.

106. *Mrs. Fairbanks,* p. 138.

107. Bliss to Twain, Hartford, July 7, 1871, MTP; Paine, p. 452, n. 1.

108. Orion to Twain, Hartford, July 4, 1871, typescript in MTP, © Mark Twain Company, 1964.

109. Bliss to Twain, Hartford, December 6, 1871, MTP.

110. Thomas W. Knox, *Overland through Asia* (Hartford, 1870), pp. 239, 20, 337; *Roughing It,* 231, 359, 397; Albert D. Richardson, *Beyond the Mississippi* (Hartford, 1869), pp. 607, 295, 231, 246, 495, 203, 511, 502, 372, 279, 377, 436, 216, 487; *Roughing It,* 47, 50, 76, 103, 147, 183, 196, 254, 304, 323, 380, 392, 487, 557. The frontispiece of *Innocents Abroad,* "The 'Quaker City' in a Storm," doubled as "The Steamer 'Wright'" in *Overland through Asia* and "A Steamship in a Gale" in *The American Publisher.* Illustrations from *Overland through Asia* and *The American Publisher* turned up in *A Tramp Abroad.* Tom Quartz in *Roughing It* became Peter in *Tom Sawyer,* and an illustration from *Tom Sawyer* was used in Frank Bliss's *Autobiography of Buffalo Bill.* The practice was, in other words, both common and sensible. Twain's and Orion's objections must be based, rather, upon a claim by Bliss that the illustrations were new and more expensive than they actually were.

111. Washington, D. C., *Daily National Republican,* May 2, 1871, p. 2; reprinted in the *Boston Transcript,* May 5, 1871, p. 2, and in the *Chicago Tribune,* May 11, 1871, p. 2.

112. *The American Publisher,* I (July, 1871), 4; reprinted in the *New York Tribune,* July 3, 1871, p. 5, and in the *Boston Transcript,* July 5, 1871, p. 2.

113. Orion to Twain, Hartford, March 11, 1871, MTP.

114. Twain related the story in his letter to Charles H. Webb, Buffalo, November 26, 1870, CWB.

115. Twain to Bliss, Buffalo, January 27, 1871, MTP, © Mark Twain Company, 1964; Bliss to Twain, Hartford, April 22, 1871, MTP.
116. *Business Man*, p. 118.
117. Bliss to Twain, Hartford, May 17, 1871, MTP.
118. Twain to Orion, Elmira, [June, 1871], MTP, © Mark Twain Company, 1964.
119. *Love Letters*, p. 166.
120. Bliss to Twain, Hartford, April 22, 1871, MTP.
121. *The American Monthly: A Mirror of the Age*, I (February, 1873), 33.
122. Twain to Bliss, [Elmira], March 4, 1873, CWB, © Mark Twain Company, 1964.
123. Clara Clemens, *My Father, Mark Twain* (New York, Harper and Brothers, 1931), p. 47.
124. Orion to Twain, Hartford, March 11, 1871, MTP, © Mark Twain Company, 1964.
125. Twain to Orion, [Elmira], March 7, [1872], MTP, © Mark Twain Company, 1964.
126. Twain to Bliss, Elmira, March 20, 1872, MTP, © Mark Twain Company, 1964.
127. Twain to Webb, Hartford, April 8, [1875], typescript in MTP, © Mark Twain Company, 1964.
128. Orion to Twain, Hartford, May 17, 1872, MTP, © Mark Twain Company, 1964.
129. Twain to Annie Moffett, Elmira, May 17, 1872, typescript in MTP.
130. Twain to Bliss, Elmira, March 20, 1872, MTP, © Mark Twain Company, 1964.

CHAPTER III

In addition to the specific works cited in the following notes, I have found Frank C. Willson's "That 'Gilded Age' Again: An Attempt to Unmuddle the Mystery of the Fifty-Seven Variants," *Papers of the Bibliographical Society of America*, XXXVII (1943), 141–56, and Walter Blair's "On the Structure of *Tom Sawyer*," *Modern Philology*, XXXVII (August, 1939), 75–88, especially helpful. Pascal Covici, Jr., *Mark Twain's Humor* (Dallas, Southern Methodist University Press, 1962), pp. 125–27, discusses *The Gilded Age* and *Tom Sawyer* in the contexts of romance.

1. Twain to Reid, Hartford, April 22, 1873, printed in Royal Cortissoz, *The Life of Whitelaw Reid* (New York, Charles Scribner's Sons, 1921), I, 274; *Twain-Howells Letters*, p. 246; *Business Man*, p. 286.

2. See Arlin Turner, "James Lampton, Mark Twain's Model for Colonel Sellers," *Modern Language Notes*, LXX (December, 1955), 593–94.

3. *Business Man*, p. 120.

4. Paine, pp. 476–77.

5. Fragment in MTP, © Mark Twain Company, 1964.

6. Ernest E. Leisy, "Mark Twain's Part in *The Gilded Age*," *American Literature*, VIII (1937), 445–47, and Bryant Morey French, "The *Gilded Age* Manuscript," *Yale University Library Gazette*, XXXV (July, 1960), 35–41. The forthcoming volume in the Manuscript Edition of Mark Twain will examine the extant manuscript and provide, in the "Textual Variants," a full key to the collaboration.

7. *Mrs. Fairbanks*, p. 170.

8. *Love Letters*, p. 182.

9. *Mrs. Fairbanks*, p. 171. Warner wrote a chapter "disposing of Laura by sending her into Western retirement and obscurity" (Leisy, p. 44).

10. Until the publication of the Manuscript Edition of Mark Twain, Professor French's "The *Gilded Age* Manuscript" is the best description available. Warner's outline is in MTP.

11. Twain to Bliss, Home, May 3, 1873, typescript in MTP, © Mark Twain Company, 1964.

12. Twain to Orion, Home, Monday [May 5, 1873], in MTP, © Mark Twain Company, 1964.

13. Twain to Bliss and Warner, London, July 16, 1873, both at Yale, © Mark Twain Company, 1964. The contract for *The Gilded Age* is also at Yale.

14. Paine, p. 489; *Love Letters*, p. 364.

15. Twain to Bliss, March 4, 1873, CWB, © Mark Twain Company, 1964.

16. A receipt for $150 for an illustration, "A Spray of Box," from William S. Smedley is in Yale.

17. *New York Tribune*, April 23, 1873, p. 4.

18. *Mrs. Fairbanks*, p. 171; *Letters*, p. 205; *Twain-Howells Letters*, p. 62.

19. Sellers' correspondence with Warner is printed in my "Escol Sellers from Uncharted Space: A Footnote to *The Gilded Age*," *American Literature*, XXXIV (March, 1962), 107–13.

20. The letters are in Cortissoz, I, 273–75.

21. *Twain-Howells Letters*, pp. 374, 390.

22. Twain to Warner, Under Way, Sat. A.M. [May, 1873], typescript in MTP, © Mark Twain Company, 1964.

23. *Twain-Howells Letters*, p. 294.

24. *Autobiography*, II, 69–70.

25. New York *Daily Graphic*, December 23, 1873, p. 351.

26. Bliss collected these together in an advertising broadside, a copy of which is now in MTP.

27. *Literary World*, IV (January, 1874), 126.

28. *Chicago Tribune*, February 1, 1874, p. 9; November 27, 1875, p. 9.

29. *Business Man*, p. 300.

30. A. L. Vogelback, "The Publication . . . of *Huckleberry Finn* in America," p. 264; Jacob Blanck, *Bibliography of American Literature* (New Haven, Yale University Press, 1958), II, 185.

31. *Business Man*, p. 255.

32. Denis Woodfield, "The 'Fake' Title-Page of *The Gilded Age*: A Solution," *Papers of the Bibliographical Society of America*, L (1956), 292–96.

33. Copies of the prospectus are in CWB, FCW, and NYPL. Pages reproduced from the book: 17–34, 36–40, 43–49, 51, 57, 59, 65, 68, 72, 77, 81, 91, 95, 98, 105, 108, 110, 114, 115, 124, and 145.

34. *Galaxy*, XVII (March, 1874), 428; *Old and New*, IX (March, 1874), 386.

35. Bernard DeVoto, *Mark Twain's America* (Boston, Little, Brown & Company, 1932), p. 286.

36. *The American Monthly*, I (September, 1873), 97.

37. *Letters*, p. 215. In the *New York Tribune*, October 28, 1874, p. 8, Bliss gave sales of *The Gilded Age* as 58,000; actually he hadn't sold that many even by the end of 1879.

38. Twain to Bliss, January 22, 1870, typescript in MTP, reprinted in *Mrs. Fairbanks*, p. 144.

39. Twain to Bliss, Buffalo, October 13, 1870, typescript in MTP, © Mark Twain Company, 1964.

40. Contract of December 29, 1870, Yale.

41. Twain to Webb, Buffalo, November 26, 1870, Yale, © Mark Twain Company, 1964.

42. Twain to Bliss, Buffalo, December 22, 1870, Yale, © Mark Twain Company, 1964; Bliss to Twain, Hartford, December 29, 1870, MTP.

43. Twain to Bliss, Buffalo, January 3, [1871], MTP, quoted in *Mrs. Fairbanks*, p. 144.

44. *Mrs. Fairbanks*, pp. 143–44.

45. Twain to Bliss, Buffalo, January 3, 1871, MTP, © Mark Twain Company, 1964.

46. Twain to Bliss, [January] 24, 1871, typescript in MTP, © Mark Twain Company, 1964.

47. Twain to Osgood, Elmira, Sunday, 1872, typescript in MTP, © Mark Twain Company, 1964.

48. Twain to Bliss, Elmira, March 21, [1872], typescript in MTP, © Mark Twain Company, 1964.

49. Twain to Bliss, Saybrook, August 7, 1872, Yale, © Mark Twain Company, 1964.

50. *Love Letters*, p. 183. The French version had appeared in *Revue des Deux Mondes*, C (July 15, 1872), 313–35.

51. *Mrs. Fairbanks*, pp. 183–84.

52. *Twain-Howells Letters*, p. 863.

53. Twain to Osgood, Friday, [1875], CWB, © Mark Twain Company, 1964.

54. Twain to Osgood, February 12, [1875], typescript in MTP, © Mark Twain Company, 1964.

55. "From 'Hospital Days'" is a different kind of mystery—a short anecdote Twain included in *Sketches* even though it apparently belonged to Jane Stuart Woolsey. The best summary of the problem is in *Twain-Howells Letters*, pp. 863–64.

56. *Twain-Howells Letters*, p. 99.

57. At Yale there is a letter from the Library of Congress to Twain (April 15, 1876) advising that copyright still required the deposit of two copies to be complete. Twain wrote Bliss asking him to forward the copies immediately. But when the humorist saw a copy of *Innocents Abroad* offered for sale by Joseph Knight Company in 1894, he wrote Frank Bliss asking if Elisha had failed to deposit copyright volumes of *Innocents*, too (Twain to Frank Bliss, December 9, 1894, Yale).

58. *Twain-Howells Letters*, p. 99.

59. *Ibid.*, p. 62; Twain to Bliss, November 5, 1875, MTP, © Mark Twain Company, 1964; *Mrs. Fairbanks*, p. 201.

60. *New York Tribune*, September 21, 1875, p. 6.

61. Twain to Webb, Hartford, April 8, [1875], MTP, © Mark Twain Company, 1964.

62. *The Big Bonanza*, ed. Oscar Lewis (New York, Alfred A. Knopf, Inc., 1947), p. xix.

63. Wright to Twain, Virginia City, February 7, 1876, Yale.

64. A copy is in Yale.

65. *Twain-Howells Letters*, p. 123.

66. Two typical examples are printed in Milton Meltzer, *Mark Twain Himself* (New York, Thomas Y. Crowell Company, 1961), pp. 58, 128.

67. The prospectus reprints the following pages of the text of the first edition: 17–19, 21, 26, 28–30, 33, 35, 44, 47, 49, 51, 52, 54, 56, 58, 60, 63, 65, 66, 69–72, 74, 77, 81, 82, 84, 85, 87, 90, 91, 94, 96, 98, 101, 102, 104, 106, 109, 111, 113, 121, 123, 126, 129, 133, 135, 153, 154, 158, 159, 162, 164, 169, 171, 182, 192, and 208.

68. *Business Man*, p. 190.
69. In a clipping in Yale.
70. Frank Bliss to Twain, Hartford, February 21, 1893, Yale; Twain to Frank Bliss, Firenze, March 9, 1893, Yale.
71. Walter Blair, "Review of *Mark Twain at Work,*" *American Literature*, XV (January, 1943), 448–49. The Sandwich Island notebook entry is reprinted in Walter Blair, *Mark Twain & Huck Finn* (Berkeley, University of California Press, 1960), p. 52. The story of the Temperance Society is in *Mark Twain's Travels with Mr. Brown*, ed. Franklin Walker and G. Ezra Dane (New York, Alfred A. Knopf, Inc., 1940), p. 146. The Congressional dinner speech and the Robin Hood games on Holliday's Hill are mentioned in *Mark Twain's Letters to Will Bowen*, pp. 17–21. The three rehearsals of the Sunday school scene are in Minnie M. Brashear, *Mark Twain, Son of Missouri* (Chapel Hill, University of North Carolina Press, 1934), p. 168; Clara Clemens, *My Father, Mark Twain*, pp. 9–12; and *The Gilded Age* (Hartford, 1873), pp. 479–83.
72. Reprinted in Bernard DeVoto, *Mark Twain at Work* (Cambridge, Mass., Harvard University Press, 1942), pp. 25–44.
73. *Ibid.*, p. 7.
74. See *Mrs. Fairbanks*, p. 173, and DeVoto, *Mark Twain at Work*, p. 4.
75. *Letters*, pp. 218–19. The hint of another intermediate stage, in the winter of 1871–1872, is suggested in the note on the first page of the manuscript, "Put in thing from Boy-lecture." This is a reference to a lecture of that year which Orion announced in the *American Publisher*, I (July, 1871), 4: "He has *two* new lectures, one an appeal in behalf of Boy's Rights, and the other one entitled simply 'D.L.H.'" See also Paul Fatout, *Mark Twain on the Lecture Circuit* (Bloomington, Indiana University Press, 1960), p. 151.
76. Brander Matthews, *The Tocsin of Revolt and Other Essays* (New York, Charles Scribner's Sons, 1922), p. 265.
77. "Memoranda," *Galaxy*, IX (May, 1870), 726, reprinted in *Mark Twain at Your Fingertips*, ed. Caroline T. Harnsberger (New York, 1948), pp. 30–31, and in McElderry, ed., *Contributions to the Galaxy*, p. 46.
78. *Letters*, p. 224.
79. *Eruption*, p. 197.
80. *The Art of the Novel*, ed. Richard P. Blackmur (New York, Charles Scribner's Sons, 1934), p. 23.
81. *Twain-Howells Letters*, pp. 87–88, 91.
82. I have examined the manuscript of the novel at greater length in "The Composition and the Structure of *Tom Sawyer*," *American Literature*, XXXII (January, 1961), 379–92. The impli-

cations of the outline note upon the composition of *Adventures of Huckleberry Finn* are suggested in Hamlin Hill and Walter Blair, *The Art of Huckleberry Finn* (San Francisco, Chandler Publishing Company, 1962), pp. 2–3. For an alternative interpretation of the note see Albert Stone, *The Innocent Eye: Childhood in Mark Twain's Imagination* (New Haven, Yale University Press, 1961), p. 89.

83. Matthews, *The Tocsin of Revolt*, p. 266.

84. Among the many editions which indomitable Mrs. Gay published, the "Seventh," printed for the author by Goodwyn and Company, Memphis, 1871, is the only one I have seen which matches exactly the pagination of the torn leaves in Twain's manuscript. In 1882 Twain told a Miss Noyes that a ceremony at her school had provided the inspiration for the scene (Hartford, February 23, 1882, MTP, quoted in Walter Blair, *Mark Twain & Huck Finn*, pp. 395–96). But in 1864 he had toyed with the basic idea: See *Mark Twain of the Enterprise*, ed. Henry Nash Smith with the assistance of Frederick Anderson (Berkeley, University of California Press, 1957), pp. 134–38.

85. *Twain-Howells Letters*, pp. 91, 95, 110–11.

86. *Ibid.*, p. 112.

87. DeVoto, *Mark Twain at Work*, pp. 9–18, and Ferguson, *Mark Twain: Man and Legend*, pp. 180–82.

88. Deleted from MS page 72, © Mark Twain Company, 1964.

89. Twain to Bliss, Elmira, November 5, 1875, quoted in *The Twainian*, II (March, 1943), 2.

90. *Twain-Howells Letters*, p. 121.

91. *Ibid.*, p. 128.

92. Frank Bliss to Twain, Hartford, April 11, 1876, in "Scrapbook, 1872–1878," p. 30, MTP.

93. Twain to Bliss, November 5, 1875, quoted in *The Twainian*, II (March, 1943), 2; Twain to Bliss, March 19, 1876, typescript in MTP, © Mark Twain Company, 1964.

94. *Twain-Howells Letters*, pp. 131–32.

95. Twain to Bliss, Elmira, June 24, [1876], Yale, © Mark Twain Company, 1964.

96. Bliss to Twain, Hartford, July 18, 1876, MTP.

97. Twain to Bliss, Elmira, July 22, 1876, MTP, © Mark Twain Company, 1964.

98. Twain to Bliss, August 8, [1876], MTP, © Mark Twain Company, 1964.

99. The notes now form a part of the Georgetown University manuscript, in the Riggs Memorial Library.

100. Exhaustive and illuminating on the subject of Canadian

pirates is Gordon Roper's "Mark Twain and His Canadian Publishers," *American Book Collector,* X (June, 1960), 13–29.

101. Twain to Conway, Hartford, January 5, [1876], typescript in MTP, © Mark Twain Company, 1964.

102. Conway to Mrs. Conway, Hartford, January 18, [1876], typescript in MTP.

103. Twain to Bliss, Elmira, August 8, [1876], MTP, © Mark Twain Company, 1964.

104. *Twain-Howells Letters,* p. 132; Twain to Stoddard, Hartford, September 26, 1876, typescript in MTP, © Mark Twain Company, 1964; Warner to Webb, Hartford, October 27, 1876, typescript in MTP.

105. A copy of the *Tom Sawyer* prospectus, in CWB, contains these pages from the first edition: 17, 28, 47, 55–58, 60, 63–64, 72–73, 79, 81, 85–86, 88, 91, 93–95, 98, 101–3, 107–10, 113, 115, 117, 134, 139, 146, 149, 146–48, 156, 158, 160, 167, 168, 173–74, 176–77, 181, 161, 164–65, 183–84, 186–91, 194, 198–99, 205, 207–9, 212–14, 217, 220, 224, 226, 233, 234, 236, 245, 247, 249, 261, 266, and 271.

106. On July 23, 1876 (see Johnson, *A Bibliography of the Works of Mark Twain,* p. 30), June 29, p. 7, June 30, p. 6, and July 6, p. 4, all cited in A. L. Vogelback, "The Literary Reputation of Mark Twain in America" (unpublished doctoral dissertation, University of Chicago, 1938), pp. 36–37.

107. Circular in the collection of Mr. Cyril Clemens, Kirkwood, Missouri.

108. *Facts. By A Woman* (Oakland, Pacific Press Printing House, 1881), *passim.*

109. See Foner, *Mark Twain: Social Critic,* p. 44.

110. These figures are more elaborately explained in my "Mark Twain's Quarrels with Elisha Bliss," *American Literature,* XXXIII (January, 1962), 455.

111. Slote to Twain, New York, February 2, 1878, in "Scrapbook, 1872–1878," pp. 35–36, MTP.

CHAPTER IV

1. Twain owned $5,000 of American Publishing Company stock in 1873 when Bliss notified him of a 10 per cent, $500 dividend (Hartford, January 7, 1873, MTP). On May 19, 1881, he sold 200 shares to Frank Bliss (receipt in CWB).

2. *Twain-Howells Letters,* p. 236.

3. Quoted in Vogelback, "The Publication and Reception of *Huckleberry Finn,*" pp. 267, 265.

4. Quoted in Herbert Feinstein, "Mark Twain and the Pirates,"

Harvard Law School Bulletin, XIII (April, 1962), 11. Wanamaker said of the agents, "The books he sells are not made to be read. They are made to sell to people who have barely learned to read and very little beyond that" (*ibid.,* p. 13).

5. See *Twain-Howells Letters,* p. 145.

6. *Ibid.,* pp. 208, 250.

7. *Ibid.,* p. 193.

8. *Ibid.,* pp. 191, 193, 200–202, 219–20, 223, 225, and 286.

9. March 8, 1878, contract in MTP.

10. Twain to Bliss, Buffalo, November 28 and December 2, 1870, and Bliss to Twain, Hartford, November 30 (all in MTP). Twain to Riley, December 2, 1870, reprinted in Irving Underhill, "Diamonds in the Rough . . . ," *The Colophon,* Part 13 (Spring, 1930).

11. Copies in Yale and MTP.

12. MTP. A check from Frank Bliss to Twain, December 20, 1870 (in NYPL), covered part of the advance.

13. Bliss to Twain, February 13, 1879, MTP.

14. Notebook 14, p. 1, MTP.

15. *Mrs. Fairbanks,* pp. 226–27, 231.

16. Frank Bliss to Twain, Hartford, March 26, 1879, MTP.

17. Twain to Frank Bliss, April 15, 1879, NYPL, © Mark Twain Company, 1964.

18. Bliss to Twain, Hartford, April 1, 1879, MTP.

19. Frank Bliss to Twain, Hartford, May 29, 1879, MTP; and Twain to Frank Bliss, Paris, June 10, 1879, Yale, © Mark Twain Company, 1964.

20. *Eruption,* p. 147; Twain to Frank Bliss, Paris, May 10, 1879, MTP, © Mark Twain Company, 1964; Frank Bliss to Twain, Hartford, June 12, 1879, MTP; and Frank Bliss to Twain, Hartford, June 27, 1879, MTP.

21. See *Twins of Genius,* ed. Guy A. Cardwell (East Lansing, The Michigan State University Press, 1953), p. 95.

22. *Letters,* p. 320.

23. *Twain-Howells Letters,* p. 231.

24. Twain to Frank Bliss, Heidelberg, July 13, 1878, typescript in MTP, © Mark Twain Company, 1964.

25. Twain to Frank Bliss, Lucerne, August 20, 1878, NYPL, © Mark Twain Company, 1964.

26. *Mark Twain's Notebook,* ed. Albert B. Paine (New York, Harper and Brothers, 1935), p. 149.

27. *Letters,* pp. 339–40.

28. *Samuel Langhorne Clemens, Some Reminiscences and Some Excerpts from Letters and Unpublished Manuscripts,* ed.

Jervis Langdon (n.p., n.d.), p. 10, and Twain to Twichell, Munich, January 23, 1879, Yale.

29. *Twain-Howells Letters,* p. 249.

30. *Letters,* p. 349.

31. *Ibid.*

32. *Twain-Howells Letters,* pp. 249–50.

33. Most of this material was later published as "omitted from *A Tramp Abroad.*" Ritter's story showed up in *Life on the Mississippi,* but Walter Blair's study of inks and paper Twain used suggests it was written in the period of *A Tramp Abroad.* See "When Was *Huckleberry Finn* Written?" *American Literature,* XXX (March, 1958), 1–25. Other "rejected" material included "The French and the Comanches," printed in *Letters from the Earth,* ed. Bernard DeVoto (New York, Harper and Brothers, 1962), pp. 183–89, which is the major portion of DV 67 (MTP), a history of France.

34. *Notebook,* p. 138.

35. The final page, reproduced as the cover illustration of *The Month at Goodspeed's,* XI (April, 1940), was dated "Munich, Bavaria, Nov. '78."

36. Franklin Rogers, *Mark Twain's Burlesque Patterns* (Dallas, Southern Methodist University Press, 1960), pp. 154–55.

37. *Twain-Howells Letters,* p. 248.

38. Albert E. Stone, Jr., "The Twichell Papers and Mark Twain's *A Tramp Abroad,*" *Yale University Library Gazette,* XXIX (April, 1955), 156.

39. Paine, p. 650.

40. DeVoto, *Mark Twain's America,* pp. 244–45.

41. *The Big Bonanza,* ed. Oscar Lewis, pp. xviii–xix.

42. DeVoto, *Mark Twain's America,* pp. 245–46.

43. Henry Nash Smith, "Introduction," *Roughing It* (New York, Harper and Brothers, 1959), p. xiii.

44. The phrase is Twain's. See *Twain-Howells Letters,* p. 236.

45. *Mrs. Fairbanks,* p. 226.

46. Twain to Frank Bliss, Paris, May 10, 1879, MTP, © Mark Twain Company, 1964.

47. *Mrs. Fairbanks,* p. 230.

48. Twain to Aldrich, Paris, May 25, [1879], MTP, © Mark Twain Company, 1964. Manuscript pages 1955 to 1963 are from Chapter XLV, now in CWB.

49. *Business Man,* p. 137.

50. Quotations from the *New York Times,* September 3, 1879, reprinted in the *Chicago Tribune,* September 6, 1879, p. 16. Paine,

p. 649, quotes interviews from the New York *Sun;* and Blair, *Mark Twain & Huck Finn,* p. 165, from the *New York Herald.*

51. *Mrs. Fairbanks,* p. 226.

52. Twain to Frank Bliss, Paris, May 10, 1879, MTP, © Mark Twain Company, 1964.

53. Frank Bliss to Twain, Hartford, May 30, 1879, MTP, and Twain to Frank Bliss, Paris, June 10, 1879, typescript in MTP, © Mark Twain Company, 1964.

54. Frank Bliss to Twain, Hartford, June 27, 1879, MTP.

55. Twain to Frank Bliss, Elmira, September 8, 1879, typescript in MTP, © Mark Twain Company, 1964.

56. Hartford, November 1, 1879, MTP.

57. The manuscript (Paine 127), is in MTP; quoted portions © Mark Twain Company, 1964.

58. *Twain-Howells Letters,* p. 269; Paine, p. 650.

59. *Twain-Howells Letters,* p. 280.

60. *Ibid.,* p. 287.

61. *Business Man,* p. 140.

62. *Ibid.,* p. 143.

63. *Notebook,* pp. 143–44; he thus identifies the Odessa anecdote in the volume.

64. The only copy of this 1879 prospectus I have located is in the possession of Mr. Franklin Meine, Chicago.

65. Chatto & Windus to Twain, London, May 3, 1880, MTP. See also *Twain-Howells Letters,* p. 302.

66. The lower figure is quoted in Paine, p. 665; the higher, in *Business Man,* p. 249.

67. Twain to an unknown recipient, April 23, [1880], CWB, © Mark Twain Company, 1964.

68. Twain to Frank Bliss, March 20, [1880], NYPL, © Mark Twain Company, 1964.

69. *Letters,* p. 379.

70. Twain to Frank Bliss, March 20, [1880], NYPL.

71. Copy at Yale.

72. To an unknown person, April 23, [1880], NYPL, © Mark Twain Company, 1964.

73. Twain to English printers, Hartford, April 20, [1880], NYPL, © Mark Twain Company, 1964.

74. In Notebook 15 (July 26, 1880, to December 3, 1880), MTP. Twain's check for the first quarter's sales was $19,000 (*Twain-Howells Letters,* p. 320); Frank Bliss to Twain, Hartford, September 13, 1880, MTP.

75. Twain to Orion, October 24, 1880, MTP.

76. *Mark Twain the Letter Writer,* ed. Cyril Clemens, p. 17; *Business Man,* pp. 147–48.

77. *Mark Twain to Uncle Remus*, ed. Thomas H. English (Atlanta, Emory University Library, 1953), p. 10.

78. Twain to Frank Bliss, Hartford, May 30, 1881, typescript in MTP, © Mark Twain Company, 1964.

79. Dan Whitford to Twain, New York, July 11, 1881, MTP.

80. Quoted in Feinstein, p. 13.

81. See *Business Man*, pp. 174, 185, and Notebook 16 (January 16, 1882, to September 20, 1882), MTP.

82. Cardwell, *Twins of Genius*, p. 95. See also *Business Man*, pp. 203–4, 223, 232.

83. *Business Man*, pp. 221–22, and Blair, *Mark Twain & Huck Finn*, p. 356; *Eruption*, p. 172, and the unpublished autobiographical dictation of July 17, 1906, MTP. Vogelback, "The Publication and Reception of *Huckleberry Finn*," pp. 260–61, quotes the New York *World's* story of the 60 per cent figure.

84. Autobiographical dictation of July 17, 1906, MTP, © Mark Twain Company, 1964.

85. See *Business Man*, pp. 211, 248, and 263.

86. *Eruption*, pp. 154–55.

87. The first annual report was discussed in Twain to Osgood, Hartford, March 7, 1881, typescript in MTP. See also my "Mark Twain's Quarrels with Elisha Bliss," pp. 453–56.

88. Dickinson, "Marketing a Best Seller," p. 115.

89. Ferguson, *Mark Twain: Man and Legend*, p. 159.

90. Quoted in the 1872 *Innocents Abroad* prospectus, in my possession.

91. *The Big Bonanza*, p. xix.

92. Quoted in the 1872 *Innocents Abroad* prospectus.

93. Quoted in the 1879 *A Tramp Abroad* prospectus.

94. *Mrs. Fairbanks*, p. 227.

95. *Business Man*, pp. 349, 389.

96. Henry Nash Smith, "Introduction," *Roughing It*, pp. xi–xii; *Love Letters*, p. 166.

97. Albert Kitzhaber, "Mark Twain's Use of the Pomeroy Case in *The Gilded Age*," *Modern Language Quarterly*, XV (March, 1954), 56.

98. Blair, "On the Structure of *Tom Sawyer*," p. 79.

99. Blair, *Mark Twain & Huck Finn*, pp. 220–25, and Louis J. Budd, "The Southward Currents Under Huck Finn's Raft," *Mississippi Valley Historical Review*, XLVI (September, 1959), 222–37.

100. Twain to Frank Bliss, Heidelberg, July 13, 1878, typescript in MTP, © Mark Twain Company, 1964; *Letters*, p. 591.

101. *Eruption*, pp. 202–3.

102. Willard Thorp, "Pilgrim's Return," and Dixon Wecter, "Mark Twain," *Literary History of the United States* (New York,

The Macmillan Company, 1948), pp. 838, 921. Carl Van Doren, *The American Novel, 1789–1939* (New York, The Macmillan Company, 1940), p. 138.

103. Wecter, in *LHUS*, p. 922.

104. *Mrs. Fairbanks*, p. 152; Wecter, in *LHUS*, p. 922.

105. All quotations are from William Dean Howells, *My Mark Twain* (New York, Harper and Brothers, 1910), pp. 130, 108–9, 121, and 133.

106. Wecter, in *LHUS*, p. 925.

107. Smith, "Introduction," *Roughing It*, p. xiii.

108. Henry Nash Smith, "Mark Twain as an Interpreter of the Far West: The Structure of *Roughing It*," in *The Frontier in Perspective*, ed. Walker D. Wyman and Clifton B. Krober (Madison, Wisconsin, University of Wisconsin Press, 1957), p. 208.

109. Van Doren, *The American Novel, 1789–1939*, p. 138.

INDEX